7

# Introduction to the Public Key Infrastructure for the Internet

ISBN 0130609277

90000

9 780130 609274

# Introduction to the Public Key Infrastructure for the Internet

Messaoud Benantar

PRENTICE HALL PTR
UPPER SADDLE RIVER, NJ 07458
WWW.PHPTR.COM

Editorial/production supervision: *Mary Sudul*
Composition: *FASTpages*
Acqusition Editor: *Victoria Jones*
Editorial Assistant:  *Michelle Vincenti*
Marketing Manager: *Debby vanDijk*
Manufacturing Manager: *Maura Zaldivar*
Cover Design: *Design Source*
Cover Design Director: *Jerry Votta*
Series Design: *Gail Cocker-Bogusz*

© 2002 Prentice Hall PTR
Prentice-Hall, Inc.
Upper Saddle River, NJ 07458

The publisher offers discounts on this book when ordered in bulk quantities.
For more information, contact
Corporate Sales Department,
Prentice Hall PTR
One Lake Street
Upper Saddle River, NJ 07458
Phone: 800-382-3419; FAX: 201-236-714
E-mail (Internet): corpsales@prenhall.com

Printed in the United States of America

10 9 8 7 6 5 4 3 2 1

ISBN 0-13-060927-7


Pearson Education LTD.
Pearson Education Australia PTY, Limited
Pearson Education Singapore, Pte. Ltd
Pearson Education North Asia Ltd
Pearson Education Canada, Ltd.
Pearson Educación de Mexico, S.A. de C.V.
Pearson Education — Japan
Pearson Education Malaysia, Pte. Ltd
Pearson Education, Upper Saddle River, New Jersey

*This book was written in memory of my parents
and is dedicated to my sisters.*

# Contents

# Preface

Modern secret key cryptography draws strength from the secrecy of keys. This characteristic is not arrived at by choice, rather it is an imposed one. Consider the case of shedding secrecy around a particular cryptographic algorithm. First, the algorithm becomes unavailable for public scrutiny. In the absence of technical scrutiny, the algorithm may hide its weaknesses and thus serves the undesirable principle of security by obscurity. Further yet, such a hiding of the strength or the weakness in a cryptographic algorithm cannot go on for an indefinite period of time. Sooner or later someone will arrive at reverse-engineering the processing logic embedded in a software or a hardware cryptographic module. The outcome will indeed signal the end of that particular algorithm.

Secret keys require distribution to communicating partners and the more often a secret key is distributed the more likely it is to become compromised. Distribution of long-term secret keys goes against the core premise of secret key cryptography, otherwise known as symmetric key cryptography. Transport of secret keys requires the establishment of secure channels. Human transport can be a solution but is certainly one that does not lend itself to large scale distributions. Online distributions require highly secure cryptographic channels, and thus the bootstrapping nature of the secret key distribution problem arises.

In order to alleviate the extent of the secret key distribution problem, the concept of central key distribution (KDC) entity emerged as a somewhat of a natural progression. This entity represents the sole agent that is trusted by every other entity. It plays the role of both the keeper of secret long-term keys and the distributor of short-term session keys intended for use between two communicating entities. This latter role is dubbed as the introduction of entities to one another and is accomplished using cryptographic channels established between each respective entity and the third party agent based upon a shared long term secret key. Albeit this approach has evolved into the most elegant third party key distribution center, it lacks the flexibility of today's Internet ubiquitous computing paradigm.

Now we're back to the future, to exploiting the concept of public key cryptography that had emerged long before concepts such as the KDC existed. In the basic yet far-reaching concept of public key cryptography, encryption keys come in related pairs, private and public. The private key remains concealed by the key owner, while the public key is freely disseminated. The premise is that it is computationally infeasible to compute the private key by knowing the public key. Data encrypted by the public key can only be decrypted by the private key. With such an appealing characteristic, public key cryptography finally seemed to hold the promise of solving the secret key distribution problem. It certainly did so with the elegant key exchange scheme such as Diffie-Hellman's. Public key Public key cryptography, however, is intended to achieve not only key exchange protocols but to render various security services such as digital signatures, non-repudiation and data enciphering using the well known public key algorithms such as RSA.

The premise of freely disseminating a public key comes with a cost; that of trust. Security services that are based on public key cryptography rely on the single foundation of trusting that a particular public key material is indeed bound to its legitimate user. A promising solution for public key trust-establishment lies in the digital certification provided by X.509 which is adopted as an Internet standard. This book is intended to be a single source covering the major aspects of the Internet public key certification.

# Secret Key Cryptography

This chapter is a brief introduction to the basics of secret key cryptography. We begin by discussing data-scrambling techniques used in early cryptographic systems, then we elaborate on the concepts employed in modern cryptosystems. We describe well-known contemporary algorithms, and finally we discuss the security services enabled through secret key cryptography. ∎

## Introduction

Confidentiality is a data security property. Its primary goal is to confine knowledge of information that the data represents within a particular set of entities (such as human or a programmable electronic system) having the ability to interpret the data. The process of achieving this confinement property, otherwise known as secrecy, is by way of scrambling the plaintext form of data into a reversible representation that perhaps has no syntax and certainly should have no semantics.

Long before the advent of electronic systems, different methods of data-scrambling transformations, known in contemporary terms as the science of cryptography, were used. A cryptographic transformation of data is a deterministic procedure by which data, in its plaintext form, is disguised to result in a ciphertext representation that does not reveal the original data. Similarly, the ciphertext can be reverse-transformed in a deterministic fashion by a designated recipient so that the original data can be recovered.

# Background

Early cryptographic algorithms [KAHN67, BECK82] manipulated the plaintext input character by character using the methods of substitution and transposition. A substitution operation, also referred to as a permutation, replaces a character of the input stream by a character from the alphabet set of the target ciphertext. A transposition, on the other hand, replaces a character from the input stream by another character of that same input, resulting in shuffling character positions and preserving all characters of the plaintext in the final ciphertext. An example of a substitution is the famous Caesar cipher which is said to have been used by Julius Caesar to communicate with his army. The cipher replaces each character of the input text by the third character to its right in the alphabet set augmented with the blank character. Formally, this transformation consists of adding 3 to the position of the input character then taking *modulo 26* to yield the substituting character. If we assign numerical equivalents of *0-25* to the 26-letter alphabet A-Z, the transformation sends each plain character *P* onto *f(P) = P + 3 modulo 26*. Figure 1.1 shows how this simple transformation is applied to the input "RETURN TO BASE" to yield the ciphertext "UHWXUQ WR EDVH".

A transposition cipher, generally, consists of first breaking the plaintext into separate blocks. A deterministic procedure is then applied to shuffle characters across different blocks. Figure 1.2 illustrates a character transposition example in which the secret message "RETURN TO BASE" is split into two blocks consisting of "RETURN" and "TO BASE" then characters are shuffled across the two blocks in a cyclic fashion to result in the ciphertext of "ROTBRS TE UANE".

Another example of a simple transposition cipher is writing the plaintext along a two-dimensional matrix of fixed rows and columns then simply transposing the matrix. Figure 1.3 illustrates the plaintext of "RETURN TO BASE" inserted into a 2 by 9 matrix which is then transposed to result in a columnar transposition cipher. To decrypt the ciphertext, the inverse transposition is applied by first rearranging the ciphertext into a 9 by 2 matrix then taking the transpose as shown in Figure 1.3

```
plain Message:        RETURN TO BASE
enciphered Message:   UHWXUQ WR E DVH
```

**FIGURE 1.1**
A simple substitution cipher

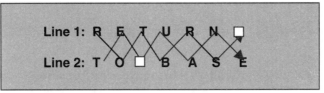

Enciphered message: **RO TBRS TE UANE**

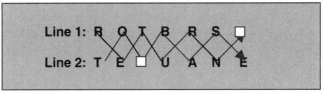

Deciphered message: **RETURN TO BASE**

**FIGURE 1.2**
An example of a transposition ciphering/deciphering transformation

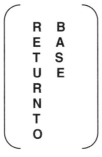

**FIGURE 1.3**
A columnar transposition cipher

Generally, transposition ciphers are easy to break but composing them by setting the result of one transposition as the input of another one, greatly enhances the ciphering against attacks.

Even though it employs a very basic algorithm, the substitution example points to the concept of secret key cryptography (the number of positions to shift right). Keeping the key secret while divulging the algorithm will, in this case, lead to recovering the plaintext through an exhaustive process of the key space which simply consists of the set of integers {1, 2, 3, 4, ..., 26}. The strength of the methods used in this era rested on the secrecy of the encryption algorithm itself. Note that in our simple example revealing the encryption algorithm leads almost immediately to the compromise of any data that it protects.

With the advent of electronic computers, early modern cryptography [KONH81, BECK82, DENN83] carried on these same concepts, employing transposition and substitution transformations. The primary difference is that these transformations now apply at the bit level of the binary representation of data instead of characters only. A common such transformation is the **XOR** operation that we discuss next.

# Basic XOR

The XOR operation denoted by + is a bit-wise function that maps an element of {0, 1}x{0,1} onto the set {0, 1} as follows:

$$0 + 0 = 0$$
$$0 + 1 = 1$$
$$1 + 0 = 1$$
$$1 + 1 = 0$$

If we take the second operand to be a key value, the XOR operation can be thought of as being simply a bit-level substitution based upon the bit values of the key. With such assumption, XOR sends a 0 or 1 to itself when the corresponding key bit is 0 and inverts a 0 into a 1 and a 1 into a 0 when the corresponding key bit is 1. XOR exhibits the following properties.

$$a + 0 = a$$
$$a + a = 0, \text{ and thus}$$
$$a + b + b = a$$

The last property implies that using a fixed key value, the XOR operation can be applied to encipher a plaintext, which can then be recovered by simply applying the XOR operation to the ciphertext and the same key value. This property has led to the proliferation of many variants of weak encryption methods that solely rely on the simple XOR operation and thus are easily breakable.

Assume that a fixed-length key, $K$, is used for the XOR of some plaintext blocks. Knowing a block of plaintext, $P$, and its XOR transformation directly leads to $K$, by way of XORing the plaintext with the corresponding ciphertext.

```
C = P + K
P + C = P + P + K
      = K
```

Similarly, by knowing two ciphertext blocks alone one can XOR them together to yield the XOR of the corresponding plaintext blocks as follows:

```
C1 + C2 = P1 + K + P2 + K
        = P1 + P2
```

Examining the bit patterns of $P1 + P2$ can easily result in recovering one of the plaintexts. The latter can then be XORed with its ciphertext to yield the keystream.

By transforming one bit at a time the XOR operation lends itself well to a class of encryption algorithms known as stream ciphers. In contrast, block ciphers divide a plaintext into identical size blocks, generally of length greater or equal to 64 bits, then apply the same encryption transformation to encrypt each block at a time. Stream ciphers are geared for use in situations where memory buffering is limited or when characters are individually transformed as they show up at an endpoint of a transmission medium. Because they generally transform plaintext bits independently from one another, error propagation remains limited in the event of transmission anomaly.

## The one-time XOR pad

Despite the simplicity of the XOR operation and the weakness of encryption algorithms that use it with fixed keys, there is a way of making the sole use of such basic operations result in a perfect encryption scheme. If the keystream digits are randomly generated and each keystream is used only once, the resulting ciphertext referred to as a one-time pad yields a perfect cipher. Such a cipher is provably secure against attacks in which a code breaker has knowledge of a set of ciphertexts. Figure 1.4 is a graphic illustration of the simple XOR-based one-time pad cipher.

The security of the one-time pad is due to the uncertainty in attempting to guess the keystream is equal to that of directly guessing the plaintext. Note that the length of the keystream for the one-time pad is equal to that of the plaintext being encrypted. Such a property makes it difficult to maintain and distribute very long keystreams which has led to the development of stream ciphers whereby the keystream is pseudorandomly generated from a fixed secret key that is manageable.

The bit-level one-time pad applies equally well at the character level. In fact, historically a one-time pad was applied to characters when it was first invented by Major Joseph Mauborgne and Gilbert Vernam. Each keypad character is applied to only one plaintext character. The receiving entity uses the same keypad to decrypt the cipher and then destroys the key.

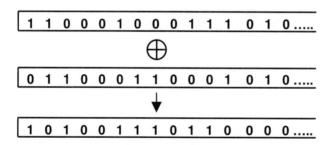

**FIGURE 1.4**
A simple one-time pad based on the XOR operation

# About the Key Space

A secret key, also known as a symmetric key, enciphering function $E$ in which encryption and decryption use the same key $K$ transforms a plaintext $P$ into a ciphertext $C$. Similarly, this encryption transformation can be inverted by the decryption function $D$ as illustrated in Figure 1.5.

The strength of modern secret key encryption methods rests in the secrecy of the encryption key, not in the algorithm being used. Breaking such cryptographic systems, therefore, can be achieved using the process of exhaustive

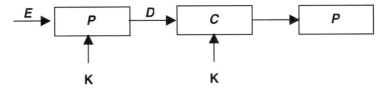

**FIGURE 1.5**
Symmetric key encryption and decryption

searches over the key space. A key space is the set of all possible key values that a particular enciphering algorithm admits. A transposition example over the English alphabet when thought of as an arbitrary permutation over the alphabet set will consist of *26!* Keys, each corresponding to one permutation. While further constraining the permutation method to one that simply maps each letter in the alphabet to one which is at a fixed number of positions to its right (with a wrap around), and by enciphering each letter at a time (block length = *1*), the key space narrows down to the much smaller set of *26* elements containing the integers *{1,2,3,...,26}*. Adding further complexity to this simple permutation transformation by making the block length equal to 3, and mapping each $(p_1p_2p_3)$ block into $(e_1e_2e_3)$ where each letter has its own mapping to a letter at a fixed position to its right, yields a key space with a size of $(26!)^3$.

Most common secret key cryptographic systems use fixed-size keys that are randomly generated. These systems can certainly be exposed to the exhaustive search of the key space. A necessary, although not sufficient, condition for any cryptographic system to be secure is that the key space be large enough to preclude exhaustive search attacks. Ironically, a speedy performance of any such enciphering methods will aid in the brute force, exhaustive, search attack.

## Common Secret Key Algorithms _____

All of the widely known secret key-block algorithms exhibit the cryptographic properties desired in a block cipher. Foremost is the fact that each bit of the ciphertext should depend on all bits. Changing any key bit should result in a 50 percent chance of changing any resulting ciphertext bit. Furthermore, no statistical relationships can be inferred between a plaintext and its corresponding ciphertext. Detailed descriptions of most common secret-key cryptographic algorithms can be found in [SCHN96, MENE96].

# DES

Modern secret key cryptographic systems are most notably known through the Data Encryption Standard (DES) algorithm [MEYE82]. DES, a symmetric cipher in which the same key is used for encryption and decryption, was developed by IBM cryptographers in the early 1970s and has been a U.S. government standard since 1976 for the protection of sensitive but unclassified electronic information. The algorithm is a block cipher, in which a 64-bit input block is transformed into a corresponding 64-bit output ciphertext. It employs a 56-bit length key expressed as a 64-bit quantity in which the least relevant bit in each byte is used for parity checking. Figure 1.6 illustrates a high level abstraction of DES.

DES, in its standard form, iterates over 16 rounds in each of which data is manipulated, using a combination of permutation and substitution transformations along with standard arithmetic and logical operations such as XOR, based on the key value.

Recently, and mainly because of the increased speed of computing systems, DES has come under brute force attack on several occasions demonstrating its vulnerability to exhaustive searching of the key space [WIEN94]. Triple-DES is simply the DES algorithm applied three times using either two or three keys. With two keys, triple-DES proceeds by encrypting a block of data using the first key and using the second key to decrypt the previous encryption. The first key is once more used to encrypt the result from the second step.

The three-key triple-DES uses a separate key for each of the three steps. The number of possible keys in triple-DES is $2^{112}$, compared to a key space of size $2^{56}$ for DES.

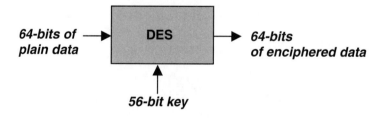

**FIGURE 1.6**
Abstraction of the DES algorithm

## IDEA

Although less visible than DES, the International Data Encryption Algorithm (IDEA) has been classified by some of the contemporary cryptographers as the most secure and reliable block-algorithm [LAI91, ETH92]. Like DES, IDEA encrypts data in 64-bit input blocks; for each it outputs corresponding 64-bit cipher block. It employs the same algorithm for encryption and decryption, with a change in the key schedule during encryption. Unlike DES, IDEA employs 128-bit secret key and dominantly uses operations from three algebraic groups: XOR, addition modulo $2^{16}$, and multiplication modulo $2^{16} + 1$. These operations are combined to make 8 computationally identical rounds followed by an output transformation resulting in the final ciphertext.

## AES

Recently nominated as a candidate to become the Advanced Encryption Standard (AES) [NIST01], a replacement of DES by the U.S. government, Rijndael is an iterated block cipher with a variable block length and a variable key length both of which can independently be 128, 192, or 256 bits. Rijndael's simple and elegant design makes it efficient and fast on modern processors. While it only uses simple whole-byte operations on single- and 4-byte words, and requires a relatively small amount of memory for its implementation. It is suitable for implementations on a wide range of processors including 8-bit hardware for power and space-restricted hardware such as smart cards. It lends itself well to parallel processing and pipelined multi-arithmetic logic unit processors. The Rijndael algorithm is a departure from the traditional so-called Feistel ciphers. Typically in such ciphers parts of the bits in its intermediate states are transposed unchanged. The Rijndael algorithm does not adopt the venerable Feistel structure. Instead, each round of transformations is composed of three distinct invertible transformations that treat each bit of the intermediate state of the cipher in a uniform and similar way.

# Security Services of Secret Key Encryption _____

Secret key encryption can be used to achieve data confidentiality, data integrity, and origin authenticity.

## Confidentiality

Using a secret key algorithm to encipher a data content allows entities with the right secret key only to decrypt and retrieve the original form of the disguised data. Reliability of the confidentiality service afforded by secret key cryptography depends upon the strength of the encryption algorithm, and, more importantly, is dependent upon the length of the key used. Recall that the key length directly affects the size of the corresponding key space. A longer lifetime of a secret key also may contribute to diminishing the assurance in its use for a confidentiality service. The longer a key is used the more likely an exhaustive key search attack will succeed. Most modern security protocols make use of secret keys that remain valid for the lifetime of a particular communications session only.

A confidentiality service enabled through a computationally secure cryptographic algorithm allows users to transmit private information over open networks. Similarly such information can be stored in accessible media without concerned for compromise. Computationally the cost of data confidentiality depends upon the encryption algorithm used and is evidently proportionate to the size of data to be enciphered.

# Secret Key Cryptography and Nonrepudiation  _____

Secret key cryptography alone is not sufficient to prevent the denial of an action that has taken place such as the initiation of an electronic transaction. Despite the fact that one can apply data confidentiality between two communicating entities, the fundamental flaw of a nonrepudiation scheme that is based on secret key cryptography alone is inherent to the fact that the secret key is dispensed to more than one party.

# Origin Authenticity  _____

Data origin authentication is inherently supported by secret key cryptography provided that the key is shared by two entities only. When three or more parties share the same  key, origin authenticity can no longer be provided by secret key cryptography alone. Various secret-key based authentication protocols have been developed.

Figure 1.7 illustrates the steps of a simple secret-key authentication protocol executed by entities $A$ and $B$. Authentication is established by presenting the

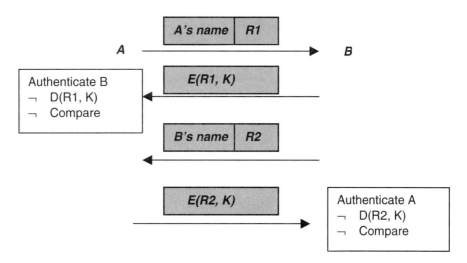

**FIGURE 1.7**
A basic secret-key authentication protocol

proof of possessing the secret key *K*. In order for *A* to authenticate *B*, it first generates a random value *R1*, keeps a copy, and sends *B* a message that contains *R1*. *B* applies *E(R1, K)* to encrypt *R1*, forms a message with *B*'s identity and the encrypted value; then sends it to *A*. In turn, *A* applies *D(R1, K)* to decrypt *R1* and compares the decrypted value with the one it had generated. Similar steps are used to authenticate *A* to *B* with *B* being the initiator and using its own *R2* value.

Authentication protocols such as the one we just described, require careful and thorough reviews. This simple protocol is flawed and is susceptible to what is known as a reflection attack in which an eavesdropper *V* may masquerade as entity *A* and authenticate to *B* as such. *V* takes advantage of the fact that *B* is willing to encrypt any challenge value. *V*, therefore pretending to be *A*, generates *R2* and asks *B* to encrypt it. *B* replies with a random value *R1* for *V* (pretending to be *A*) to encrypt so that it authenticates itself. Meanwhile *V* starts another authentication session with *B* and picks the same value, *R1*, received from the pending authentication session and sends it to *B*, which replies with *R1* encrypted. Now *V* goes back to the first session and sends *B* this encrypted value, therefore authenticating itself to *B* as entity *A*.

One way of fixing this protocol is to insist on always having different values for the challenge from the initiator and that from the responder.

# Data Integrity

At a much lesser cost than encrypting a plaintext in its entirety, both services of data integrity and origin authentication can be afforded by a secret cryptographic scheme using a Message Authentication Code (MAC). Its main component is the digest function.

## Hash Functions

By definition a hash function is a deterministic function that maps a message of arbitrary length to a fixed length string (e.g., 128 or 160 bits) commonly known as a message digest [MERK79, PREN93]. Hash functions are considered to be one of the fundamental primitives in modern cryptography. For a function $H$ to be a hash function, it should satisfy the following properties:

- For an arbitrary input $p$, it is easy to compute $h = H(p)$
- It is computationally infeasible to compute the inverse $p = H^{-1}(h)$, a property that attributes the hash function the one-way hash function name
- It is also computationally infeasible to determine $p'$ such that $H(p) = H(p')$, a property know as collision resistance

The collision resistance characteristic of a hash function is further enhanced by having the function satisfy a property whereby the probability that a randomly picked stream of bytes is mapped to a known $n$-bit hash-value is $2^{(-n)}$.

The fundamental premise here is that the hash value becomes, depending upon the strength of the hashing algorithm, a compact representation of the original data; hence hash value is sometimes referred to as fingerprint. In modern cryptography hash functions are commonly used in providing digital signatures of documents, data integrity, and data origin authentication.

MD5 [RIVE92] and SHA-1 [SHS95] are the most widely used cryptographic hash functions. MD5 yields a 128-bit hash value; SHA-1 results in a 160-bit digest. SHA-1 appears to be a cryptographically stronger function as it presents an enhancement over MD5 and is more resistant to brute force attacks. On the other hand, MD5 edges SHA-1 in computational performance.

The combination of a hash function and a secret key cryptographic scheme yields a MAC, which enables both data integrity and data origin authenticity. In contrast to imply using a hash function to digest a message as is the case in Modification Detection Codes (MDC), the keyed MAC hashing function yields a value that can only be verified by an entity having knowledge of the secret key.

## MAC Examples

One simple method of turning a one-way hash function into a MAC is to encrypt the resulting hash value with a secret-key block algorithm. Similarly, a MAC can be computed by solely using a symmetric block algorithm in a mode such as the cipher block chaining (CBC) [FIPS81]. In this mode we start with a randomly chosen block of data as an initial vector. We perform the XOR of the initial vector with the first block to be encrypted. Then we encrypt the block. The procedure is repeated for the next block using the block that was encrypted last as an initial vector. The cascading nature of this chained feedback is shown in Figure 1.8. The last ciphertext block is encrypted once more in CBC mode, yielding the final MAC value. Known instances of this procedure employ DES and triple DES resulting in DES-MAC and Triple-DES-MAC, respectively.

## HMAC

Other methods of constructing MACs rely solely on keyed one-way hash functions. One simple example would be to prefix or suffix the data to be digested with a secret key. The result is then subjected to the hashing transformation. Another variation consists of prefixing and suffixing the data to

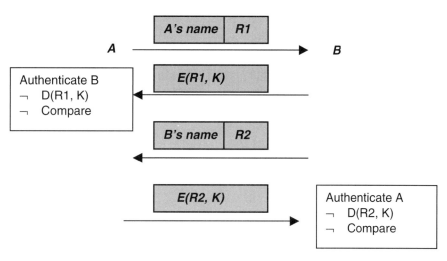

**FIGURE 1.8**
Feedback chaining in a CBC-based MAC algorithm

be digested with the key. Additionally, a more reliable version of such a method includes the length of the data to digest while computing the hash value.

A common method in this category is the keyed hashing for message authentication known as HMAC [KRAW97]. The HMAC algorithm is described using a generic iterative hash function $H$. In practice, however, it has been employed mostly with MD5 and SHA-1.

Let's denote by $b$ the block length of the underlying hash function's input block (64 for both MD5 and SHA-1). The following inner and outer padding values are defined:

- *innerPad* = the byte 0 x 36 repeated $b$ times
- *outerPad* = the byte 0 x 5C repeated $b$ times.

To compute HMAC over an input $p$ we perform:

$$H((K \text{ } XOR \text{ } outerPad) \text{ } | | \text{ } H( \text{ } (K \text{ } XOR \text{ } innerPad) \text{ } | | \text{ } p)),$$

where | | denotes string concatenation. This computation breaks into the following steps:.

1. Append zeros to the end of $K$ to create a $b$ byte string
2. XOR the $b$ byte string computed in step (1) with *innerPad*
3. Append the stream $p$ to the $b$-byte string resulting from step (2)
4. Apply $H$ to the stream generated in step append (3)
5. XOR the $b$ byte string computed in step (1) with *outerPad*
6. Append the $H$ result from step (4) to the $b$ byte string resulting from step (5)
7. Apply $H$ to the stream generated in step (6) and output the result

The effective contribution to the final hash value is accumulated in accordance to function $H$. The procedure is then iteratively applied to each of the remaining blocks.

# Secret Key Distribution and Management

This chapter looks at the scalability of managing secret cryptographic keys. Secret-key cryptographic channels inherently require key distribution to the involved parties so that messages encrypted at one end can be decrypted by the intended recipient. Managing and distributing secret keys in a secure fashion is a problem that increases in complexity with the size of the community involved, the scope of the local security policies, and the patterns involved in the communications.■

## Introduction

Naturally the security services offered through a secret-key cryptographic system require that secret keys be distributed to two or more entities before such services can be used. The key distribution process is also referred to as secret key establishment. Naturally, this process requires distribution through a secure means whether online or out-of-band so as to guard against potential eavesdropping threats. After being distributed, long-term secret keys necessitate secure management processes.

Certainly the key should remain protected while in its storage medium either locally or over a network as well as while being transmitted during the process of a further distribution. Equally important is building and maintaining the key-sharing relationships dictated by the communication patterns adopted by a community of users. Additional key management details may, for instance, require a cryptographic confirmation following the process of a key establishment between two entities. Also, key management processes should support the possibility of updating old key values while supporting countermeasures in the event of a key compromise.

The complexity of these key management functions is proportionate to the type of local policies being enforced. More importantly they depend in great part upon the patterns or webs of communications that a particular community follows. In this chapter we illustrate topologies of the keying relationships that support this assertion.

# Sharing Secret Keys: Topology Effect

Assume that a group of $n$ people decides to use a symmetric cipher in order to establish a cryptographic communications channel among its members. Different scenarios of secret key distribution may arise within the group as a result of the key establishment process. There are four scenarios.

## One key for all

In this scenario the group members share a single secret key and use it for the encryption and the decryption of exchanged messages. The shared secret key requires $n$ distributions, and each user needs to manage a single key. A breach in the key results in all communications among the group members being compromised. Additionally, data origin authentication may not be reliably achievable because a single key is being shared by all entities, thus group members might masquerade under one another's identity. Nonrepudiation services are certainly not achievable in this scenario. Figure 2.1 illustrates the basic scheme in which a single key is shared by all of the community members.

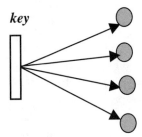

**FIGURE 2.1**
A single secret key shared by all members of a community. Four key distributions are needed

## One key for each user

In this scenario each member of the group decides to use a separate key and thus needs to distribute it $n-1$ times, resulting in a total of $n(n-1)$ key distributions for the whole community. Each member needs to manage his/her key in addition to $n-1$ others for a total of $n$ keys. This scenario is amenable to achieving data origin authentication, but not to nonrepudiation. Since each member of the community knows all the secret keys being used, he/she can mount an eavesdropping attack on communications destined for other community members. The fact that the same secret key of one user is divulged to the rest of the members, makes masquerading of one user under another user's identity a potential security threat.

We model the communication patterns within a community by a directed graph in which the vertices represent the set of users. A directed edge between node $a$ and node $b$ represents the fact that a key distribution step needs to be initiated from $a$ to $b$. The total number of key distributions required would simply be the total number of edges of this directed graph or twice the number of edges in the corresponding undirected graph. Figure 2.2 illustrates this fact for a community of five users.

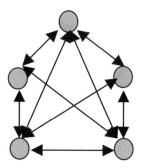

**FIGURE 2.2**
Each entity shares a distinct secret key with the rest of the group members. Arrows indicate the directions of key distributions

## One key for each pair of users

In a third scenario each pair of the group members decides to share a distinct secret key.

The corresponding graph representation would be a complete undirected graph. The total number of edges of this graph—and therefore the number of key distributions required—would be $n(n-1)/2$. Additionally $n-1$ keys (one key shared with each other user) need to be stored and managed by every user as illustrated in Figure 2.3. Compromising one key results only in the communications between the underlying pair of users breached.

| (bob, alice) | $K_1$ |
|---|---|
| (bob, elyes) | $K_2$ |
| . . . | |
| (bob, karim) | $K_{n-1}$ |

**FIGURE 2.3**
Managing the keying relationship by each user when each pair of users is sharing a single key

## A separate key for each user

In another scenario each user may use a distinct key to communicate with each member of the group, resulting in a total of $n(n-1)$ key distributions (twice the number of edges in the indirect graph representation). Additionally, now each user needs to manage $n-1$ keys that are used to communicate with each other user while each other user will trust him/her with one key for a total of $n-1$ additional keys. In total each user needs to manage $2(n-1)$ keys as illustrated in Figure 2.4. This number is twice as many as is required in the case of sharing distinct keys across each pair of users.[1]

Figure 2.5 depicts three variations in the communication patterns that can take place within a group of seven users. Each member of the group is represented by a node of a graph; with the edge adjacency in the graph representing two-way communication links among the members. Assuming that each user maintains a distinct secret key, the total number of key distributions in each scenario will be equal to twice the number of edges of the corresponding graph. Therefore, in **(a)** 14 key distributions are required; in **(b)** where users are partitioned along a bipartite graph, will require 24 key distributions; in the case of a complete graph as in **(c)** where each user needs to communicate with the rest of the group, 34 key distributions are needed.

---

1. Note that this scenario does not have any practical advantage over sharing distinct keys across each pair of users.

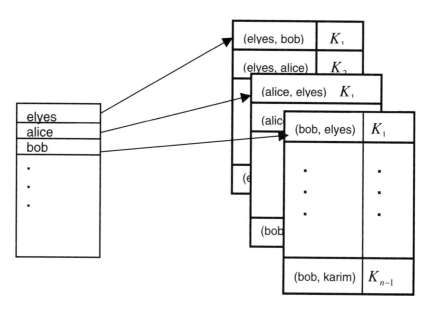

**FIGURE 2.4**
Managing separate keys for each member of a community

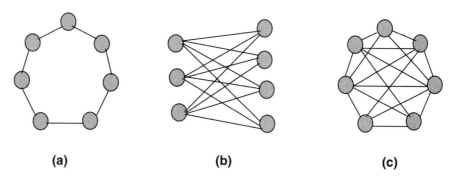

**(a)**                                      **(b)**                                      **(c)**

**FIGURE 2.5**
Secret key distribution is directly proportionate to the underlying communication pattern

These scenarios point out that the number of secret key distributions is increasingly proportionate to the number of communication links among the group of users. As we have seen, the policies that drive the keying relationships among a group of users may also contribute to the complexity of key distribution. Upon renewal of a secret key, the key distribution process takes place over again.

Naturally, the more frequently a secret key is to be distributed, the more it becomes likely to be the subject of a compromise. A key can be compromised while it is maintained on a storage medium or while in transmission during a distribution. The distribution and exposure of long-term secret keys to management processes, in essence, act against the core premise of the symmetric key cryptography in that the strength of such systems lies in the secrecy of the key.

# Central Secret Key Management

Advances in software systems have mitigated the security risks posed by secret key distribution and management operations. One such advance proposes a solution that adopts a central repository of keys, managed by a single server commonly referred to as the Key Distribution Center (KDC). Here each of the communicating entities divulges its secret key to the KDC only, resulting in a number of key distributions equal to the size $n$ of the community involved in using such a system. Each participating entity becomes no longer concerned with the management of secret keys including its own.

Figure 2.6 illustrates the novel concept introduced in the third-party key distribution center. Third party indicates the neutrality of the server with respect to each entity in the system. Each entity trusts only the KDC and distrusts the rest of entities except when access is brokered through the KDC.

The mere presence of a KDC alone, however, is not sufficient to disseminate the secret keys across the community of users. A security protocol is needed to introduce the communicating parties and perform the brokering step. In a way entities establish their trust in one another by way of trusting the KDC server while it acts as a broker that presents one entity to another.

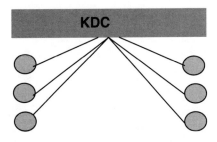

**FIGURE 2.6**
A centralized key management scheme

# The Needham-Schroeder Scheme _____

The Needham-Schroeder scheme described in [NEED78] presented a novel method for achieving the secure introduction of entities that we alluded to in the previous section. As a result of the entity introduction proposed by this scheme, authentication as well as the rest of the cryptographic security service are achieved by using a temporary secret key. This key is generated by the KDC for a short duration, and is pertinent to a single communication session binding two entities.

Here is a summary of the protocol steps executed by two entities, **A** and **B**, along with the KDC to arrive at a session key. Preceding these protocol steps is a setup procedure in which both **A** and **B** establish secret keys $K_a$ and $K_b$, respectively, with the KDC. We denote by $K_{a,b}$ a key that is shared between $a$ and $b$. We denote by $E_{a,b}$ some secret key encryption procedure that uses a key shared between entities $a$ and $b$.

- To initiate the protocol sequence, entity **A** signals its intention to do so by requesting attention from the KDC. It sends a message that contains the identity of **A** and **B** and a random number, $N_a$.

$$\boxed{\text{A} \mid \text{B} \mid N_a}$$

$$\text{A} \longrightarrow \text{KDC} \qquad (1)$$

- KDC generates a session key, $K$. It then forms a message containing $K$ and the identity of **A**; and encrypts it with $K_{b,kdc}$ (shared with **B**). The result is further concatenated with **A**'s random number $N_a$, **B**'s identity, and the session key $K$, and finally encrypted using $K_{a,kdc}$.

$$\boxed{E_{a,kdc}\ (N_a, B, K,\ E_{b,kdc}(K,A))}$$

$$\text{KDC} \qquad (2)$$
$$\text{A} \longleftarrow \qquad\qquad\qquad$$

- **A** uses its own key and decrypts the message received in the previous step, thus unveiling the session key, $K$. It then verifies that the random nonce, $N_a$, is the same as what was sent to the KDC in the first step and sends **A** the portion of the message that the KDC encrypted with **B**'s secret key.

$$\boxed{E_{b,kdc}(K,A)}$$

**A** ——————————————▶ **B**                    (3)

- **B** uses its own key that it shares with the KDC, $K_{b,kdc}$, and decrypts the message received in the prior step, thus unveiling the session key, $K$. It then generates a random value $N_b$, encrypts it using $K$, and sends it to **A**.

$$\boxed{E_K(N_b)}$$

**A** ◀—————————————— **B**                    (4)

- **A** decrypts the message of the previous step, computes $N_b\text{-}1$; encrypts it with $K$, and sends it to **B**.

$$\boxed{E_K(N_b\text{-}1)}$$

**A** ◀—————————————— **B**                    (5)

- **B** decrypts the previous message and verifies that it indeed received the value $N_b\text{-}1$. This step is used to prevent against message replay attacks.
- Now $K$ can be used to encrypt any data that **A** and **B** may exchange over the established channel.

## Kerberos

Later advancement in the third-party authentication protocols came in as a variant of the Needham-Schroeder scheme in what is known as the *Kerberos* protocol. This widely deployed security protocol has proven to be one of the best third-party authentication schemes ever devised. Its concepts are directly derived from the Needham-Schroeder protocol we discussed in the previous section. Ironically, Kerberos development has been given much more credit and attention in the security literature than the originators of the trusted third-party concept. Its credit is due to taking the concept of a trusted third-party key management a step further, making it more amenable to practical implementations. This feature is mainly expressed in its core enhancement to the Needham-Schroeder scheme by way of adding the time stamp and the lifetime constructs to a session key. In doing so it sets a time constraint on a session key so that the effect of a compromise becomes limited.

Kerberos certainly encompasses more than an authentication protocol. The completion of its steps results in a secure distribution of a session key. The latter forms the basis in establishing a cryptographic channel between entities without having to divulge any long-term keys. Entities using the Kerberos protocol authenticate each other without having to rely on the local host operating system, or requiring physical security of the underlying hosts running the applications. The entities work under the assumption of an open network in which traveling packets can be read, modified, and inserted at will.

Kerberos Version 5 has been integrated in a number of operating systems and has become an Internet standard [KOHL83]. With all its protocol elegance and security, it still has shortcomings in today's pervasive paradigm of computing over the Internet. For one thing, the use of the third-party KDC server requires its online availability to the communicating parties for the introduction step to take place. Additionally, the presence of a secure time source is needed to guarantee the reliability of generated session keys. Most importantly, the requirement for the online presence of the KDC server does not lend itself to the paradigm of ubiquitous Internet computing. The KDC, in maintaining all the secret keys, becomes a single point of a catastrophic failure once it is compromised.

# A Note about Secret Key Distribution

The problem with secret key distribution is not as much related to the extent of the number of distributions needed to propagate the keys as it is to finding a reliably secure channel for achieving the distribution task [ANSI85, BALE85]. Because of the recursive nature of this problem, secret key cryptographic systems alone cannot resolve the key distribution issue. In the next chapter we examine public key cryptography that exhibits a novel characteristic that deals away with the key distribution problem found in secret key cryptography.

# Public Key Cryptography

3

We present the foundations of public key cryptography and outline the mathematical processes behind such cryptosystems. Then we discuss some of the common public key cryptographic algorithms. Subsequently, we elaborate on the services that public key systems offer and how they compare to secret key cryptosystems. Finally, we introduce the concept of trusting a public key as a prelude to the fundamental topic of the book. ■

## Foundations of Public Key Cryptography _____

Public key cryptography emerged in the mid-1970s with the work published by Whitfield Diffie and Martin Hellman [DIFF76a] as well as by Ralph Merkle [MERK78]. The concept is simple and eloquent yet it has had far reaching impacts on the science of cryptography and its applications as a whole. Public key cryptography is based on the notion that encryption keys come in related pairs, private and public. The private key remains concealed by the key owner while the public key is freely disseminated. Data encrypted using the public key can only be decrypted using the associated private key and vice versa.

In the following we consider a simple example that illustrates the dual key concept of public key cryptographic systems. We restrict our plaintext to the 26 letter English alphabet plus the blank character—a total of 27 characters. We then assign numerical equivalents to our plaintext alphabet sequentially from the integral domain of [0...26] with the blank assigned the numerical 26. We consider our encryption function, $E$, to be the affine transformation that takes in a plaintext character $P$ and maps it into a ciphertext, $C$, as follows:

$$E(P) = (a*P + b) \bmod 27 = C$$

with $a$ and $b$ being fixed integers. Solving for $P$ in terms of $C$ in the prior equation yields the inverse transformation, decryption $D$.

$$D(C) = (\text{a'}*C + \text{b'}) \bmod 27, \text{ where}$$

$$a' = a^{-1} \bmod 27, \text{ and}$$

$$b' = -a^{-1}*b$$

For $a$ to be invertible while computing in $\mathbf{Z}/27\mathbf{Z}$ it is necessary and sufficient to have $a$ and 27 relatively prime. That is to say there is no number which divides both $a$ and 27 but for the trivial divisor of 1. Note that this condition guarantees a one-to-one mapping between P and C. $\mathbf{Z}/27\mathbf{Z}$ is the set of equivalence classes (residue classes) with respect to the relationship of congruence *modulo* 27.

The parameterized affine transformation in the example and its inverse can be used for a basic public key cryptosystem with the private and public keys being $(a, b)$ and $(a', b')$, respectively. An example would be to have $a = 2$ and $b = 1$, $(a', b') = (14, -14)$. A special scenario arises when setting $a = 1$ which yields a shifting transformation with a shifting constant of $b$ in the range [0...26]. This yields

$$(a, b) = (a', b') = (1, b)$$

which is the case of a symmetric key cryptographic system). We had encountered this type of transformation earlier in Chapter 1.

In practice, however, such a public key cryptographic system is easily defeated even with its generalization to longer blocks instead of single characters. A block of size $s$ yields a ciphering transformation that maps each block to a value in the range $[0...N^s-1]$ where $N$ is the size of the alphabet. The weakness of this algorithm rests in the ease by which a decryption key can be deduced from an encryption key in a deterministic fashion, using very simple operations (multiplication and additions *modulo* $(N^s-1)$). But first and foremost is the fact that the encryption function admits a deterministic inverse function.

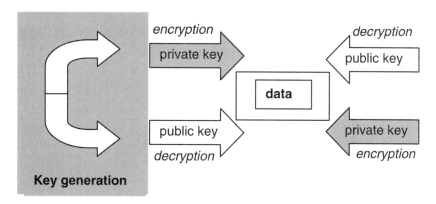

**FIGURE 3.1**
The public key encryption concept

The key premise behind public key cryptography is that it should be computationally infeasible to compute the private key by simply knowing the public key. Figure 3.1 illustrates this novel concept of public key cryptography.

Modern public key cryptography derives from eloquent mathematical foundations that are based on the one-way trapdoor functions existing in the abstractions of number theory. Encryption is the easy one-way trapdoor, decryption is the hard direction. Only with knowledge of the trapdoor (the private key) can decryption be as easy as encryption. Two of these currently known trapdoor one-way functions form the basis of modern public key cryptography and we discuss them in the next sections.

## The Problem of Factoring Large Numbers

The first of the well-known trapdoor one-way functions is based on the ease of multiplying two large prime numbers; while the reverse, factoring a very large number, is a far more complex task. Factoring an integer $n$ is the process of finding a series of prime factors, such that their products yields $n$. A prime number, by definition, is one that has no divisors other than 1 and itself; otherwise a number is called composite. Factoring large numbers (over *1,024* bits) is known to be computationally infeasible with today's computers and technology. Modular arithmetic renders the multiplication of such numbers a far easier task. Consequently, the one-way trapdoor problem here is to make a very large number public knowledge, and secretly maintain its prime factors. Note that the trapdoor function discussed here requires deciding on whether or not a randomly picked very large number is prime. Primality testing is a much easier task than the actual factorization [GORD85].

A number of methods have been devised to determine the primality of an odd number $N$. The most trivial of which is to run through the odd numbers starting with 3 and determine if any of such numbers divides $N$. The process should terminate when we reach $\sqrt{N}$. Due to the time complexity that this method requires, in practice it is stopped much earlier before reaching $\sqrt{N}$, and is used as a first step in a series of more complicated primality test methods.

With this in mind, we now summarize the widely adopted Rivest-Shamir-Adleman (RSA) public key algorithm.

## RSA Algorithm

The following are the steps needed to arrive at the public/private key pair of the RSA cryptosystem.

- Randomly pick two large prime numbers $p$, and $q$ (*100* to *200* decimal digits). We compute the product $n = p*q$.
- Compute $\varphi(n) = (p-1)*(q-1) = n + 1 - p - q$.
- *Randomly select another number e* that is relatively prime to *(n)*; i.e., the great common divisor of $e$ and $\varphi(n)$ is equal to 1.
- Then use the extended Euclidean algorithm to compute the multiplicative inverse, *d, of e modulo* $\varphi(n)$.

*The numbers e* and $n$ define the public key and are known as the *exponent* and the *modulus*, respectively; $d$ and $n$ define the private key. Both encryption and the inverse function of decryption simply consist of modular reduction operations that map an element of $\mathbf{Z}/n\mathbf{Z}$ to another element of $\mathbf{Z}/n\mathbf{Z}$, where $\mathbf{Z}/n\mathbf{Z}$ is the set of residue classes *modulo n*. For any block of plaintext $T$, the following equations hold:

$$C = f(T) = T^e \bmod n, \text{ and}$$

$$T = f^{-1}(C) = C^d \bmod n$$

Computing both $f(T)$ and its inverse is optimized using modular reduction techniques  such as the method of exponentiation by the repeated squaring method that we discuss in the next section.

In simple terms the RSA algorithm centers around three numbers, the public exponent, $e$; the private exponent, $d$; and the modulus, $n$. The private and public values make use of the common modulus value and each is the exponential inverse of the other under the modulus $\varphi(n)$. A block of plaintext whose numerical equivalent is less than the modulus is raised to the power $e$ *mod n* in order to yield the ciphertext. Conversely, when the ciphertext is raised to the power $d$ modulo $n$ it results in recovering the plaintext.

# Computing Modular Exponentiations

To encrypt or decrypt a message the RSA algorithm interprets a block of data in either plaintext or ciphertext form as a very large number which is then raised to a large power. Note here that the length of the block is appropriately sized and should be less than the modulus. Computing such exponentiations would be very time-consuming if it were not for an eloquent property that the operation of exponentiation in modular arithmetic exhibits. This property is known as the modular exponentiation by the repeated squaring method. For instance, when raising an integer $a$ to the eighth power, instead of performing seven multiplications and one large modular reduction, we perform three smaller multiplications and three simple modular reductions:

$$a^8 \bmod n = ((a^2 \bmod n)^2 \bmod n)^2 \bmod n$$

The ease of such exponentiation operation remains applicable even with the exponent not being a power of 2.

Consider the following example of computing

$$399^{157} \bmod 457$$

First note that

$$157 = 128 + 16 + 8 + 4 + 1$$

Now we perform the following iterative computations:

$399 \bmod 457 = 399$ which represents $399^1 \bmod 456$

$399^2 = 159201$ and $159201 \bmod 457 = 165$ which represents $399^2 \bmod 457$

$165^2 = 27225$ and $27225 \bmod 457 = 262$ which represents $399^4 \bmod 457$

$262^2 = 68644$ and $68644 \bmod 457 = 94$ which represents $399^8 \bmod 457$

$94^2 = 8836$ and $8836 \bmod 457 = 153$ which represents $399^{16} \bmod 457$

$153^2 = 23409$ and $23409 \bmod 457 = 102$ which represents $399^{32} \bmod 457$

$102^2 = 10404$ and $10404 \bmod 457 = 350$ which represents $399^{64} \bmod 457$

$350^2 = 122500$ and $122500 \bmod 457 = 24$ which represents $399^{128} \bmod 457$

Therefore

$$399^{157} \bmod 457 = 24 * 153 * 94 * 262 * 399 \bmod 457$$

Because

$$(a * b) \bmod n = ((a \bmod n) * (b \bmod n)) \bmod n$$

this computation, in turn, can be split into:

$$24 * 153 \bmod 457 = 16 \text{ and } 94 * 262 * 399 \bmod 457 = 158$$

And finally yielding

$$399^{157} \bmod 457 = 16 * 158 \bmod 457 = 243$$

Breaking the RSA algorithm is conjectured to be equivalent to factoring the product of two large prime numbers. This is because one has to extract the modulus from the public key value and proceed to factor it. With the complexity of the fastest known factoring algorithm being in the order of

$$e^{((\log n)^{1/3} \, * \, (\log \log n)^{2/3})}$$

where $n$ is the total number of the binary bits in the modulus. This roughly means every additional 10 bits make the modulus 10 times harder to factor. With the state of factoring numbers where it is today, it is strongly believed that keys with 2,048 bits are far secure in the future. The fastest known factoring algorithm to date is the number field sieve.

## Computing Discrete Logarithms in a Large Finite Field

The second well-known trapdoor one-way function that exists in number theory is the ease of computing a function $f$ that consists of raising a number to a power in a large finite field, while the inverse function, $f^{-1}$, of computing discrete logarithms in such a field is known to be a much harder problem. A finite field, also known as a Galois field, denoted by GF($p$) is the field of integers modulo a prime number $p$, and thus each element, $a$, of GF($p$) is guaranteed to have a multiplicative inverse $a^{-1}$ that is also in GF($p$) such that

$$a * a^{-1} = 1 \bmod p$$

The time complexity required for the computation of $f(x) = a^x = y$ in $\mathbf{Z}/p\mathbf{Z}$ is polynomial in $\log x$. Computing $x = f^{-1}(y) = \log_b(y)$ given $y$ is a much harder task known as the discrete logarithm problem. Here both $x$ and $y$ are constrained to be elements of the discrete set $\mathbf{Z}/p\mathbf{Z}$ as opposed to the much easier continuous problem in the set of real numbers for instance; hence the use of discrete in qualifying this problem.

The one-way trapdoor function as defined by the discrete logarithm problem can be stated as follows:

> Knowing $a$ and $x$ it is an easy operation to compute $a^x$ in $\mathbf{Z}/p\mathbf{Z}$ (using the repeated-squaring method). On the other hand if we keep $x$ secret and hand someone the value $y$ that we know is of the form $a^x$ and ask to determine the power of $a$ that gives $y$; they can use up all the computing resources they have available but will indefinitely fail to hand back a response.

A number of modern public key cryptographic algorithms are based on the discrete logarithm one-way trapdoor function. Because of the simplicity that they exhibit, we use ElGamal cryptographic system [ELGA95] and the Diffie-Hellman key exchange algorithm [DIFF76b] as representatives of the discrete logarithm process.

## ELGamal Cryptosystem

Here the private deciphering key, $x$, is a randomly chosen number from a very large finite field GF($p$) such that $0 < x < p\text{-}1$. Similarly, a second number, $g$, is randomly picked in GF($p$). The public key becomes the value $g^x$ computed over GF($p$). Encrypting a block of plaintext $T$ consists of picking a third random number $k$; we then compute, in GF($p$), the pair of ciphers

$$(C_1, C_2) = (g^k, Tg^{xk})$$

Note here that computing $g^{xk} \bmod p$ does not require knowledge of the secret $x$.

To decrypt the ciphertext $(C_1, C_2)$, we compute

$$T = C_2/C_1^x \bmod p$$

Since in GF($p$) we have

$$Tg^{xk}/(g^k)^x = T$$

It is worth noting that this cryptosystem results in a ciphertext that is twice the size of its plaintext. ElGamal algorithm originated as a signature scheme and can therefore be used for both digital signatures and encryption.

## The Diffie-Hellman Key Exchange System

The Diffie-Hellman key agreement algorithm is an eloquent procedure for use by two entities in order to establish a secret cryptographic key over a public network without the risk of exchanging secrets. Indeed it presents an eloquent solution to the secret key distribution problem. The security of the algorithm relates to the one-way trapdoor function found in the discrete logarithm problem. The mathematics encompassed in the algorithm is fairly simple. First the two entities agree on a large prime number, $n$, and a second number $g$ such that $g$ is primitive *mod n*. The last property ensures that every element in $Z/pZ$; i.e., from 1 through $p-1$ can be expressed as

$$g^a = b \bmod p \text{ for some integer value } a.$$

These two values, $g$ and $n$, can be exchanged over a public network. Each of the entities, **A** and **B**, then proceeds to generate a secret key according to the following steps.

---

**A** randomly picks a large value $x$ and sends **B**

$$X = g^x \bmod n$$

**B** picks a random large integer $y$ and sends **A**

$$Y = g^y \bmod n$$

A deduces the secret key by computing

$$K = Y^x \bmod n = (g^y \bmod n)^x \bmod n = g^{xy} \bmod n$$

**B** computes the same key value from

$$K = X^y \bmod n = (g^x \bmod n)^y \bmod n = g^{xy} \bmod n$$

---

The result is that **A** and **B** now have established a shared secret key without having to exchange secret information. This goes deep into using classical secret key cryptography without having to be concerned over secret key distribution. Note the security of this key agreement process is based upon the fact that it is computationally infeasible to compute $g^{xy}$ by simply knowing the public values $g^x$ and $g^y$.

## Elliptic Curves Cryptographic Systems

Elliptic curves over finite fields have been proposed for use with existing public key cryptographic systems [KOBL87, MILL86]. Given a point $P$ over an elliptic curve $E$, and an integer $a$, the one-way function here consists of the ease of computing the product $a*P$ ; while the inverse of finding $a$ such that $a*P$ results in a point over $E$ is intractable. One straightforward application of this one-way function to Diffie-Hellman is for two entities **A** and **B** to publicly agree on a point $P$ over $E$. To generate the key, the initiating entity, **A**, picks a random large integer $a$, computes $a*P$ over $E$ and sends it to the entity **B**. The latter performs a similar computation and sends entity **A** the result of $b*P$. Both entities then compute the secret key

$$K=a*b*P$$

which is a point over $E$.

# The Fate of Secret Key Cryptography _____

The advent of public key cryptography did not signal the end of secret key cryptography. Rather, it has evolved into an interesting aspect of conveniently complementing one cryptographic method by the other. Public and secret key cryptography together make the core of most cryptographic protocols in use today. Such a marriage gave rise to what is known as *hybrid* cryptographic systems. Here a public key system is used for the distribution of a secret key, which can be a long-term key or might be specific to a particular communications session. Thereafter, the securely distributed secret key is used to encrypt and decrypt a communications channel between two end points of a security protocol. The performance of secret key cryptography over that of public key, and the appeal of key distribution inherent to public key cryptography, are the main driving reasons behind the wide adoption of these hybrid systems. Most notable and elegant of such systems is the Diffie-Helleman key exchange algorithm used for secret key agreement over a non-secure channel.

# Public Key Cryptography Services_____

## Confidentiality

Obviously public key cryptography from its origins enables data encipher-ing. The strength of enciphering depends upon the specific algorithm that is used as well as the length of the keys adopted. In general, the strength of each algorithm is directly related to the type of the one-way trapdoor func-tion used. The ones we have discussed, namely factoring a very large num-ber and computing the discrete logarithm problem, are known to be reliable processes within the scope of current computing means and, to a broader extent, the theoretic knowledge available today.

RSA is the most widely used public key encryption algorithm. The premise of the privacy service here is achieved by way of encrypting data using the recipient's public key, and the fact that decryption can only be done by way of using the recipient's private key. Thus, only the recipient with knowledge of the private key is able to decrypt the enciphered data. It is worth noting that such a privacy service strongly depends on the assurance in the fact that a public key legitimately belongs to the recipient.

## Data Origin Authenticity

This service is inherently achieved by way of encrypting data using the pri-vate key. Because the private key is assumed to remain confined to the owner, decrypting data using the matching public key automatically proves the iden-tity of the originator. Performing encryption using the public key and decryp-tion using the private key does not yield origin authenticity. In practice, however, digital signatures are the preferred method of achieving data origin authenticity, thereby avoiding the encryption of large amounts of data.

## Data Integrity

Confidentiality amounts to encrypting data using a publicly available key. Naturally, an eavesdropper may intercept the data, substitute new data for the old, and encrypt it using the same public key. By simply applying a public key algorithm to achieve privacy in this manner does not necessarily yield data integrity. Alternatively, in this scenario, data integrity can be achieved by way of encrypting the data using the private key and thus decryption will take place only using the matching public key. This procedure, however, does not yield message privacy. Figure 3.2 illustrates the relationship between data privacy and integrity when a public-key encryption is used.

Data origin authentication, integrity, and privacy services can coexist using public key encryption and digital signatures as we discuss next.

## Nonrepudiation

With the fundamental premise that the private key remains in the confines of its owner, decrypting a message using the associated public key leaves no possibility for the originator to deny involvement. Denial, however, can always take place on the basis that a private key has been compromised. A strong nonrepudiation service as such is one that never exposes the private keys it manages, even to the owner. Tamperproof hardware modules for burying private keys become necessary in building any nonrepudiation service. Nonrepudiation as such, however, may be hard to become legally binding.

## Key Distribution

Public key cryptography can be used for secret key establishment over a public network. Simply put, the secret key now constitutes the data that needs to be distributed with a privacy requirement. Thus, the secret key is encrypted using the public key of the target entity. The receiving entity uses its private key to decrypt the enciphered key, thus having established a com-

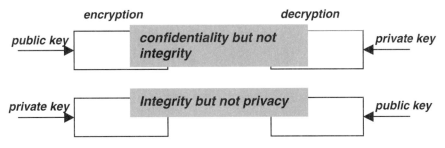

**FIGURE 3.2**
Achieving data privacy versus integrity when using a public key encryption algorithm

mon secret key with the sending entity. Note here that authenticating the identity of the sending entity is a strong security requirement. A breach in such a key establishment mechanism risks exposing the entire crypto-graphic channel that follows key establishment.

## Diffie-Hellman

The Diffie-Hellman algorithm is a classical choice for secret key establish-ment, the generalization of which extends quite easily to a community of $n$ users. Consider a scenario in which three entities **A**, **B**, and **C**, need to share a common secret key using the Diffie-Hellman process.

- First, **A**, **B**, and **C** exchange the public values $g$ and $n$; then each gener-ates private values $x$, $y$ and $z$, respectively (Figure 3.3a).
- As illustrated in Figure 3.3b, entity **A** computes $X$ and sends it to entity **B**. In turn, entity **B** computes $Y$ and sends it to **C**; entity **C** computes $Z$ and sends it to **A**.
- In the second round each respective entity makes use of its private value as well as the quantity that it had received from its peer during the previous step. This quantity is then raised to the power of the pri-vate value that only the respective entity knows, and then communi-cated to the neighboring peer in a circular fashion (Figure 3.3b).
- Now each entity, knowing its own secret value, computes the shared secret (bottom of Figure 3.3b).

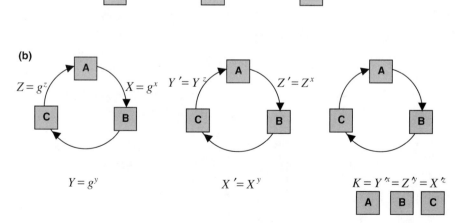

**FIGURE 3.3**
Diffie-Hellman key agreement performed by a group of three entities

The generalization of this scheme to a population of $n$ users extends in the same manner as we illustrated for three users. First the entities can be pictured around a circle with each entity communicating with its immediate peer in a clockwise fashion. The loop illustrated in Figure 3.3b is then performed $n-1$ times. In each iteration, the quantity last received from the peer is raised to the power of the private value, then communicated to the next peer.

## Diffie-Hellman Through a Public Directory

One other aspect of applying the Diffie-Hellman key agreement protocol within a community of users is to have each entity publish its public Diffie-Hellman component to a publicly accessible directory. Entity **A** wishing to establish a secret key with entity **B**, looks up the Diffie-Hellman public value for entity **B** out of the directory, then computes the key. Likewise, entity **B** retrieves the Diffie-Hellman public component of **A** and computes the same secret key. This scheme enables the members of a community to establish secret keys with one another without exchanging any secrets as opposed to exchanging $n(n-1)/2$ secret keys like we saw in the previous chapter. Figure 3.4 depicts the Diffie-Hellman process via a public directory.

Note that the Diffie-Hellman key agreement scheme does not have identity authentication embedded into it. One has to rely on an additional authentication mechanism while engaged in this key agreement protocol. Simply put, entity **A** is not assured of the identity of entity **B** with which it had just entered into a key agreement exchange.

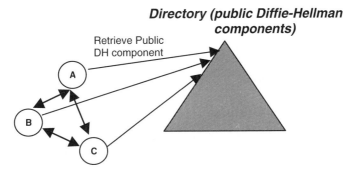

**FIGURE 3.4**
Achieving Diffie-Hellman key agreement using a public directory

## Authenticated Key Exchange

The Encrypted Key Exchange (EKE) algorithm proposed by Bellovin and Merritt embeds entity authentication in a key agreement protocol, and thus prevents against a masquerading entity coming into the key agreement exchange. This provides assurance in establishing a secure channel only between legitimate entities. The steps of the EKE are summarized as follows:

- We assume entities **A** and **B** share a single password, $p$.
- **A** generates a public key pair; uses $p$ along with a symmetric algorithm to encrypt the public key portion and sends **B** its identity as well as the encrypted public key.
- **B** uses $p$ to decrypt the public key; generates a session key, $K$, encrypts it with the public key and sends it to entity **A**.
- **A** uses the private key to decrypt the session key.

Subsequently the two entities enter into a challenge/response exchange encrypted using the newly established session key. The EKE algorithm can be used to leverage the Diffie-Hellman key exchange by way of encrypting the public value of one entity using a one-way transform of the shared password.

Recently, the Internet Engineering Task Force (IETF) through RFC2875 [PRAF00] recommended an algorithm that provides for the proof of possession of the private keys when the public key is to be used for a Diffie-Hellman key agreement process. Specifically this RFC applies to the scenario in which a public Diffie-Hellman key is requested for certification via the Public Key Cryptographic Standard (PKCS#10) messaging format from RSA, Inc. Traditionally, PKCS#10 assumes that the public key being requested for certification corresponds to an algorithm capable of signing data. Although the recommendation applies to a specific context, it can be generalized for any Diffie-Hellman key exchange.

## Kerberos and Public Key Encryption

The Kerberos community has drafted a proposal to the IETF that defines a public key-based alternative to obtaining a master session key. Specifically the proposal addresses the use of public keys during the initial authentication with the KDC server. Extensions to the original Kerberos protocol have been proposed to allow a client to make use of his/her public key along with a digital signature instead of the conventional secret key. Upon receipt of this request, the KDC verifies the signature and issues a ticket granting ticket (TGT) for the client as before. The protected portion of the reply message carrying the TGT is now encrypted utilizing either a Diffie-Hellman derived key or the user's public key. This message is authenticated through the public key signature of the KDC.

The advantages provided by leveraging Kerberos with public key cryptography include simplified key management (i.e., the KDC is no longer required to securely manage a potentially large number of secret keys). For each principal the KDC provides the flexibility of having to maintain a conventional secret key, a public key, or both. Additionally, such a scheme maintains Kerberos as a viable key distribution protocol even with the advent of public key cryptography and its applications.

# Digital Signatures

The advent of public key cryptography combined with one-way hash functions gave rise to the digital signing of a document that inherently enables data origin authentication and withstands repudiation. Using the private key of a public key pair to encrypt a data stream automatically binds the subject with whom the key is associated to the data. The cost of encrypting an entire document in order to simply establish this binding can be prohibitive. Fortunately, the alternative is eloquent and computationally affordable as it does not require encrypting an entire document. Two of the well-known digital signature algorithms are RSA and DSA.

## RSA Signature

The RSA digital signature algorithm proceeds along two main steps

- Using one of the common hashing algorithms such as MD5 or Secure Hash Algorithm (SHA-1), a document is first digested into a much smaller representation, a hash value.

- Encryption is applied to the hash instead of an entire document

Provided there is no need for a confidentiality service, the signed document is then transmitted in its cleartext form and the signature is provided to the recipient for verification.

Figure 3.5 illustrates the RSA signature computation and verification procedures.

## DSA Signature

Other types of digital signatures rely on algorithms that are solely designed for signing but not encryption. An example is the standard Digital Signature Algorithm (DSA) that is a U.S. government standard [DSS94]. DSA computes a signature over an input of arbitrary size, and makes use of a one-

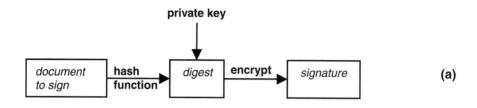

**(a)**

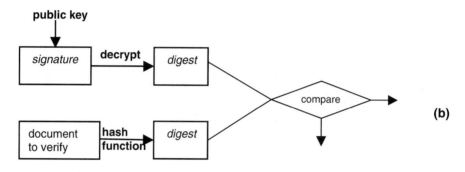

**(b)**

**FIGURE 3.5**
(a) generating a RSA signature; and (b) verifying the signature

way hash function specified in the standard as SHA-1. It uses five public parameters and a private key. The key length in DSA is extended to 1,024 bits after it was originally limited to 512 bits only.

The final signature over a plaintext P consists of two 160-bit integers $(r, s)$ with

$$r = (g^k \bmod p) \bmod q$$
$$s = (k^{-1} (hash(P) + xr)) \bmod q$$

The verification step is performed using the public components of the DSA key in conjunction with the value $s$, and the message. A successful verification leads to finding the quantity $v$ equal to the signature value $r$ using the following formulae.

$$w = s^{-1} \bmod q$$
$$u_1 = (hash(P) * w) \bmod q$$
$$u_2 = rw \bmod q$$
$$v = ((g^{u_1} * y^{u_2}) \bmod p) \bmod q$$

where $p$ is a prime number ranging from 512 to 1024 bits (a multiple of 64). $q$ is a 160-bit prime factor of $p$-1; $k$ is a random number less than $q$ generated by the signer, and $x$ (the private key) is an integer less than $q$; $y$ is a $p$-bit number that sastisfies $y = g^x \bmod p$ while $g$ is computed as

$$g = h^{(p-1)/q} \bmod p$$

with $h$ being an integer less than $p$-$1$ such that

$$h^{(p-1)/q} \bmod p > 1$$

DSA implementation can be speeded up by precomputing the value $r$ as it does not depend on the signed data. Figure 3.6 illustrates signing and verification procedures used in the DSA.

## Hybrid Public Key Services

Combining digital signatures and encryption in public key cryptography can yield elegant and reliable schemes for simultaneously achieving most of the security services offered by public key cryptosystems. Consider the following scenario in which entity **A** wishes to communicate with entity **B** over a cryptographic channel with the intent of achieving data integrity, privacy, and origin authentication.

- Entity **A** computes a digest of the message, encrypts it, and signs the message.

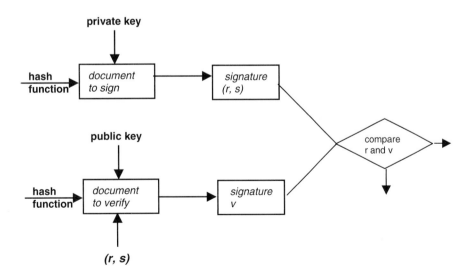

**FIGURE 3.6**
Signature generation and verification using the DSA scheme

- Entity **A** concatenates the message and its signature with well-defined delimiters, then encrypts the result with **B**'s public key and sends the message to **B**.

- Entity **B** uses its private key to decrypt the message, achieving data privacy.

- Entity **B** extracts both the signature and the data from the message, then proceeds to verify the signature on the message using **A**'s public key, therefore achieving data integrity, origin authentication, and non-repudiation.

The signature in this scenario is wrapped inside a confidentiality envelope allowing each of the communicating entities to use its own private key and the other entity's public key as illustrated in Figure 3.7.

Note here that the use of a time stamp, or a random nonce for instance, in these protocol steps would prevent against replaying messages by eavesdroppers.

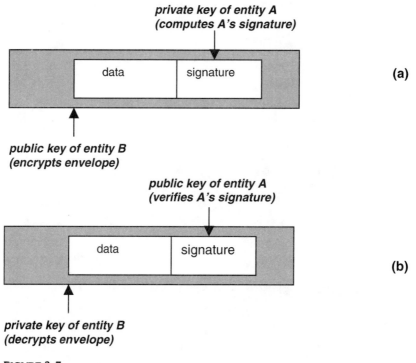

**FIGURE 3.7**
(a) Computing a cryptographic envelope and (b) opening the envelope

# Trusting a Public Key

From the outset, public key cryptography seems to eloquently solve the key distribution and management problem introduced by secret key cryptography. Anyone can use the public key to encrypt data, but only the owner of the private key can decrypt it. The community of users in our example that had concerns over key distribution issues, now can adopt a public key cryptographic system for securing its communications, dispelling concerns over key distribution and simply sharing a repository that maintains the public keys of its members.

Consider the scenario in which Elyes and Aicha, two members of this community, wish to communicate with each other through a secure channel. Elyes looks up the public key for Aicha from the repository of keys, then uses it to encrypt and send a message to Aicha. A third person, Alice, wants to listen in on this communications channel mounting the attack illustrated in Figure 3.8. Before any communication takes place, in step 1, Alice replaces the public key of Aicha in the key repository with her own public key. In step 2, while Elyes thinks he retrieved the public key of Aicha, he in fact now has the public key of Alice. In step 3 Elyes uses the key he retrieved in step 2, encrypts a message and sends it to Aicha. In step 4, Alice intercepts the mes-

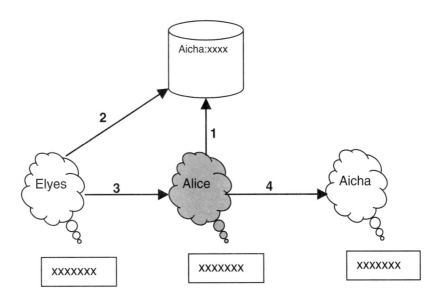

**FIGURE 3.8**
Implanting a public key value by a third-party eavesdropper

sage, uses her private key to successfully decrypt it, reads the message and then re-encrypts it using the public key of Aicha, and forwards the message. Finally, Aicha receives the message and decrypts it using her private key unaware of the eavesdropping.

The weakness that facilitated such an attack is due, in great part, to using a public key without securely verifying that it indeed belongs to the designated party. This raises the fundamental question of how a secure binding can be achieved between a publicly available key and its holder so that a user of a public key, referred to as a *relying party*, can securely verify the existing binding prior to using the key.

One promising answer to the issue of assurance in a public key lies in the certification process that a *Public Key Infrastructure* (PKI) can provide. At the heart of a PKI is the digital signature technology that we introduced earlier. Parties relying on public keys confine their trust in a single entity, known as the *Certificate Authority* (CA). Before a user's public key is disseminated the underlying high assurance CA uses its own private key to digitally sign the user's key, which is then distributed to a public repository. The concept of a verifiable public key certification can be traced back to the work published in [KOHN78].

A relying party securely installs the public key of the trusted CA and uses it to verify the signature of each user's public key that might thereafter be used. Only upon a successful verification does the reliant party initiate a communications channel. This simple method of certification thwarts an attacker who does not have a public key signed by the same CA as that of the two communicating parties but fails when the attacker is in possession of a key signed by the same CA.

In order to yield a reliable assurance, a comprehensive public key certification process necessitates more security elements than simply signing an encryption key. These elements are embodied in the data construct that is to be certified. For the Internet realm this construct is called a *X.509 Version 3* certificate, and the secure infrastructure that makes it is the Public Key Infrastructure for X.509 (PKIX); while the repository in which certificates are finally kept is based on the standard Lightweight Directory Access Protocol (LDAP) service. Details of this infrastructure follow in the next chapters.

# Public Key Establishment— the PKIX Way

We begin with a background introduction of the evolution of X.509 from its inception at the International Telecommunications Union (ITU) to its adoption by the Internet standard body. Then we briefly review the basic elements of an Internet public key infrastructure. We devote almost half of the chapter to learning the ASN.1 syntax. The second part of the chapter covers the core data constructs of the Internet PKI, an X.509 certificate, and accompanying Certificate Revocation List (CRL). ■

## Introduction

While the problem of secret key establishment, as we have discussed it, evolves around the security of distributing an encryption key to an entity, the public key establishment problem relates to the security of the binding that exists between a subject and a public key material. Public encryption keys, intended for distribution over secure and nonsecure channels, can be stored in public directories. An established public key is one that exhibits the property of being securely and unambiguously associated with its legitimate owner. This association should remain valid no matter the transport over which the key is being communicated, the storage medium in which it resides, or an execution run time that is processing the key.

In the world of the Internet, public key establishment is defined and maintained through the X.509 digital certification performed by a trusted third party known as the CA. The output of the certification process is a data construct in the form of an X.509 certificate representing a cryptographic binding between the public key and its holding subject. The core element of such certification is the digital signature technique. The Key PKIX is the Internet public key establishment infrastructure. The Abstract Syntax Notation One (ASN.1) is the notational language used in describing PKIX constructs. We devote nearly half of this chapter to learning about the ASN.1 basics to familiarize you with PKIX and other ASN.1 definitions that we will encounter in the rest of the book.

# Background

A digital signature over a public key value alone represents a primitive form of certification. It is prone to masquerading, and does not carry any information identifying the subject nor the authority responsible for the signature. Furthermore, a basic form of signing public keys as such leads to the proliferation of keys in a way that does not lend itself to management applications. In addition to the public key value, a comprehensive public-key certification process needs to include other identifying attributes over which a digital signature can be computed.

Due to the importance of public key certification to rapidly evolving Internet computing, the Internet Engineering Task Force (IETF) initiated work within the IETF security area to specifically tackle the standards issues in the field of public key infrastructures. As a result, the PKIX working group was created.

IETF is an international community of network designers, operators, vendors, and researchers concerned with the evolution of the Internet architecture and its related operational standards. IETF is organized into technical areas grouped by related subject matters (e.g., security). The technical work is performed at the working group levels. The procedure adopted by the IETF is similar to many other standards bodies. First, an internet draft is issued describing a specific technology matter in a way similar to a detailed specification. The draft is then made public so that it can be read and commented on. Based upon feedback, the draft may then be moved to become a recommended standard authored as a Request For Comments (RFC) or may remain as an informational document or be obsolete.

# PKIX Certificates and Certificate Revocation Lists ____

In 1995 a well-known structure in the form of an X.509 Version 3 certificate was adopted by the PKIX working group for the realization of the Internet PKI digital certification. X.509 is a construct which originally evolved at the ITU. X.509 Version 3 defines a widely accepted basis for a digital certificate which is generic enough to be adopted by a wide range of security protocols and applications.

The core aspect of the generalized X.509 V3 certificate lies in its inclusion of an extensions field. The latter provides for a standard yet flexible way of interpreting dynamic attributes that a certificate user may be associated with. As such, it has been used to accommodate the needs of several Internet protocols and applications. Similarly, a profile for the CRL Version 2 has been advanced by the PKIX working group as a standard format for the identification of certificates that are no longer valid or simply revoked by a designated CA, generally the one that had issued them. By way of including an extensions field, the CRL V2 profile is also generic enough to enable a wide range of Internet security protocols.

# Elements of PKIX _____

From a simplistic perspective, a PKIX can be defined as a mixture of software agents,  policies, and procedures as well as human interactions with such environments. The purpose is to manufacture, distributem and manage two data constructs: the X.509 version 3 certificate and the X.509 version 2 CRL. The first establishes a provable binding of a public cryptographic key to a certain subject; the second vouches for the reversal of the binding established by an issued certificate and essentially certifies against it. By definition a PKI consists of the following components:

- One or more CAs that issue and revoke Public Key Certificates (PKCs).
- One or more registration authorities (RAs) that vouch for the binding between public keys as well as a number of other attributes, and the identities of certificate holders known as subjects.
- Certificate holders that are issued certificates and can sign and encrypt digital documents or engage in key agreement protocols.
- Clients that interact with the infrastructure to request certificates, initiate certificate revocation requests, or validate certificates and CRLs

by computing certification paths starting with a known public key of some trusted CA.

- Repositories that store and make available certificates and certificate revocation lists.
- Possibly one or more certificate validating agents.

Before we indulge into the details of PKIX constructs, we will briefly review ASN.1, a notational language used to describe PKIX data types. ASN.1 is an ITU standard and has been widely adopted as a data definition language (DDL) for the description of networking protocols and data types associated with Internet standards [CCIT98].

# ASN.1: The PKIX Definition Language _____

ASN.1 is a DDL developed by the International Organization for Standardization (ISO) in the mid-1980s. ISO, formed in 1945 and headquartered in Geneva, Switzerland, is a worldwide federation of standards bodies from some 130 countries. It addresses standards in most technical fields including information technology (IT).

Standards in the IT field are carried jointly with the International Electrotechnical Commission (IEC) by an ISO/IEC Joint Technical Committee referred to as JTC1. The driving force behind the adoption of ASN.1 is the benefits that the abstraction principle brings to software engineering and the IT field in general. Such abstractions allow system designers to hide the details and make component designs independent of implementation processes. One of the most complex of such systems is the ISO Open Systems Interconnection (ISO/OSI) described in X.200. ISO/OSI is a layered architecture that governs the interconnection of computer systems. It spans the physical layer up to the application layer at the user level. Each layer defines its object in abstract terms independently of other layers.

ASN.1 found its early adoption by OSI when it became the abstraction language of the objects that make up each OSI layer. To achieve a consistent way of transferring those objects across the communicating layers an encoding scheme that translates ASN.1 objects into a bit-string representation was needed. The answer came in the encoding scheme known as basic encoding rules (BER).

On a lighter note, originally the abbreviation was ASN1 but it was often mistyped as ANS1 and then misread as ANSI which is the acronym for the American National Standards Institute. The abbreviation was then modified to ASN.1 to clear up the confusion. It is also worth noting that the One in the abbreviation was used as a recognition by ISO that there could well be other notations for abstract syntax definitions. Similarly, the BER encoding was denoted as basic leaving it open for other encoding schemes to be developed for the mapping of ASN.1 constructs.

## ASN.1 View Through an Example

ASN.1 adopts simple syntax and lexical rules in a way similar to high-level programming languages such as the C family. It is purely a data definition language and thus contains no control statements. It has a relatively small set of keywords, and, like most computer languages, is recursively defined. ASN.1 defines a set of basic, also called primitive, types from which it builds constructed ones.

The next example illustrates the use of ASN.1 keywords and data types. We consider a merchant automating his/her sales points with a back-end system managing the inventory. Customers issue orders at the points of sales and return at a later time with a confirmation number in order to pick the merchandise.

```
Module-CustomerOrders  DEFINITIONS  AUTOMATIC TAGS ::=
BEGIN
  CustomerOrder ::= SEQUENCE {
    customerInfo    Customer,
    paymentInfo     PaymentMethod,
    timeAndDate     TimeAndDate,
    orders          Orders,
    timeofOrder     GeneralizedTime
  }

  Customer ::= SEQUENCE {
    name            PrintableString  (SIZE (1..20)),
    address         Address
  }

  Address ::= SEQUENCE {
    street          PrintableString (SIZE(1..60))  OPTIONAL,
    city            PrintableString (SIZE(1..30)),
    zipCode         INTEGER
  }

  PaymentMethod ::= CHOICE {
    cash            NULL,
    check           NumericString (SIZE(12)),
    credit          IMPLICIT [0] CreditOrDebitCard,
    debit           IMPLICIT [1] CreditOrDebitCard
  }

  CreditOrDebitCard ::= SEQUENCE {
    type            CardType,
    number          NumericString (SIZE(20),
    expiration      NumericString (SIZE(6))   -- MMDDYY
  }

  CardType ::= ENUMERATED {
    amex(0),
    visa(1),
    discover(2),
    diners(3)
  }

  TimeAndDate :: CHOICE {
    two-digit-year    UTCTime,
```

```
      four-digit-year   GeneralizedTime
}

Orders ::= A SET OF { ItemAndQuantity}

ItemAndQuantity ::= SEQUENCE {
   itemNumber     PrintableString (SIZE (12)),
   quantity       INTEGER
}
   -- other definitions may follow
END -- end of Module-CustomerOrders
```

In turn the server responds with the following information:

```
ResponseInfo ::= SEQUENCE {
   confirmationNumber INTEGER,
   status                 OrderStatus
}

OrderStatus  ::= SEQUENCE {
   itemNumber     PrintableString (SIZE (12)),
   fullfilled     BOOLEAN
}
```

Information about a customer's order defines the data payload that is transmitted to the central warehousing unit. The use of ASN.1 to describe this payload makes it independent of the data transfer syntax adopted by the underlying communications protocol.

The abstract data type of a **CustomerOrder** is defined by a structure-like data type formally called a **SEQUENCE** in ASN.1 notation. In turn, this sequence consists of three ordered abstract data types: **Customer**, **Payment-Method**, and **Orders**.

Note:

- Variable names precede their types in ASN.1 declarations, as opposed to most existing programming languages.
- Variable names always begin with lower-case letters; data type names begin with an upper-case letter.
- ASN.1 keywords such as **SEQUENCE, SET, SET OF, CHOICE, ENU-MERATED, INTEGER, NULL,** and **OPTIONAL** are all in capital letters (there are some exceptions but they all begin with an upper-case letter).
- Variables can be given names with the ASN.1 assignment operator ::=.
- An ASN.1 comment is delimited by a pair of hyphens -- or a pair of hyphens and a line break as in the code sample.

The keyword **OPTIONAL** is used to indicate that the underlying data field may or may not be present. In the absence of this keyword, however, the presence of a value for the corresponding data field becomes a requirement.

## Structured ASN.1 Types

Structured ASN.1 types constitute the basis for defining abstract data types that are composed of other components. Each component in turn may recursively refer to other constructed types. For instance the **Customer** type in the example in the previous section is also defined as a constructed type made of **name** and **address** components.

ASN.1 defines four structured data types: **SEQUENCE**, **SEQUENCE OF**, **SET** and **SET OF**.

- **SEQUENCE** is an ordered list of one or more elements, each of which can be of any ASN.1 type.
- **SEQUENCE OF** is an ordered list of zero or more elements all referring to the same data type.

Note that a **SEQUENCE OF** may be an empty set. Essentially, **SEQUENCE OF** refers to a repetitive structure of a variable size whose elements are drawn from a single data type. While a **SEQUENCE** is a fixed size constructed type that uses multiple types for its entries, also referred to as components and sometimes elements. You may encounter a definition similar to the following in several ASN.1 specifications including those that relate to PKIX.

**MySequence ::=  SEQUENCE SIZE (1..MAX) OF  MyType**

The **SIZE (1..MAX)** constrains an instance of **MySequence** to have at least one component.

- **SET** is an unordered collection of one or more elements. Thus, it is the ordering of elements is what distinguishes a **SEQUENCE** from a **SET**.
- **SET OF** is an unordered collection of zero or more elements, all of which are of the same type.

**SET OF** underscores a repetition of the same data type that is of variable size; while a **SET** is a fixed-size construct.

## Selection in ASN.1

The **CHOICE** keyword denotes a selection among one or more alternatives. It is analogous to the **union** keyword in the C family of languages, and offers the flexibility of choosing one type among a set of possible types. In the example an order can be associated with cash, check, a credit card, or a debit card mode of payment. For any order, the mode of payment is required to have only one of these values. Related to the **CHOICE** is the **ANY** keyword, which denotes an arbitrary value of an arbitrary type, where the arbitrary type is possibly defined in the registration of an object identifier or integer value.

## Basic ASN.1 Types

A number of primitive types are built in ASN.1. Such types make the building blocks for the definition of constructed types. In the end each ASN.1 data type is broken into a series of primitive data types. The following is a list of the ASN.1 basic types.

### BOOLEAN

A data of this type may assume either one of the two abstract values **TRUE** or **FALSE**. These value notations are built-in symbolic names in ASN.1. This type is used to assert the answer to a yes or no question such as the **fullfilled** status of an order as in the previous example.

### INTEGER

This type denotes an integer of positive or negative value. ASN.1 integers are theoretically unbounded. In practice, however, they are always of fixed size. An ASN.1 integer can be declared to have a set of distinguished values and as such it becomes analogous to the **ENUMERATED** type although there is a clear syntactic difference between the two types as we discuss shortly. In that respect the **CardType** in the previous example can also be defined as

```
CardType ::= INTEGER {
    amex(0),
    visa(1),
    discover(2),
    diners(3)
}
```

Similarly, a range constraint can be placed on an integer value such as

```
CardType ::= INTEGER (0..3)
```

Like for all ASN.1 basic types a default value may also be designated in the declaration statement. The **quantity** variable in our example may be declared to have a default value of **1** as follows.

> **quantity    INTEGER  DEFAULT  1**

## ENUMERATED

This type refers to an integer variable that is required to take values from a distinguished set of values. The distinction between the **ENUMERATED** and the **INTEGER** types lies in their respective syntax. An **INTEGER** declaration is not required to be followed by a set of distinguished values. One other difference relates to the ASN.1 scope rules. For instance in the above example the name **visa** is scoped within the **PaymentMethod** data type and thus can also be used elsewhere within the module.

## REAL

This type designates a real value. The syntax for a **REAL** type declaration is straightforward and does not allow for any options. A declaration for a **REAL** value assignment, however, can be qualified with the base under which the value is to be represented such as base 10 or base 2 as in the following definition:

> **myRealValue ::= {mantissa 3, base 10, exponent 7}**

## BIT STRING

The **BIT STRING** type denotes an arbitrary string of variable-length binary bits. Note the required space in the symbolic name of this type. A **BIT STRING** may also refer to a particular set of named bits such as:

> **myBitString  BIT STRING { version1(0), version2(1) } DEFAULT {version2}**

## OCTET STRING

This type denotes an arbitrary string of octets, a variable-length stream of 8-bit quantities. Its use allows for the encapsulation of a data stream. The semantics interpretation of the latter are only relevant to a particular context in which the octet string is used.

## NULL

The **NULL** keyword a symbolic reference to the integer value of zero.

## OBJECT IDENTIFIER

Commonly referred to as **OID**, this type is used to identify another ASN.1 object. It consists of a sequence of integer components that uniquely refer to an abstract construct such as a particular algorithm.

In order to achieve worldwide unambiguous identification of data constructs, many ASN.1 object identifiers draw their values from specific standards such as PKIX. Allocation of OIDs follows a tree structure with global authorities responsible for the top-level arcs, while local authorities are responsible for lower arcs. A global authority may be an international standards body for instance, while a local authority can be a particular company or organization.

# ASN.1 Character String Types

ASN.1 makes use of a number of predefined string data types. A subset is listed below

- **PrintableString**: an arbitrary string from the following character set

  **A,B, ...,Z**
  **a,b, ...,z**
  **0,1, ...,9**
  **(space)'()+,-./:=?**

- **IA5String**: denotes the International Alphabet 5, which is the same as ASCII and includes the nonprinting control characters. For instance IA5 includes the character '**@**' which is not part of the **PrintableString**.

- **T61String**: also referred to as **TeletextString** and is an arbitrary string of T.61 characters (8-bit extension of the U.S. ASCII character set).

- **BMPString**: stands for the Basic Multilingual Plane String. It models the BMP of ISO/IEC/ITU 10646-1, a two-octet (**USC-2**) encoding form, which is identical to Unicode 1.1. **BMString** is encoded and decoded in big-endian form. The Universal Character Set (UCS) encompasses most of the world's character sets and defines two multioctet encoding, a 4-octet encoding (UCS-4) and a 2-character encoding (UCS-2). Currently there are no characters defined outside of the UCS-2 plane.

- **UTF8String**: Universal Transformation Format using 8 bits was introduced in 1998 and can be used to represent any existing character. It is essentially a transformation of UCS that leaves the representation of 7-bit ASCII characters unchanged (with the highest bit set to zero). UTF8 representation of non-ASCII characters has the highest bit of the first octet set to 1. Characters are represented in UTF8 using variable-length streams ranging from 1 to 6 octets. UTF8 is recommended as the character set of choice for full internationalization. The whole BMP set will encode at most 3 bytes using UTF8.

- **NumericString**: refers to an arbitrary string of numeric characters including the space character: 0,1,2,...,9,SPACE.
- **VisibleString**: is the ASCII character set without control characters.

Although the symbolic names of these character data types are not all written in upper-case letters they are in fact reserved ASN.1 words.

## Date/Time Types

ASN.1 defines two types for the date/time constructs, **UTCTime** and **GeneralizedTime**.

- **UTCTime** stands for Coordinated Universal Time, also known as Greenwich Mean Time (GMT). It is intended for use by applications that span multiple time zones and for which local time alone is not adequate. **UTCTime** specifies the year through the two low order digits and time to the precision of one minute or one second. It may contain the character Z (for Zulu, or GMT) or a time differential. The following is the form of the UTC time with the GMT reference that includes a precision up to the seconds.

    **YYMMDDHHMMSSZ**

    Where YY is the year (00-99), MM for the month (01-12), DD for day (01-31); while HHMMSS represents hours (00-23), minutes (00-59), and seconds (00-59). A sample of other forms may be

    **YYMMDDHHMM+HHMM** or
    **YYMMDDHHMMSS-HHMMSS**

    Both of the last forms use a time-differential representation in which the first part represents local time and the portion following the differential operator (either + or -) is the time that needs to be added or subtracted from the local time in order to yield the UTC value.

- **GeneralizedTime** is used for variable precision representation of time. It has the same overall format as **UTCTime** including the use of time differentials. **GeneralizedTime** has the advantage of representing the year using 4 digits instead of 2.

# ASN.1 BER Encoding

ASN.1 specifies a data abstraction framework that can be used by system designers to describe different system components without being constrained by physical implementations. ASN.1 level of abstraction enables the representation of data objects in a way independent of the control modules in the underlying operating systems and applications. Thus, a change in this representation should not affect those control modules.

Ultimately ASN.1 abstractions become physical entities with values that need to be communicated across system boundaries. Such is the case with the historical development of ASN.1 going back to the OSI networking model. In OSI, data abstractions become data constructs communicated across network layers and therefore ASN.1 abstractions need to be converted into encoded constructs. The need for interoperation has lead to the development of a common ASN.1 data transfer syntax for which ISO has chosen the method of BER.

The essence of BER is that an ASN.1 construct can be represented in a three-field form, namely:

- a Tag indicating the type of data
- the Length field containing the number of 8-bit quantities (bytes) allotted for the data value
- the Value field itself

This representation is commonly abbreviated as TLV. The use of the term basic reflects recognition that other encoding rules could indeed exist. Figure 4.1 illustrates the TLV/BER encoding.

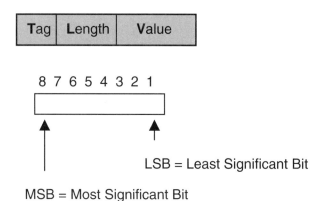

**FIGURE 4.1**
BER encodings are based on the TLV principle

## The Tag Field

The BER encoding unambiguously identifies each encoded data value with a tag field. The scope in which a tag value appears is a key element in resolving ambiguities. Excluded from this tagging mechanism are two types: **CHOICE** and **ANY**. The reason is evident. The first is simply used as a notation for a set of possible alternatives and thus the chosen alternative in itself is encoded. The ambiguity is resolved by way of assigning distinct tags to all of the choice elements. Similarly, the data that fills in for **ANY** will be the item of concern to the encoding scheme.

A tag is encoded as a combination of two things: a *class* and a nonnegative number (a *tag number*). Four classes are defined.

- **Universal**, for types that maintain the same semantics in all applications; these types are limited to the ones defined in X.208.
- **Application**, for types whose meaning is specific to an application, such as X.500 directory services. Types in two different applications may have the same application-specific tag and different meanings.
- **Private**, for types that have semantics defined within a specific enterprise.
- **Context-specific**, for types whose meanings are scoped by a particular structured type. **Context-specific** tags are used to distinguish between component types with the same underlying tag number that may arise within some structured type. Components within two different constructed types may have the same tag and different meanings. The context in which these components appear is what distinguishes them.

Each of these four tag classes is encoded using the lower two digits of the tag field (from left to right). Class encoding is as shown in Table 4.1. Standard tag numbers are shown in Table 4.2.

**TABLE 4.1**
Class encoding in the Tag field

| Class | Bit 8 | Bit 7 |
|---|---|---|
| Universal | 0 | 0 |
| Application | 0 | 1 |
| Context-specific | 1 | 0 |
| Private | 1 | 1 |

**TABLE 4.2**
Standard tag numbers

| Type | Tag Number |
|---|---|
| BOOLEAN | 1 |
| INTEGER | 2 |
| BIT STRING | 3 |
| OCTET STRING | 4 |
| NULL | 5 |
| OBJECT IDENTIFIER | 6 |
| ObjectDescriptor | 7 |
| EXTERNAL and InstanceOf | 8 |
| REAL | 9 |
| ENUMERATED | 10 |
| Embedded-pdv | 11 |
| UTF8String | 12 |
| Reserved for future use | 13–15 |
| SEQUENCE/SEQUENCE OF | 16 |
| SET/SET OF | 17 |
| NumericString | 18 |
| PrintableString | 19 |
| T61String | 20 |
| VideoString | 21 |
| IA5String | 22 |
| UTCTime | 23 |
| GeneralizedTime | 24 |
| GraphicString | 25 |
| VisibleString | 26 |
| GeneralString | 27 |
| Reserved for future use | 28-30 |

Encoding of tags can be done in two ways:

- **Short form**. Here only 1 octet (byte) is used to encode the tag portion. Bits 8 and 7 specify the class as shown in Table 4.2. Bit 6 is called the primitive/constructed (P/C) bit and is used to distinguish a primitive from a constructed type; 0 for a primitive (e.g., an **INTEGER**) and 1 for a constructed value (e.g., a **SEQUENCE**). Bits 5-1 are used for the tag number, which can range from 0 to 30.

- **Long form**. This representation of tags can take two or more octets. For the first octet, bits 8 to 6 have the same meaning as for the short form. Bits 5 to 1 of that same octet are all set to 1. Second and following octets give the tag number. Bit 8 in these following octets is set to 1 except in the last octet where it is set to zero. Most existing standards produce tag numbers below 128 which consume only 2 octets.

Figure 4.2 illustrates the encoding of the tag field.

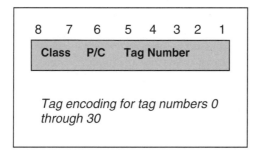

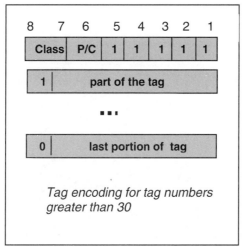

**FIGURE 4.2**
BER encoding of the Tag field

Several factors contribute to the encoding of ASN.1 tags. The following lists the most important of these.

- The ASN.1 type of the value.
- The context and the scope in which the value is defined. We will later discuss how the context of a definition may override the **UNIVERSAL** tagging in order to resolve ambiguities.
- The extent of the tag number portion of the Tag field.

## The Length Field

Three possible forms can be used in encoding the Length field:

- **Short**. This form is used when the value field has length ranging from 0 to 127 octets. Only 1 octet is needed to represent the length. Bit 8 of this octet is set to zero.
- **Long**. This form is used for representing the length of a Value field that contains more than 127 octets. The first octet has bit 8 set to 1 to indicate the long form. Bits 7 to 1 contain the number of following octets that represent the length of the value.
- **Indefinite**. This form is mainly used with constructed values. Like in the long form, bit 8 is set to 1. Bits 7 to 1, however, are all set to 0. Following this octet will be a series of octets from the Value field. The end of the value octets is signaled by the presence of one delimiting pair of zero octets. It is the decoder's responsibility to determine the length of the value octets. It should be noted here that a Value field may always end with a pair or a series of zero octets. In this case, the last pair of zeroes is what should be considered the delimiter. Note also that in practice a pair of zero octets can never represent a TLV encoding and thus it is safe to designate it as a delimiter.

Figure 4.3 illustrates encoding of the Length field part of the TLV BER encoding. The short form is the easiest and fastest to encode and decode.

The Indefinite form is easy to encode but a decoder will have to determine the length by running down the stream of octets until the last pair of zero octets is found.

For data constructs that represent security objects, such as those resulting from applying a hashing function or a digital signature, it becomes a strict requirement that the hashed or signed object map onto a unique encoding. The reason is evidenced by the fact that constructs such as cryptographic digests and signatures have to be re-created by the receiving end when data is exchanged in order for verification to take place. BER defines a unique

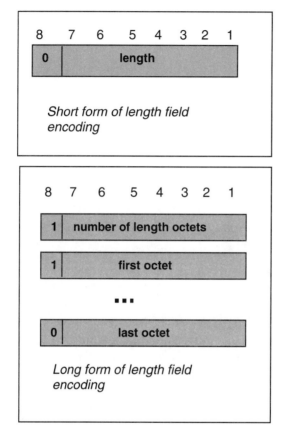

**FIGURE 4.3**
BER encoding of the Length field

encoding method in the form of the distinguished encoding rules referred to as DER. The latter simply relates to the case of a BER encoding with a definite length form and with the minimum number of octets needed to represent the length field.

## The Value Field

The Value field may contain the BER encoding of a primitive ASN.1 type such as an **INTEGER** or the encoding of a nested constructed ASN.1 object. Encoding the Value field is a recursive process in the same way the ASN.1 syntax is recursively defined. Next we discuss the value encoding of a selected set of ASN.1 types: **INTEGER, OBJECT IDENTIFIER, SEQUENCE, SET, OCTET STRING, BOOLEAN**, and **NULL**.

- **INTEGER**. This basic data type is encoded in two's complement form using the minimum number of octets. The value 0 is encoded as a single octet with all bits off. For instance the hexadecimal encoding of value of 128 looks like in Figure 4.4.

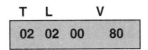

**FIGURE 4.4**
An example of **INTEGER** encoding

- **OBJECT IDENTIFIER**. Since an OID consists of a sequence of integers one might choose to represent it in the same way a **SEQUENCE OF INTEGER** is represented. This approach yields a constructed value of yet another TLV form inside of which we should also encounter the TLVs that represent each integer component. Instead of this cumbersome method, BER requires that OIDs be represented in an optimized form.

Historically all the OIDs are supposed to be descendent of the high level arcs shown in Figure 4.5. The first two arcs of any OID, descending from this tree, for all practical purposes can be encoded using a single octet. This restriction is guaranteed by way of using a simple formula to compute the number representing the first (top) and the second arcs as follows

*40\*(value of first arc) + value of second arc*

Each of the remaining arcs is first converted to base 128. Then each digit in this base is represented as a single octet with the most significant bit

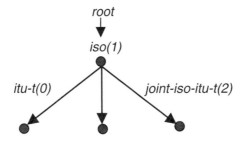

**FIGURE 4.5**
The high level arcs of standard OIDs

set to 1 with the exception of the last octet providing for a delimiter. The example which follows may help clarify these statements. Where the representation of an arc in this manner uses only a single octet, the most significant bit of this octet will therefore be set to 0.

The OIDs that PKIX deals with are all emanating from the ISO arc and thus the top level arc will always have value **1**. Assume that we need to represent the OID **{1, 2, 840, 113549}**. The first and second arcs will encode to:

*40\*1 + 2 = 42 = '2A'H*

The second arc **840 = (6 \* 128 + 48)** in base **128**. Thus the 840 component will be represented using two octets as: 86 48. Note the leftmost half of the first octet is 8 just because we need to set bit 8 to one. Applying the same procedure to the fourth component yields the hexadecimal representation of 86 F7 0D.

The BER encoding of this OID is as shown in Figure 4.6.

| T | L | V |
|---|---|---|
| 06 | 06 | 2A 86 48 86 F7 |

**FIGURE 4.6**
Example of an OID representation

- **SEQUENCE** and **SET**. Here the BER encoding begins with the outermost TLV whereby the tag is either 16 for the **SEQUENCE/SEQUENCE OF** or 17 for the **SET/SET OF**. The value field is then computed over the concatenated encoding of all elements in the sequence or the set. Each of these elements, in turn, is encoded as a nested TLV and certainly may consist of a constructed type. This process is recursively applied over each element until a primitive data type is reached.

An **OPTIONAL** field without a value assigned to it is omitted in both BER and DER encoding; while a field with a **DEFAULT** qualifier and which is assigned the default value may or may not be omitted in BER; but is required to be omitted for DER. In essence the **DEFAULT** qualifier also renders the field to an optional one. The difference here is that in the absence of the field, the default value is assumed.

The DER encoding of a **SET** mandates that the set members be ordered along the tag numbers before the encoding is determined. Note that for BER the ordering in which elements of a **SET** are encoded is irrelevant.

Any optional component that does not have a value assigned to it should be omitted from encoding. It is worth noting that in most literature an ASN.1 **SEQUENCE** or a **SET** is defined as consisting of one or more elements; while a **SEQUENCE OF/SET OF** are defined to consist of zero or more elements. While this holds true in most cases, one can also define a sequence with all elements optional, and therefore such a sequence ends up being encoded with the value field empty, thus representing a sequence of zero elements.

The BER encoding of a **SET** requires the use of distinct tags for each of the members in the set whether required or optional. By contrast a sequence in which all of the elements are required does not impose such a constraint. But in a sequence with optional elements (any that is qualified with **DEFAULT** or **OPTIONAL**) a variant of this constraint applies in that any block of optional elements is required to satisfy the above constraint as described for the **SET**. Additionally, the immediately preceding, or immediately following mandatory field, if any, must have a tag distinct from any element in the optional block.

- **OCTET STRING**. There are two forms in which an octet string can be put in a BER encoding. The first simply encodes a TLV with a tag $T = 04$ for the **OCTET STRING** type. The Length field can be either definite or indefinite, and the Value field encodes the octet stream being represented. In this way the **OCTET STRING** is said to be encoded in a primitive from. The constructed form encoding of octets consists of fragmenting the octet stream into separate blocks; each is then encoded as a primitive **OCTET STRING**. For example octets '**02002211AAABB449910101112133**'H are encoded as shown in Figure 4.7.

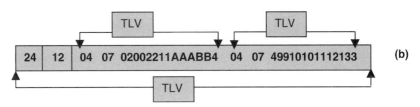

**FIGURE 4.7**
BER encoding of an OCTET STRING, (a) primitive form and (b) constructed form

Tag '24'H results from the **UNIVERSAL** tag of '04' combined with primitive/constructed bit set to one.

DER encoding of an **OCTET STRING** requires the use of the primitive form so as to guarantee a unique representation. In the case of the constructed form it is worth noting that the nested TLVs of the fragmented octet strings will always have a tag value of '04'H. This is contrary to the outermost tag that may have different tags based upon the context in which the octet string appears (we will discuss that later). The indefinite length form may be used in both the primitive as well as the constructed form.

- **CHARACTER STRING**. Each of the character string types is encoded as mandated by the corresponding character set standard. For instance a **UTF8String** encoding of an ASCII character will have bit 8 set to 0. For multibyte characters, the encoding of the value begins with the first 2 to 6 bits all set to 0 to indicate the number of octets used for the representation of the character. Each following octet has bits 8 and 7 set to 1 and 0, respectively; the remaining 6 bits participate in the encoding of the underlying character.

- **BOOLEAN**. This type is encoded as a single octet. In BER any non-zero value may be used for **TRUE**; while in DER this value is required to be encoded as '**FF**'H. The **FALSE** value always corresponds to **00**.

- **NULL**. This type is encoded with an empty value field as shown in Figure 4.8.

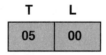

**FIGURE 4.8**
BER encoding of the NULL value

- **BIT STRING**. This is similar to an **OCTET STRING** except that the value of an octet string is always a multiple of 8-bit quantities. The length of a bit string accounts for an arbitrary number of bits that make up the value field. This number may not necessarily be a multiple of 8-bit quantities. On the other hand a bit string ought to be encoded and exchanged over a data field that is nothing but a stream of octets. Because of this, BER encoding of a bit string uses the first octet of the Value field to indicate the total number of unused bits that are in the last octet. This value can range from **0** to **7**.

In DER the unused bits are required to be all set to 0. The Length field is the total number of octets over which the bit string is represented including the octet used to represent the number of unused bits. Like for an octet string, two forms can be used to represent a bit string:

- Primitive
- Constructed

Figure 4.9 depicts the primitive representation of the bit string

'10100011100101011010111'

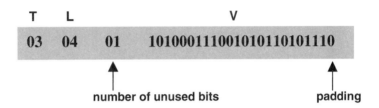

**number of unused bits**          **padding**

**FIGURE 4.9**
An example of the BER representation of a primitive bit string

# BER Encoding for IMPLICIT and EXPLICIT tagging

A BER encoding structure should guarantee that each ASN.1 object such as a protocol message be wrapped with an identifier that distinguishes it from any other ASN.1 object in the specification.

Evidently the use of universal tags alone cannot satisfy the constraint. For example consider a protocol specification in which two or more exchanged ASN.1 objects consist of a sequence type. There has to be a way for distinguishing the two sequences. In order to resolve such ambiguities ASN.1 introduces two types of tagging that, in conjunction with the context-specific, private and application specific class of tags, can be used to assign tag numbers in a nonconflicting fashion. The two types of tagging mechanisms are referred to by the reserved words of **IMPLICIT** and **EXPLICIT**.

## IMPLICIT Tagging

This type of tagging provides a parameterization scheme for the ASN.1 encoding of a tag. This scheme is defined over the tag number portion of a tag as defined by bits 5 through 1 in the short form of a tag and through a higher number of bits in the long form. Recall that a tag number is an arbitrary positive integer; zero upward. The implicit tagging provides for a way to override a tag number and furthermore extend the tag number beyond what the universal class alone defines. Such tagging has been in most cases used in conjunction with the context-specific class. It can be used in conjunction with the private and the application-specific classes as well, but with a lesser frequency. The context-specific resolves encoding ambiguities only within a defined scope. That scope or context typically consists of a **SEQUENCE**, a **SET**, or a **CHOICE**. To illustrate the ambiguity that implicit tagging resolves, consider a sequence that contains two integers as follows:

```
mySequence ::= SEQUENCE {
    firstInteger     INTEGER  OPTIONAL,
    secondInteger  INTEGER  OPTIONAL
}
```

Assume that I have a BER encoding of type **mySequence** in which **firstInteger** was omitted because it is an optional field. The tag encoding of the integer within **mySequence** will be 2 for **[UNIVERSAL 2]**. There is no way for me to tell whether the single integer I received is **firstInteger** or **secondInteger**. To resolve this ambiguity, we   take advantage of the ASN.1 implicit tagging and rewrite **mySequence** in the following manner:

```
mySequence ::= SEQUENCE {
    firstInteger      IMPLCIT[1] INTEGER  OPTIONAL,
    secondInteger   IMPLCIT[2] INTEGER  OPTIONAL
}
```

This redefinition removes the previous ambiguity as the presence of a nested TLV such as shown in Figure 4.10 (a) indicates a **firstInteger** value; the representation in Figure 4.10 (b) indicates the presence of a **secondInteger** field.

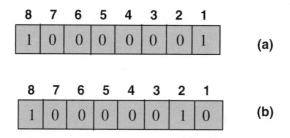

**FIGURE 4.10**
Use of IMPLICIT tagging to remove encoding ambiguity

Note how the **IMPLICIT** tag number is stated in ASN.1 by simply enclosing the overriding number within square brackets. The use of other classes such as **private** requires explicit indication of the class as in:

**secondInteger   IMPLICIT[private 2] INTEGER   OPTIONAL**

## EXPLICIT Tagging

While implicit tagging replaces or overrides a tag with one that is stated along with the **IMPLICIT** keyword; with **EXPLICIT** tagging an ASN.1 object maintains the same tagging for the object but adds an outer TLV wrapping of the object encoding. Thus, an explicitly tagged object becomes a structured type containing a single component, the original object itself. To put this in terms of the ASN.1 syntax, consider the following definition:

**myInteger   [PRIVATE 1] EXPLICIT  INTEGER,**

This is equivalent to:

```
myInteger   [PRIVATE 1] IMPLICIT SEQUENCE  {
        myInteger  INTEGER
}
```

When tagging is present in an ASN.1 definition without either keyword of **IMPLICIT** or **EXPLICIT** like in

**myInteger   [PRIVATE 1]  INTEGER,**

it means **EXPLICIT** tagging is used except when the **Module** in which the ASN.1 type is defined has implicit tagging by default. So the keyword **[class number]** alone is the same as explicit tagging with the exception noted earlier.

Generally, each alternative of a **CHOICE** type is required to be explicitly tagged when selected. In order to understand this encoding constraint, consider the definition of the **GeneralName** type which is used in numerous IETF ASN.1 specifications, including PKIX.

```
GeneralName ::= CHOICE {
        otherName            [0]    OtherName,
        rfc822Name           [1]    IA5String,
        dNSName              [2]    IA5String,
        x400Address          [3]    ORAddress,
        directoryName        [4]    Name,
        ediPartyName         [5]    EDIPartyName,
```

```
        uniformResourceIdentifier [6]    IA5String,
        iPAddress                  [7]    OCTET STRING,
        registerredID              [8]    OBJECT IDENTIFIER
}
```

and now consider the **directoryName** alternative which is in turn defined as a **CHOICE** type even when it consists only of a single alternative (perhaps to accommodate any future extensions to directory name structures)

```
directoryName          [4]    Name ,   where
Name ::= CHOICE {-- defined in X.501
           RDNSequence
}
```

In this case when **IMPLICIT** tagging is used, it would replace the **RDNSequence** tag with the [4] tag. Thus a decoder will not be able to determine which of the Name choices are used.

## Other ASN.1 Encoding Rules

A number of ASN.1-related encoding rules have emerged. Most notably the packed encoding rules (PER) that seek to minimize the number of bits over which an ASN.1 definition can be unambiguously encoded. For instance PER uses only a single bit instead of a byte (as in BER) to encode the **BOOLEAN** type. **INTEGER** types are encoded over bits instead of bytes. For example only 3 bits are used in encoding integers that are known a-priori to fall in the range [0...7]. Additionally, PER in many instances avoids the use of the Tag field or at least minimizes its space requirement a great deal. For example instead of encoding the Tag for a selected member of a **CHOICE**, PER simply encodes a bitmap representing the choice-index using the minimum bits necessary. For a choice with two alternatives, only 1 bit is used for the choice-index; while 2 bits are used for three to four alternatives. Similarly the presence or absence of optional fields in a sequence or a set is represented in a bitmap which becomes the first part of the encoding of the underlying structured type. PER is amenable to encoding and transferring data from bandwidth and storage constrained devices.

Other encoding schemes include the lightweight encoding rules (LWER), octet encoding rules (OER) and most recently the Extended Mark-up Language encoding rules (XER-XML).

# The PKIX Information Model _____

Now to turn our attention to learning about the PKIX information model. We begin by reviewing the fundamental constructs of an X.509 PKC and the CRL [HOUS99]. These two data types are at the core of the Internet PKI. We will discuss the process of validation that PKIX reliant entities in the form of end users, security protocols, systems, and applications, may perform to securely verify the validity of a certificate at the time of its use. We defer the PKIX networking topology and entity interactions as well as all the operational protocols to Chapter 6.

## The PKIX Data Constructs

The basic premise of a PKIX is the high level of assurance and confidence in a public key that it certifies. The result of this digital certification enables a provable binding between the public key material and its associated subject and the private key. In addition to the public key pair, the certified binding implicates a set of other attributes that a subject may have such as an X.500 distinguished name (DN), an electronic mail address, and so forth.

Similarly, the infrastructure can securely disassociate itself from a prior public key certification that it had established, when the certificate is no longer valid. This PKIX characteristic of being able to disassociate itself from an active certification is achieved by way of generating another construct called the CRL. A PKIX, therefore, generates two distinct, digitally signed data types:

- a Certificate
- a CRL

### X.509 Version 3 Certificate

Originally the X.509 digital certificate format was first published as part of the X.500 directory standard series. At its inception in 1988, the X.509 format was dubbed version 1. In 1993 two more fields in the form of unique identifiers were added to the version 1 format, thus resulting in the X.509 version 2 certificate. Attempts at exploiting the public key infrastructure by the Internet Privacy Enhanced Mail (PEM) protocols [KENT93] have demonstrated the deficiency in the state of X.509 at the time for a flexible support of security protocols. In response to the new requirements ISO in conjunction with IEC and ITU developed the X.509 version 3 format that was later adopted by the IETF in RFC 2459 [HOUS99].

We now begin unraveling the data elements that define an Internet digital certificate version 3. Figure 4.11 broadly depicts the content of an Internet X.509 v3 certificate.

| | |
|---|---|
| { -- *the signed portion* | |
| version number | v3 |
| serial number: | xxxxxxxxxxx |
| signature algorithm | xxxxxxxxxxxx |
| issuer name | xxxxxxxxxxxxxx |
| validity period | xxxxxxxxxx |
| subject name | xxxxxxxxxxxxxx |
| subject public key | xxxxxxxxxxxxxxxx |
| issuer unique identifier | xxxxxxxxxxxxx |
| subject unique identifier | xxxxxxxxxxxxxxx |
| extensions | xxxxxxxxxxxxx |
| } | |
| signature algorithm | xxxxxxxxxxxx |
| signature value | xxxxxxxxxxxxxxxxx |

**FIGURE 4.11**
Elements of the X.509 v3 certificate

The details of the elements illustrated in Figure 4.11 are described by the following ASN.1 specification for the X.509 v3 certificate.

```
Certificate ::= SEQUENCE {
    tbsCertificate          TBSCertificate,
    signatureAlgorithm      AlgorithmIdentifier,
    signatureValue          BIT STRING
}
```

where **tbsCertificate** (to be signed certificate) is defined by the following sequence

```
TBSCertificate ::= SEQUENCE {
    version                 [0] EXPLICIT Version DEFAULT v1,
    serialNumber            CertificateSerialNumber,
    signature               AlgorithmIdentifier,
    issuer                  Name,
    validity                Validity,
    subject                 Name,
    subjectPublicKeyInfo    SubjectPublicKeyInfo,
    issuerUniqueID          [1] IMPLICIT UniqueIdentifier OPTIONAL,
    subjectUniqueID         [2] IMPLICIT UniqueIdentifier OPTIONAL,
```

```
    extensions              [3] EXPLICIT Extensions OPTIONAL
}

Version ::= INTEGER { v1(0), v2(1), v3(2) }
CertificateSerialNumber ::= INTEGER
Validity ::= SEQUENCE {
    notBefore   Time,
    notAfter    Time
}

Time ::= CHOICE {
    utcTime         UTCTime,
    generalTime     GeneralizedTime
}

UniqueIdentifier ::= BIT STRING

SubjectPublicKeyInfo ::= SEQUENCE {
    algorithm       AlgorithmIdentifier,
    subjectPublicKey BIT STRING
}

AlgorithmIdentifier ::= SEQUENCE {
    algorithm       OBJECT IDENTIFIER,
    parameters      ANY DEFINED BY algorithm OPTIONAL
}

Extensions ::= SEQUENCE SIZE (1..MAX) OF Extension
Extension ::= SEQUENCE {
    extnID      OBJECT IDENTIFIER,
    critical    BOOLEAN DEFAULT FALSE,
    extnValue   OCTET STRING
}
```

Three fundamental elements of the certificate form the building block of the signed information that establishes the required assurance in the binding between a certified public key and its subject:

- The certificate serial number.
- The name of the issuing CA
- The subject name (owner of the certificate)

### Certificate serial number

The *serial number* is an integer assigned by the CA to the certificate at the time of issuance. There must be a one-to-one mapping between the serial numbers and the set of certificates that a particular CA issues. In simple terms the serial number of a certificate should be unique within the scope of each CA. In the eavesdropping scenario that we described in the previous chapter, the certificates of all three parties involved must be assigned different serial numbers when issued by the same CA. This property is fundamental to verifying the binding of public keys; thus, the infrastructure is required to satisfy it for the entire life cycle in which it remains in operation.

### Issuing Name

The issuer field identifies the authority that issued the certificate. To allow for further extensibility, this identifier adopts the definition of **Name** as defined by X.501 in the from of a choice as follows:

```
Name ::= CHOICE {-- defined in X.501
             RDNSequence
}
```

with

```
RDNSequence  ::= SEQUENCE OF RelativeDistinguishedName
RelativeDistinguishedName  ::= SET OF AttributeTypeAndValue
```

and

```
AttributeTypeAndValue  ::= SEQUENCE {
       type      AttributeType,
       value     AttributeValue
}
```

```
AttributeType  ::= OBJECT IDENTIFIER
AttributeValue ::= ANY DEFINED BY AttributeType
```

Thus, the issuer name is an X.500 hierarchical DN. The hierarchy is expressed using **SEQUENCE OF RelativeDistinguishedName**, the type commonly referred to as RDN. The latter is in turn expressed for generality as a **SET OF** type-value pairs. Consequently this syntax accommodates multiple attribute-value pairs for a single RDN. Each attribute type in the attribute-value pair is identified by a well-known object identifier. The value portion generally draws its syntax from the **DirectoryString** type defined as follows:

```
DirectoryString  ::= CHOICE {
        teletexString      TeletexString (SIZE (1..MAX)),
        printableString    PrintableString (SIZE (1..MAX)),
        universalString    UniversalString (SIZE (1..MAX)),
        utf8String         UTF8String (SIZE(1..MAX)),
        bmpString          BMPString (SIZE(1..MAX))
}
```

**PrintableString** and **BMPString** alternatives are most widely used, but IETF mandates that all certificates issued after December 31, 2003, adopt the **UTF8String** encoding. Figure 4.12 illustrates the structure of each RDN that defines a DN entry. Note how each entry can have multiple attributes, while each attribute can be assigned multiple values at the same time.

As an example, we consider the DN for a CA of a fictitious U.S.-based company called WebStore that certifies users within the Bookstore division of the company.

*CN=WebStore  CA, OU=BookStore, O=WebStore, C=US*

The name is expressed according to the IETF RFC 1485 for representing DNs in a user-oriented manner; with the root attribute being the country, C. In RFC 1485 the most significant component, closest to the root of the namespace, is written last.

RDN attributes generally relate to standard properties referred to via symbolic abbreviations such as *C* for country, and *O* for organization. While symbolic abbreviations of an attribute are used for externalization purposes, internally each attribute is known by its numeric OID. In the example the DN sequence is made of four RDNs: Country (*C*) at the top, Organization (*O*), Organizational Unit (*OU*), and Common Name (*CN*).

A hierarchical X.500 name as such should uniquely identify the CA within the naming space adopted. This unique identification, although relative to a

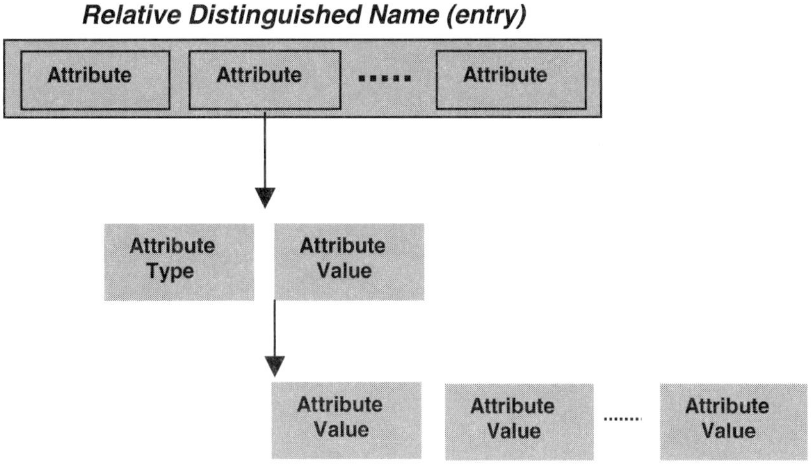

**FIGURE 4.12**
The structure of a relative distinguished name

naming space, adds to the assurance of a certificate's origin. The issuer name is common to all certificates issued by the same CA. The combination of the certificate serial number and the name of the issuing CA should suffice in uniquely identifying a certificate. When two certificates are issued by the same CA, each will carry a distinct serial number. If they are issued by two different authorities, each will be distinguished through the name of the issuing authority.

Table 4.3 lists a set of standard X.520 attribute types along with associated object identifiers. Other attributes defined by X.520 and that are commonly used in PKIX include: Domain Component (DC), Postal Code (PC) Street (STREET). Identification of these attributes emanates from the arc shown in Figure 4.13, referred to in PKIX documents by the name **id-at** defined as

**id-at     OBJECT IDENTIFIER ::= {joint-iso-ccitt(2) ds(5) 4}**

Additionally, the electronic mail address attribute (EMAIL) defined by the Public Key Cryptographic Standard 9 (PKCS#9) has been frequently used in DN components [NYST00].

**TABLE 4.3**
A set of X.520 standard attributes

| Attribute | OID |
|---|---|
| Country (C) | {2.5.4.6} |
| Organization (O) | {2.5.4.10} |
| Organizational-Unit (OU) | {2.5.4.11} |
| dnQualifier | {2.5.4.46} |
| State or Province Name (ST) | {2.5.4.8} |
| Common Name (CN) | {2.5.4.3} |
| X.520 attributes that are strongly recommended for adoption by PKIX | |
| Locality (L) | {2 5 4 7} |
| Title (T) | {2 5 4 12} |
| SurName | {2 5 4 4} |
| GivenName | {2 5 4 42} |
| Initials | {2 5 4 43} |
| Generation Qualifier | {2 5 4 44} |

**The id-at arc**

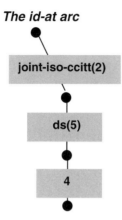

**FIGURE 4.13**
The base arc that is used in identifying X.520 attributes

The DC attribute was introduced in 1998 by RFC 2247 as a mechanism to labeling resources along the hierarchy defined by associated Internet domain names. For instance the domain name "CS.RPI.EDU" can be transformed into its distinguishing hierarchical name that looks like

**DC=CS, DC=RPI, DC=EDU**

The DC attribute is assigned the OID **{ 0.9.2342.19200300.100.4.13 }**.

An instance of the value for the generation qualifier attribute would be Jr. As a side note qualifiers such as surname, initials, and generation qualifier are less used in practice.

## Subject Name

Like for the issuer, the subject name is a hierarchical X.500 name such as

**CN=Elyes, OU=BookStore, O=WebStores, C=US**

The subject name uniquely identifies the subject of the certificate, also known as the certificate holder, within the adopted naming space.

We distinguish two cases with respect to subject names:

- **CA certificate**. The issuer name and the subject name fields should refer to the same DN value. Both the issuer and the subject name should be nonempty DNs. The CA certificate is identified by the value of a required extension field called the basic constraints extension (see details of the certificate extensions in the next chapter).

- **User certificate**. The subject name can be encoded as an empty sequence, but its presence is required. Because identifying the underlying subject is a fundamental element, the certificate is required to carry the subject alternative name extension when the subject name value is empty. In the latter case the extensions must be marked as critical. Relating examples may include a certificate that is bound to a domain name, or one bound to an email address.

As a good security practice, it is generally mandated that certificate holders within a particular enterprise are assigned distinct X.500 names. A reliable PKIX plays a fundamental role in enforcing such a distinguishing property. It becomes the responsibility of the RA/CA to enforce the property whereby a particular subject name is not issued multiple certificates that differ only in the public key value, or that certify the same public key material. Multiple certificates can be issued based upon functionally meaningful reasons such as a limitation with respect to the public key usage (e.g., one key for use in signing documents only) while another one for data enciphering only (see more about certificate extensions in the next chapter). In the absence of functionally differentiating factors such as those mentioned, a comprehensive PKIX should require the revocation of an old certificate prior to issuing a new one for the same subject.

The key to enforcing any applicable policies, such as the uniqueness of names, is the requirement that the CA maintain a repository of all the certificates it issues during its entire time of operation. The CA repository is referred to as the Issued Certificates List (ICL) which, in conjunction with a registration procedure that an enterprise PKI enforces prior to a certification request, yields a controllable way for granting certificates. It should be noted here that a reliable PKIX is one in which certificates are always issued in a controllable fashion. This is analogous to the practice of creating users in a legacy authentication registry, thereby yielding nonconflicting identities.

### Validity Period
The *validity period* of a certificate is the time interval during which the certificate maintains its validity of use provided it has not been explicitly revoked. It is represented as a sequence of two dates. The first component is the date when the certificate validity period begins; the second is the date on which the certificate validity period ends.

Time is represented according to an International standard and is computed with respect to the GMT, thus ensuring independence from the physical location of PKIX using applications. Conforming PKIX implementations are required to encode certificate validity dates through year 2049 in **UTCTime** form. Dates in 2050 or later must use the **GeneralizedTime** type. Recall that the main difference between the two types is that the former represents the year using two digits, while the latter uses four digits.

## *Signature Algorithm*

This field identifies the cryptographic algorithm used by the issuing authority in signing the certificate. In order to accommodate for a wide range of signature algorithms, the following ASN.1 definition is used:

```
AlgorithmIdentifier ::= SEQUENCE {
    algorithm      OBJECT IDENTIFIER,
    parameters   ANY DEFINED BY algorithm OPTIONAL
}
```

Note that this field is present twice in the certificate—once within the signed portion and once outside of it. The values of these two fields must be the same in both locations.

The algorithm identifier field may represent any public key signature algorithm. SHA-1 with RSA encryption is the preferred signing algorithm. Other signature algorithms include MD2 or MD5 with RSA encryption as well as the DSA. Note that all three algorithms use the padding and encoding conventions as described by the PKCS#1 specification from RSA Inc. which is also an ITEF Informational RFC [KALI98].

The object identifiers for these common signature algorithms are listed below.

- MD2 with RSA encryption
  **md2WithRSAEncryption OBJECT IDENTIFIER ::=**

    **{ iso(1) member-body(2) us(840)rsadsi(113549) pkcs(1) pkcs-1(1)  2 }**

  which is simply  **{1.2.840.113549.1.1.2}**

- MD5 with RSA encryption
  **md5WithRSAEncryption OBJECT IDENTIFIER ::=**

    **{ iso(1) member-body(2) us(840)  rsadsi(113549) pkcs(1) pkcs-1(1)  4 },**

  or  **{1.2.840.113549.1.1.4}**

- SHA-1 with RSA encryption
  **sha-1WithRSAEncryption OBJECT IDENTIFIER ::=**

    **{ iso(1) member-body(2) us(840)  rsadsi(113549) pkcs(1) pkcs-1(1)  5 },**

  or **{1.2.840.113549.1.1.5}**

- DSA
  **id-dsa-with-sha1 ID ::= { iso(1) member-body(2) us(840) x9-57 (10040) x9cm(4) 3 }**

  or **{1.2.840.10040.4.3}**

The RSA-based signature algorithms do not require use of parameters but the DSA algorithm requires a sequence of three. For end entity certificates signed using the DSA algorithm, the parameters field is omitted. In order to determine the values of those parameters, one uses the certificate of the issuing authority. The **subjectPublicKeyInfo** field of the underlying CA certificate is used to extract the DSA parameters. The parameters field when encoded in the case of RSA takes the **NULL** value.

### Signature Value

This field contains the actual value of the cryptographic signature. The signature must be computed over the DER encoding of the **tbsCertificate** portion of the certificate. Recall that DER is mandated for use here in order to yield a unique encoding of the value to be signed. Ultimately, this is the field that encodes the certificate assurance, and traces back to the issuing CA in a secure and nonreputable fashion. It is worth noting here that the CA signature, therefore, certifies the entire content of a certificate and not just the public key portion of it.

While the RSA-based signature is a contiguous bit string that is meaningful only as a single entity, the DSA signature is the DER encoding of a sequence of two values as described by the following ASN.1 object.

**Dss-Sig-Value ::= SEQUENCE {**
        **r  INTEGER,**
        **s  INTEGER**
**}**

### Subject Unique Identifier

This field is used to identify the subject of the certificate uniquely in time and location.

## Issuer Unique Identifier

This field is used to universally identify the authority that signed the underlying certificate. Both unique identifiers are optional and are not recommended for use with X.509 v3 certificates.

## Version

This field indicates the version to which the certificate format conforms. It can refer to version 1 (value **0**), version 2 (value **1**) or version 3 (value **2**).

## Subject Public Key

The subject public key information is a sequence of two fields. One represents the actual value of the public key material being certified, the other identifies the algorithm with which the key is associated such as RSA. Algorithm identification is represented using the OID data type.

While an implementation is free to certify any type of public cryptographic keys the PKIX profile specifically states the details of encoding the RSA, the DSA and the Diffie-Hellman keys.

- **RSA keys**. These are encoded with the following OID in the **algorithm** field of **SubjectPublicKeyInfo**.

  **RsaEncryption OBJECT IDENTIFIER ::=**
      **{ iso(1) member-body(2) us(840) rsadsi(113549) pkcs(1) 1  1}**
  or **{1.2.840.113549.1.1.1}**

  The public key value is the DER encoding of an **RSAPublicKey** value with the following syntax:

  **RSAPublicKey ::= SEQUENCE {**
          **modulus           INTEGER, -- n**
          **publicExponent    INTEGER  -- e**
  **}**

  RSA public keys are defined by two components: the modulus and the exponent.

  It is known that each of the exponent values: **3**, **17** and **65537** speeds up the RSA algorithm a great deal. The **X.509** standard recommends the use of **65537**. The IETF PKIX profile, on the other hand, does not endorse one value or the other. The DER encoding of the sequence above becomes the value field of the bit string representing the public key material.

- **DSA keys**. The OID identifying the DSA algorithm was stated earlier in the Signature Algorithm Section. The **parameters** field is, generally, required to be present. It consists of the DER encoding of the following ASN.1 structure.

```
Dss-Parms ::= SEQUENCE {
          p    INTEGER,
          q    INTEGER,
          g    INTEGER
}
```

In the event this parameters field is absent, the DSA parameters when found in the certificate of the issuing CA will apply to the current subject's DSA key. Otherwise, the absence of the DSA parameters implies that they are communicated to reliant entities via other means. Practically, this scenario is a remote possibility.

The DSA key material is the bit string representing the DER encoding of the following type

```
DSAPublicKey ::= INTEGER -- public key, Y
```

- **Diffie-Hellman keys**. Recall that these keys are intended for exchanging secret keys over a nonsecure channel. The OID used in identifying such keys has been defined by the ANSI X9.42 specification and is given by the following ASN.1 definition:

```
dhpublicnumber OBJECT IDENTIFIER ::=
    { iso(1) member-body(2) us(840) ansi-x942(10046) number-type(2)   1}
or {1.2.840.10046.2.1}
```

The **parameters** field is the DER encoding of the sequence:

```
DomainParameters ::= SEQUENCE {
     p                      INTEGER, -- odd prime,  p=jq +1
     g                      INTEGER, -- generator, g
     q                      INTEGER, -- factor of p-1
     j                      INTEGER OPTIONAL, -- subgroup factor
     validationParms        ValidationParms OPTIONAL
}
```

where
```
ValidationParms ::= SEQUENCE {
     seed                   BIT STRING,
     pgenCounter            INTEGER
}
```

The components that make up a **DomainParameters** type have the following semantics:

- **p** identifies the prime number defining the *Galois* field **GF(P)**
- **g** specifies the generator of the multiplicative subgroup of order g
- **q** specifies the prime factor of **p-1**
- **j** an optional element, specifies the value satisfying the equation **p=j*q+1** used to
- support the optional verification of group parameters
- **seed** an optional element, specifies the bit string parameter used as the seed for
- the system parameter generation process
- **pgenCounter** optionally specifies the integer value output as part of the system parameter prime generation process. The PKIX profile requires the presence or absence of both of the parameter generation components (**pgencounter** or **seed**). When these optional elements are absent, they are expected to be arbitrarily generated by the processing system

The **BIT STRING** value of the public key in this case wraps the DER encoding of an ASN.1 **INTEGER** type with value of:

$$y = g^x \bmod p$$

The key usage extension, when present, should reflect the fact that the certified key is intended for key agreement (see the next chapter).

### Extensions

The extensions field represents an interesting aspect of X.509 v3 certificates. It may contain zero or more extensions, each of which adds specific information about the certificate such as the intended usage from the underlying public key. A number of these extensions has been defined by the standard body. Private extensions can also be exploited within a particular enterprise. Chapter 5 is devoted to discussing the details of X.509 v3 certificate and CRL v2 extensions.

### A Sample Certificate

The following is a sample X.509 v3 certificate generated by the IBM Jonah CA, a freeware PKIX reference implementation donated to the Internet community. Note the use by the CA of SHA-1 hashing method in conjunction with the RSA encryption algorithm in signing the certificate. The certificate encodes three extensions and has already entered expiry date.

```
Certificate: {
 TBSCertificate {
  version: 2 (v3)
  serialNumber: 2
  signature: 1.2.840.113549.1.1.5 (SHA-1/RSA)
  issuer: C=US, O=IBM, OU=Jonah, CN=Jonah CA
  Validity: {
   notBefore: Fri Oct 08 13:27:03 CDT 1999
   notAfter:  Wed Apr 05 13:27:03 CDT 2000
  }
  subject: C=us, O=IBM, OU=Jonah, CN=EEhaza1008
  subjectPublicKeyInfo:    PublicKeyInfo {
   algorithm: 1.2.840.113549.1.1.1 (RSA)
   key:
    30 81 89 02 81 81 00 B9 C6 A0 99 21 5A 4B 2D A2 F1 23 C3 CC 15 8B 33 12 D7 87 26 04 47 98 1D 04
    A4 0B 81 B3 B5 D9 33 61 D5 70 38 0D B7 00 3C 65 24 C5 7A 13 F7 15 B9 DB 89 E8 0D AA B0 59 17 EB
    11 BD 2E 8C F4 70 B1 2C 49 19 DD 7B 2A D0 19 9C 74 AA F3 1D B8 1A FC 8B BF 15 9A 95 77 B5 71 02
    3F 42 34 BA 1D D2 C2 EF B6 CC 30 6F 8D BB AB 4C A5 6D F8 E2 6E 13 43 7D CF 5B 37 4B D0 17 22 77
    FB D4 C2 87 E5 8D EF 02 03 01 00 01
  }
  Extensions {
   Extension {
    extnID: keyUsage
    critical: true
    extnValue: {0}
   }
   Extension {
    extnID: subjectKeyIdentifier
    critical: false
    extnValue:    [UNIVERSAL OCTET STRING] (8 bytes)

       76 D0 74 90 60 9C 87 04
   }
   Extension {
    extnID: authorityKeyIdentifier
    critical: false
    extnValue: AuthorityKeyIdentifier {
     KeyIdentifier:
        09 7D 22 4B AA 96 40 04
    }
   }
  }
 }
 signatureAlgorithm: 1.2.840.113549.1.1.5 (SHA-1/RSA)
 signature:
  4D E2 04 53 95 A7 6F CA F3 59 9E 84 2C E6 42 22 AC F3 73 52 35 AB 13 24 94 51 7F E3 E8 FF 36 5A
  37 61 91 74 7C EB 18 16 E4 8B 5B E5 3E C1 75 9C 78 32 D7 FE E1 A3 BD 7F 56 2B F3 DB 65 A7 47 3A
  E8 0A 9B 41 52 6A 60 25 87 1D E9 46 33 19 1A 4A FC 8A 8B 3E 6C 2B 26 D6 78 69 F0 66 52 EA 3F C0
  D6 44 6E 10 F1 BD 38 DE 4B 99 33 05 2F 88 FD B2 3E E5 88 D8 A7 F7 E0 BF 13 ED FF 57 DE E1 4A 38
}
```

# Summary of Constraints Over the Certificate Fields

In this section we discuss some of the standard constraints applicable to the content of an X.509 v3 certificate. The constraints are the result of the IETF/ PKIX mandate for the syntax and semantics of certain fields such as the issuer and subject names.

For a CA certificate both the issuer and subject fields must encode non-empty distinguished names. In case of a root CA certificate (one that is at the top of a hierarchy) the issuer name and the subject name must encode the same value. While the subject name field in an end entity certificate may encode an empty value, the issuer name field is required to contain a non-empty name. In the event the subject name is empty, the presence of the subject alternative name extension is required. Such an extension must encode a nonempty alternate name, and must be marked as a *critical* extension.

The version field must indicate version 3 (value of 2) when the **extensions** field is present. Note that the ASN.1 syntax of X.509 version 3 certificate requires that the **extensions** field when present should encode at least one extension. In the absence of the **extensions** field the version must be either 2 or 1 (values of **1** and **0**, respectively). When the version field is omitted, version 1 is assumed as the default value.

Version 3 certificates should not encode the **issuerUniqueID** and the **subjectUniqueID**.

The serial number field must be unique for each certificate issued by a particular CA.

## A Compact Form of the X.509 Certificate

Excluding all the optional fields in an X.509 certificate yields the short form of the **tbsCertificate** structure that looks like:

```
TBSCertificate ::= SEQUENCE {
      version                 [0] EXPLICIT Version DEFAULT v1,
      serialNumber            CertificateSerialNumber,
      signature               AlgorithmIdentifier,
      issuer                  Name,
      validity                Validity,
      subject                 Name,
      subjectPublicKeyInfo    SubjectPublicKeyInfo,
}
```

The subject and issuer unique identifiers as well as the extensions are all omitted in the above sequence. Furthermore, the version field can be omitted in version 1 certificates.

## Proof of Private Key Possession

Another element that contributes to shaping trust in PKIX is the ability to certify a public key for an end entity without requiring the corresponding private key be communicated online or offline to the certification authority or any other entity. In most practical cases, the public and private key pair is generated at the end user side of the infrastructure with the private key remaining securely stored in the user's local environment. The underlying storage mechanism can be chosen based upon the exploiting applications. An example of such a mechanism would be the smart card token.

The PKI management protocols support the need of an infrastructure to require that end entities present proof of possessing the private key, known as POP. Verifying POP becomes a condition to fulfilling the certification. POP verification can be performed either by the RA or the CA. Generally, the RA service is considered to be a core element of the infrastructure and thus must embed a high level of assurance.

An example of achieving POP is to have the infrastructure verify the signature of a requesting end entity. An enterprise level PKIX, however, should support the assurance of possessing the private key in ways appropriate with the type of key usage specified by the requesting entity.

## X.509 Version 2 CRL

A certificate may cease to be valid for two explicit reasons. First, when the time of its use by a reliant party is out of the interval of the validity period as stated in the certificate (expired or has not entered into use yet). Second, while the validity period is still applicable, the certificate subject is no longer entitled to the certificate. In the latter case, the certificate is said to be revoked by the issuing CA.

A CRL is the vehicle by which a certification authority announces the breakup of the binding represented in a certificate. The CA periodically issues and signs CRLs updating them with recently revoked certificates. A typical X.509 version 2 CRL contains the data illustrated in Figure 4.14.

```
{ -- the signed portion
   version number            v2
   signature algorithm       xxxxxxxxxxxx
   issuer name               xxxxxxxxxxxxxx
   this update               xxxxxxxxxx
   next update               xxxxxxxxxxxxxx
   revoked certificates { -- a sequence of
      certificate serial number  xxxxxxxxxx
      revocation date            xxxxxxx
      CRL entry extensions       xxxxxxxxxxx
   }
   extensions                xxxxxxxxxxxxx
}

signature algorithm         xxxxxxxxxxxx
signature value             xxxxxxxxxxxxxxxxx
```

**FIGURE 4.14**
Elements of the X.509 V2 CRL

The form of an X.509 v2 CRL is described by the following ASN.1 specification:

```
CertificateList ::= SEQUENCE {
       tbsCertList            TBSCertList,
       signature              Algorithm AlgorithmIdentifier,
       signature              BIT STRING
}

TBSCertList ::= SEQUENCE
{
       version                Version OPTIONAL, -- if present, shall be v2
       signature              AlgorithmIdentifier,
       issuer                 Name,
       thisUpdate             Time,
       nextUpdate             Time OPTIONAL,
       revokedCertificates    SEQUENCE OF SEQUENCE {
          userCertificate        CertificateSerialNumber,
          revocationDate         Time,
          crlEntryExtensions     Extensions OPTIONAL -- if present, shall be v2

       } OPTIONAL,
       crlExtensions       [0] Extensions OPTIONAL -- if present, shall be v2
}
```

A CRL shares five data types with a certificate—a version number, a signature algorithm identifier, the issuing CA name, zero or more extensions, and a signature value. The signature is computed over the flattened DER encoding of the CRL content. Each revoked certificate is identified by its serial number. Since certificate serial numbers are unique with respect to the issuing CA, a reliable PKIX revokes certificates through the same CA entity that issued them.

The first time stamp encountered in a CRL indicates the date of issuance of the CRL; while the second one refers to the date for the next CRL update. The most notable component of the extensions field is the issuing distribution point name, a standard extension that indicates the location where the CRL is to be published. In the next section we discuss CRL distribution points in further details. We now describe details of each CRL v2 field.

## Version

Although this is an optional field, a reliable infrastructure always encodes a version number. The PKIX profile requires its presence along with the **crlExtensions** field which is also optional by X.509. Furthermore the value of this field should be integer **1** which is used to indicate version 2 of the CRL format.

## Signature

Like in the case of the certificate, this field identifies the type of algorithm used to sign the encoded CRL. Signature algorithms recommended for use by the Internet PKI were discussed earlier while profiling the X.509 certificate. The value of the algorithm identifier used here contributes to the overall CRL signature and must have the same OID value as that indicated in the subsequent **signatureAlgorithm** field.

## issuer

This field is an X.500 distinguished name that identifies the CRL issuing authority. It follows exactly the same encoding rules and recommendations as those for the issuer name field of an X.509 v3 certificate.

## thisUpdate

Indicates the date and time on which the CRL was issued. CAs conforming to the PKIX CRL profile should encode this field in **UTCTime** for dates through the year 2049 and in **GeneralizedTime** for dates thereafter.

## nextUpdate

This field indicates the date by which the next CRL is to be issued. It follows the same encoding rules as **thisUpdate**. Although optional, the presence of this field is required by the PKIX CRL v2 profile.

## revokedCertificates

This field is a structured type used to identify the certificates that have been revoked via the issuance of the underlying CRL. Most important, is the fact that each revoked certificate is identified by its serial number (the **userCertificate** field). Therefore, disseminating unique certificate serial numbers is a strict requirement for the CA over its operational life span.

The other element of information associated with each revoked certificate is the revocation date (**revocationDate**) which indicates the date in which revocation took place. There is nothing that prevents one from stating a revocation that will occur at a future time. As such, applications that seek to reliably validate a certificate need to further compare the revocation date against time of use and not just to have check for the certificate membership in a CRL.

This **revocationDate** information follows the same encoding rules as for **thisUpdate** or **nextUpdate** fields. The optional **crlEntryExtension** field is mostly ignored in the Internet PKI.

## crlExtensions

This field is optional in the X.509 standard, but is required by the PKIX CRL v2 profile. It is used to encode additional CRL attributes that are needed by various application protocols. We discuss the details of standard CRL v2 extension in the next chapter.

## Signature Algorithm

This field encodes the signature algorithm used by the issuing authority in signing the CRL. It must contain the same algorithm identifier as the signature field of the **tbsCertList** sequence. Thus, the integrity of this field is guaranteed by way of the signature value.

## Signature Value

This field represents the trust foundation that a CRL v2 carries with it. It contains a digital signature computed over the DER encoding of the **tbsCertList** field. The resulting signature value is wrapped within a **BIT STRING** to represent the signature value. Computation of the signature value is governed by PKCS#1 recommendations.

# Identification Links between a Certificate and a CRL

As illustrated in Figure 4.15 the certificate serial number is about the only field that identifies a certificate membership in the list of revoked certificates contained by a particular CRL. A collision in certificate serial numbers, therefore, may lead to erroneous decisions by validating entities. Since it is only within the confines of a particular CA that the serial number generation process can be controlled, it becomes an implicit requirement that a certificate be revoked by the same authority that had issued it. Furthermore, assuming that the serial numbers are generated in some incremental fashion, the serial number generation functions need to maintain a persistent

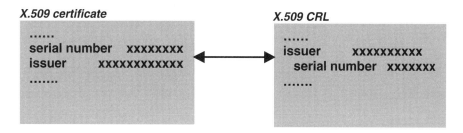

**FIGURE 4.15**
Identification links between a certificate and a CRL

representation of the current serial number over the life span of the authority. Furthermore, and due to the importance of using unique numbers for each certificate, the persistent form of the current serial number may need to be encrypted while in auxiliary storage.

Certificate membership in a CRL needs to be decided by the identification parameters as represented by the serial number as well as the issuer name. To speed up deciding a certificate membership in a particular CRL, implementations may resort to sorting the certificate serial numbers stored in the CRL.

The certificate validation process we will discuss in Chapter 6 involves further elaborate checks than simply deciding on a certificate membership within the applicable CRL.

# X.509 Certificate and CRL Extensions

This chapter discusses a fundamental aspect of X.509 v3 digital certificates and X.509 v2 certificate revocation lists, that of extensions. Without a flexible means of extending certificate and CRL attributes, PKI-enabled applications cannot take advantage of the assurance embedded in a certificate and apply it to their own specific uses. We begin by introducing the need for certificate extensions. Then we discuss the details of each currently defined certificate and CRL extension. ■

## Introduction

Extensions are the distinguishing factor in the structure of X.509 v2 CRLs and most notably that of X.509 v3 certificates. In addition to the static fields as defined by X.509, the extensions field provides a way of associating security attributes to the holder of a certificate. They represent the dynamic nature of security information that can be packed inside a certificate and add up a dimension of flexibility that can be tailored for use by different security mechanisms and protocols. The ASN.1 syntax for the **extensions** field is duplicated below.

```
Extensions ::= SEQUENCE SIZE (1..MAX) OF Extension
Extension ::= SEQUENCE {
        extnID      OBJECT IDENTIFIER,
        critical    BOOLEAN DEFAULT FALSE,
        extnValue   OCTET STRING
}
```

Recall that the **extensions** field is optional, but when present in a certificate or in a CRL it must contain one or more extensions wrapped in the **Extensions** sequence. The generic nature provided by the syntactic form of an extension is expressed in the **extnValue** field which is an octet string and therefore can be used to encode any type of information. The semantics of the encoded value are determined by the corresponding object identifier value of the **extnID** field. Additionally, an operational flag is used to indicate the importance level of an extension as represented by the boolean field of **critical**. The absence of this criticality field automatically means that the underlying extension is not considered critical. Interpretations and operational behaviors resulting from the criticality field of a particular extension are subject to recommendations by the PKIX standards as well as internal policies that an enterprise chooses to implement.

The deciding factor of the nature of an extension is its OID encoded in the **extnID** field. A set of standard extension identifiers are adopted for X.509 v3 certificates as well as X.509 v2 CRLs enumerating various extensions. Conforming PKIX implementations must allow support of these extensions, particularly those mandated by the PKIX certificate and CRL profile to be critical extensions [HOUS99]. These are:

- Key usage
- Certificate policies
- Subject alternative name
- Basic constraints
- Name constraints
- Policy constraints
- Extended key usage

OIDs used for the X.509 extensions are derived from the arc **{2 5 29}** are illustrated in Figure 5.1.

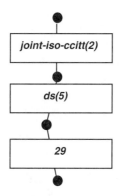

**FIGURE 5.1**
The id-ce identifying arc

# X.509 v3 Certificate Extensions _____

We begin by discussing the common extensions that can be encoded in a certificate. The syntactic form of each extension as well as its intended semantics will be presented. The overall policy guideline mandated by the PKIX standard is for an application to reject an extension that is marked critical but which it cannot interpret. Such a guideline although remaining applicable, can be overridden by local policies at their own risks.

## Key Usage

The key usage extension is a means for confining the use of the certified public key to only certain cryptographic functions. An example would be to use the public key for the sole purpose of verifying signatures. Attempting to use the key to encipher or decipher data must not be allowed. The mere presence of a key usage extension may not necessarily indicate any restriction. Value of **0** for this extension does not assert any particular limitation. It is interpreted for a general-purpose key (recall that the nature of the key as determined by the **subjectPublicKeyInfo** field of the certificate dictates the scope of this generality). Similarly, the extension may assert multiple uses of the key. It is highly recommended that when this extension, when present, to be marked critical.

The key usage extension is assigned the following identifier:

**id-ce-keyUsage   OBJECT IDENTIFIER ::= { id-ce 15 }  --  { 2.5.29.15 }**

and its value has the following syntax:

```
KeyUsage ::= BIT STRING {
        digitalSignature (0),
        nonRepudiation (1),
        keyEncipherment (2),
        dataEncipherment (3),
        keyAgreement (4),
        keyCertSign (5),
        cRLSign (6),
        encipherOnly (7),
        decipherOnly (8)
}
```

Navigating the bit string value from left to right we encounter 9 bits (0 thru 8) which are defined by the PKIX standard. Asserting each of these bits is based upon these interpretations:

- **digitalSignature**. This bit is generally used in end-entity certificates to indicate that the certified key is to be used for digitally signing documents or messages. End entities must not have certificate signing bit (5) or CRL signing bit (6) asserted. These two bits are reserved for CAs. The nonrepudiation bit includes the signing function as well. This bit can be asserted for any entity including a CA.
- **nonRepudiation**. This bit is used to assert the nonrepudiation service when verifying digital signatures using the underlying public key.
- **keyEncipherment**. This bit is asserted for a public key that is used to encrypt secret keys intended for distribution.
- **dataEncipherment**. This bit is asserted when the subject public key is used for encryption of user data, other than cryptographic keys. Naturally secret keys also can be considered to define a data payload and, thus, can be enciphered by keys having only the **dataEncipherment** bit asserted. Key usage separation, however, is recommended as it provides a proper means to managing public keys along their designated uses.
- **keyAgreement**. This bit is asserted when the subject public key is to be used while engaging in a key agreement protocol such as in Diffie-Hellman.
- **keyCertSign**. This bit may be asserted in a CA certificate only (it is a good practice to always assert it in this case). It represents a strong indication that the underlying public key belongs to a certificate authority. However, as we discuss later, this is not the means by which to distinguish a CA certificate from a user certificate.
- **cRLSign**. Similarly, this bit is asserted when the underlying public key is used for verifying a CRL signature. Thus, it is only asserted in CA certificates.
- **encipherOnly**. Asserting this bit is intended for use only in conjunction with the **keyAgreement** bit. When both of these bits are asserted the underlying public key may be used only for encrypting data while engaging in a key agreement protocol. The **encipherOnly** bit has no meaning when the **keyAgreement** bit is not asserted.
- **decipherOnly**. Similarly, this bit is used in conjunction with the **keyAgreement** bit only and has no significance otherwise. It means that the underlying public key may be used only for deciphering data while performing key agreement protocol steps.

## Extended Key Usage

This extension applies to the functional purpose for which the certified public key is issued. It can be used in lieu of the key usage extension or alongside it. It designates the key usage purpose with a higher level construct using the **OBJECT IDENTIFIER** type instead of a low-level construct of the bit string used in the key usage extension. The OID identifying this extension as well the syntax of the extension's value are described by the following ASN.1 definitions.

**id-ce-extKeyUsage  OBJECT IDENTIFIER  ::=  {id-ce  37} -- { 2.5.29.37 }**

**ExtKeyUsageValue ::=  SEQUENCE SIZE (1..MAX) OF KeyPurposeId**
**KeyPurposeId      ::=  OBJECT IDENTIFIER**

Depending upon an organization's policy, this extension can either be critical or noncritical. When both key usage and extended key usage extensions are present and both are critical, the use of the certificate must be consistent and reconcile between the two extensions.

The key purpose (**kp**) OIDs emanate from the arc:

**id-kp   OBJECT IDENTIFIER  ::=  { id-pkix 3 }**

as depicted in Figure 5.2.

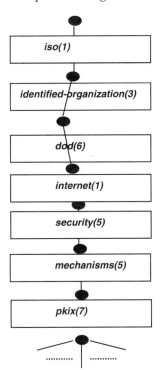

**FIGURE 5.2**
The id-pkix identifying arc

The PKIX certificate and CRL profile standard defines a number of OIDs for the extended key usage extension intended for use by Internet applications. Table 5.1 lists a set of these extended key usage OIDs, describes the intended use, and the equivalent key usage bit settings. TLS is the PKI-based Transport Layer Security protocol, an IETF standard described in RFC 2246 intended to provide privacy and data integrity between two communicating applications. TLS is based on version 3 of the Secure Socket Layer protocol (SSL), an industry de facto standard for securing TCP/IP-based communications.

**TABLE 5.1**
Standard extended key usage values

| Symbolic name | OID value | Description | Equivalent key usage |
|---|---|---|---|
| id-kp-serverAuth | {id-kp  1} | TLS web server authentication | digitalSignature, keyEncipherment, or keyAgreement |
| id-kp-clientAuth | {id-kp 2} | TLS web client authentication | digitalSignature and/or keyAgreement |
| id-kp-codeSigning | {id-kp 3} | Signing of downloadable executable code | digitalSignature |
| id-kp-emailProtection | {id-kp 4} | E-mail protection | digitalSignature, nonRepudiation, and/or (keyEncipherment or keyAgreement) |
| id-kp-timeStamping | { id-kp 8 } | Binding the hash of an object to a time from an agreed-upon time source | digitalSignature, nonRepudiation |

## Basic Constraints

The basic constraints extension is the standard method for distinguishing a CA certificate from an end entity certificate. It must appear in every CA certificate to assert the fact that the certificate is that of a signing authority. Furthermore, the basic constraints extension must be marked critical. Asserting a CA certificate is represented by a boolean field that must be set to **TRUE**. The following is the ASN.1 definition for the value of the basic constraints extension.

```
id-ce-basicConstraints OBJECT IDENTIFIER ::= { id-ce 19 } -- { 2.5.29.19 }
BasicConstraints ::= SEQUENCE {
        cA                      BOOLEAN DEFAULT FALSE,
        pathLenConstraint    INTEGER (0..MAX) OPTIONAL
}
```

Additionally the basic constraints extension may contain an optional field, **pathLenConstraint**, to indicate the maximum length of a certificate validation path that can emanate from this certificate. The CA associated with the certificate may be directly issuing certificates to end entities and not involved in any hierarchical trust scheme. In this case the **pathLenConstraint** value should be set to **0**.

When the CA is participating in a hierarchy, the value of **pathLenConstraint** should be set to a maximum allowable depth of a hierarchy in which the CA might participate. In the absence of the **pathLenConstraint** there is no limit to the length of a trust path emanating from this CA.

It is recommended that this extension be omitted from user certificates. There is no purpose in encoding the basic constraints extension in end-entity certificates. Doing so extends the size of a certificate without serving a purpose.

## Subject Alternative Name

While the subject name field identifies the holder of the certificate expressed in the form of a hierarchical X.500 name, the subject alternative name extension allows for other forms of identities, such as an electronic mail address to be associated with the certificate holder. Because the identity of a subject is an information that binds directly with the public key being certified, it is required that policies consider using strict validation methods to ensure entities are not masquerading under the identity of one another.

In the event the subject name field is encoded as an empty sequence (recall that this is a required field), the subject alternative name must appear in the certificate and be marked as a critical extension. Furthermore, it must contain a nonempty name identifying the subject; i.e., the sequence of **GeneralNames** must contain at least one element. The subject alternative name extension is identified by:

```
id-ce-subjectAltName OBJECT IDENTIFIER ::= { id-ce 17 } -- { 2.5.29.17 }
```

and its value has the following ASN.1 type:

**SubjectAltName ::= GeneralNames**

**GeneralNames    ::= SEQUENCE SIZE (1..MAX) OF GeneralName**

where

**GeneralName ::= CHOICE {**
       **otherName**                  **[0] OtherName,**
       **rfc822Name**               **[1] IA5String,**
       **dNSName**                   **[2] IA5String,**
       **x400Address**              **[3] ORAddress,**
       **directoryName**            **[4] Name,**
       **ediPartyName**             **[5] EDIPartyName,**
       **uniformResourceIdentifier [6] IA5String,**
       **iPAddress**                 **[7] OCTET STRING,**
       **registeredID**              **[8] OBJECT IDENTIFIER**
**}**

**OtherName ::= SEQUENCE {**
       **type-id**      **OBJECT IDENTIFIER,**
       **value**        **[0] EXPLICIT ANY DEFINED BY type-id**
**}**

**EDIPartyName ::= SEQUENCE {**
       **nameAssigner [0] DirectoryString OPTIONAL,**
       **partyName**     **[1] DirectoryString**
**}**

Commonly used subject alternative names are Internet-style names such as an electronic mail address, an Internet Protocol (IP) address, a domain name service (DNS), or a Uniform Resource Identifier (URI). In the following we discuss some restrictions that apply to each of the commonly used alternative names.

- **Internet mail address**. This name (**rfc822Name** alternative) follows the format of "**addr-spec**" as defined by RFC 822 [CROC82]. It has the form of **local-part@domain** with no significance attached to the case.
- **IP address**. For IP version 4 (IPv4) the address must be encoded using four octets in network byte order as specified by RFC 791 [DARP81]. IPv6 addresses are encoded using 16 octets as specified by RFC 1883 [DEER95].
- **Domain name service**. A DNS name must be encoded as an **IA5String** as specified by RFC 1034 [MOCK87a]. In Figure 5.3, a hierarchical domain descending from the **EDU** subdomain is represented as **CS.RPI.EDU**. Note that while upper and lower case letters are allowed in domain names, no significance is attached to the case.

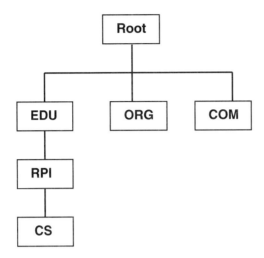

**FIGURE 5.3**
An example of a domain name hierarchy

## Issuer Alternative Names

This noncritical extension is used to assign identities to a CA in addition to the distinguished name by which it is known. Recall that the CA name in a certificate, whether as an issuer or as a subject name, must contain a non-empty value. The format of this extension is the same as that of the subject alternative name.

## Name Constraints

This critical extension is recommended for use in CA certificates only. The purpose is to put a constraint on the naming space from which all distinguished names of certificates emanating from this CA are to be drawn. These restrictions may apply to the subject name field as well as the subject alternative name extension. The name constraint extension is specified by the following ASN.1 definitions:

```
id-ce-nameConstraints    OBJECT IDENTIFIER ::= { id-ce 30 } – { 2.5.29.30 }
NameConstraints ::= SEQUENCE {
        permittedSubtrees    [0] GeneralSubtrees OPTIONAL,
        excludedSubtrees     [1] GeneralSubtrees OPTIONAL
}
```

Restrictions are specified in terms of two optional fields of the **NameCon-straints** sequence, namely **permittedSubtrees** and **excludedSubtrees**. The former is used to specify permitted name forms, while the latter specifies name forms that are excluded from the naming space. Matching a subject name within an **excludedSubtree** automatically disqualifies it from certification by the underlying CA.

Allowed and disallowed subtree forms are chained in a sequence structure as specified in the following:

```
GeneralSubtrees ::= SEQUENCE SIZE (1..MAX) OF GeneralSubtree
GeneralSubtree ::= SEQUENCE {
    base            GeneralName,
    minimum [0]     BaseDistance DEFAULT 0,
    maximum [1]     BaseDistance OPTIONAL
}

BaseDistance ::= INTEGER (0..MAX)
```

Note that the fields **minimum** and **maximum** of the **GeneralSubtree** sequence are not used by PKIX-conforming infrastructures. Instead, the imposed name constraints are determined from the name alternative chosen for the **GeneralName**. In the following we discuss rules governing name forms for a subset of **GeneralName** choices as mandated by the PKIX certificate and CRL profile standard.

- **RFC822 Name**. This constraint applies to the e-mail address when designated as a subject alternative name. For implementations that embed the **EmailAddress** attribute as part of the subject directory name and omit the subject alternative name, the constraint is required to be applied in the same manner to this attribute. The constraint simply requires adhering to the **addr-spec** form of RFC 822.

- **DNS Name**. Acceptable DNS forms are expressed as foo.bar.com or any of its sub-domains such as www.foo.bar.com.

- **Directory Name**. This constraint applies to the form of the subject DN as well as to the subject alternative name extension of type **directoryName**. The constraining rules apply to DN comparison procedures. The main elements of these comparison rules as outlined by the PKIX standard are:

  ✓ The same attribute values encoded in different types (e.g., **PrintableString** and **BMPString**) may be assumed to represent different strings.

✓ Attribute values in types other than **PrintableString** are case sensitive (so that matching of attribute values as binary objects can be directly performed).

✓ Attribute values in **PrintableString** are compared after removing leading and trailing white spaces. Internal substrings of one or more consecutive white space characters must be converted into a single space.

- **URI**. URI restrictions apply to the host part of the name when it is present in the scheme; e.g., in an HTTP URL. The restriction also applies to the host and the domain name. A URI name constraint that begins with a period "." as is in .bar.com means that domain names as such must be expanded with any other subdomain such as foo.bar.com or www.foo.bar.com.

- **IP Address**. The constraining form for an IP address is as specified for the subject alternative name extension we discussed previously. There is a difference, however, in the number of octets used to represent the address. For IPv4 the constraint for the address field must be encoded over 8 octets as described in RFC 1519 indicating a range of addresses. For example IP addresses for a class B subnet of 192.9.0.0 can be constrained to be in the range 192.9.0.0.255.255.0.0. A class B subnet is one that has two octets representing the network ID in an IP address. Similarly, for IPv6 such a constraint represents address ranges using 32 octets.

## Authority Key Identifier

With the proliferation of public key infrastructures, one might encounter a situation in which the public key of a particular signing authority is to be selected among multiple keys. In fact that same CA may be in possession of multiple signing keys such is the case after performing a CA key update, also referred to as CA key rollover. The CA also could be using separate keys for signing certificates and CRLs, or it might be participating in a hierarchy scheme that a validating entity encounters along a trust path. In order to efficiently build a trust path in this case, the authority key identifier (AKID) can be useful in determining the appropriate certificate or CRL signing keys. It is recommended that an AKID value be unique for each particular key it identifies. Because other methods can be used in identifying signing keys, the AKID extension must not be marked critical. The following are the ASN.1 definitions for the AKID extension.

```
id-ce-authorityKeyIdentifier OBJECT IDENTIFIER ::= { id-ce 35 } – { 2.5.29.35 }
AuthorityKeyIdentifier ::= SEQUENCE {
      keyIdentifier                    [0] KeyIdentifier OPTIONAL,
      authorityCertIssuer              [1] GeneralNames OPTIONAL,
      authorityCertSerialNumber        [2] CertificateSerialNumber OPTIONAL
}
KeyIdentifier ::= OCTET STRING
```

AKID may use a unique octet string as in the case of the **keyIdentifier** field or may use a combination of a name and certificate serial number as indicated by the last two fields of in the sequence **AuthorityKeyIdentifier.** The **keyIdentifier** value is generally derived from the public key value being identified through a cryptographic means. Although implementations may choose to use proprietary methods for the computation of AKID values, the PKIX certificate and CRL profile standard recommends two ways for achieving such computation:

- The **keyIdentifier** is composed of the 160-bit SHA-1 hash of the value of the **BIT STRING** representing the **subjectPublicKey** structure (excluding the tag, length, and number of unused bits).

- The **keyIdentifier** is composed of a 4-bit type field with the value 0100 followed by the least significant 60 bits of the SHA-1 hash of the value of the **BIT STRING subjectPublicKey.**

Note that the wording in the standard is less specific in the second method as to whether or not the fields containing the tag, length, and number of unused bits in the TLV form representing the key are to be included in the hashing process.

## Subject Key Identifier

This extension, named for short SKID, is intended for similar reasons as for the AKID extension. The goal is to be able to quickly and accurately identify a subject public key among multiple keys. When dealing with a hierarchical scheme of trust, a subject may indeed be a certificate authority as well.

Figure 5.4 illustrates how the AKID and the SKID extensions interleave in the process of computing a trust chain in which there is one root CA, one intermediate CA and an end user. Values of the AKID and the SKID extensions in a self-signed certificate should be identical. The equality relationships between the AKID and SKID values are depicted in the figure using arrow links. Note that these equalities may be best satisfied during the issuance of certificates by way of extracting the SKID value from the certificate of the signing authority and storing it as the AKID of the certificate being issued.

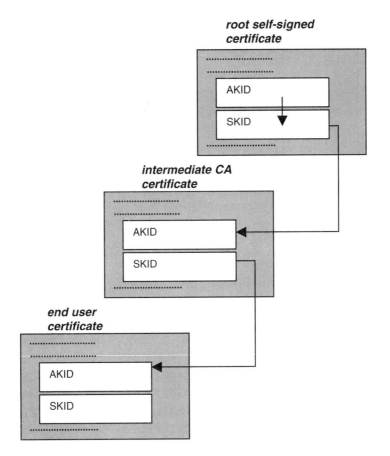

**FIGURE 5.4**

Chaining the AKID and SKID values. Equal values are shown linked with arrows

## The CRL Distribution Points

Reliable PKI-based applications are required to verify the validity of a certificate at the time of its use, in particular whether or not the certificate has been revoked. Conceptually, this verification step is a simple one; it consists of finding out if the certificate has become a member of any applicable CRL. Such a simple yet time-sensitive task necessitates a number of cooperating elements for its achievement. Foremost is the location from which one would fetch the applicable CRL. With the "globalization" paradigm of today's Internet computing, interacting applications are not necessarily tightly coupled within a specific environment.

CRL distribution points (DPs) is an X.509 v3 certificate extension used to indicate the location of the revocation information as it relates to the certificate. It represents a bridge between the certificate and its deciding CRL. The CRL DPs extension also addresses the issue of scale that can arise over a long period of time in an enterprise that deals with revoking large numbers of certificates. By distributing CRLs across multiple locations, validating applications are able to offload smaller portions of CRLs. Similarly CRL DPs can be used to indicate alternate CRL locations, thus improving on the availability of the revocation information.

The format of a CRL DP name is generalized enough to allow for various types of network hosting services. It provides two naming alternatives for the location of CRL information:

- a full name in the form of a **GeneralName**
- a distinguished name relative to the DN of the CA; i.e., a subtree emanating from the CA's entry in an X.500-based directory.

Generally using the full name is the preferred means for designating CRL locations over the Internet. For instance it can be a URI in the form of an LDAP URL, or some other service identified by its IP address.

The format of the CRL DPs extension is specified by the following ASN.1 definitions.

```
id-ce-cRLDistributionPoints OBJECT IDENTIFIER ::= { id-ce 31 }
cRLDistributionPoints ::= { CRLDistPointsSyntax }
CRLDistPointsSyntax ::= SEQUENCE SIZE (1..MAX) OF DistributionPoint
DistributionPoint ::= SEQUENCE {
        distributionPoint   [0] DistributionPointName OPTIONAL,
        reasons             [1] ReasonFlags OPTIONAL,
        cRLIssuer           [2] GeneralNames OPTIONAL
}

DistributionPointName ::= CHOICE {
        fullName                    [0] GeneralNames,
        nameRelativeToCRLIssuer     [1] RelativeDistinguishedName
}
ReasonFlags ::= BIT STRING {
        unused (0),
        keyCompromise (1),
        cACompromise (2),
        affiliationChanged (3),
        superseded (4),
        cessationOfOperation (5),
        certificateHold (6)
}
```

A CRL distribution point is designated using three parameters:

- the location of the CRL
- its issuer
- the revocation reasons for which the CRL is constructed, if any

Note that the **BIT STRING** representation for the revocation reason implies that multiple revocation reasons can be accommodated in one single CRL. Most of the above reason codes are self-explanatory. The **certificateHold** is used to suspend a certificate, which can be resumed at a later point. This non-critical extension can appear in an end entity as well as a CA certificate. It is recommended for use by the PKIX standard as a means for validating applications to locate the revocation information associated with the certificate.

A number of criteria can be used to group revoked certificates under one single CRL distributed at a particular location. One approach that seeks to balance the CRL size would equally split revoked certificates across multiple CRLs starting with a single CRL then rolling over to the next one once the current CRL is fully populated. Other criteria may split revoked certificates based upon the revocation reasons. A CRL that contains no reason flags is assumed to maintain revocation information due to any possible reasons.

CRL DPs may also be used to enable for redundant CRL locations so that certificate validation is not affected by a CRL hosting server that becomes unavailable. CRLs can be stored in a LDAP server as attributes of the issuing CA. Figure 5.5 illustrates three CRLs located at three distribution points all in the form of a directory name,

**CN=CRL DP0, OU=Security, O=IBM,C=US**
**CN=CRL DP1, OU=Security, O=IBM, C=US, and**
**CN=CRL DP2, OU=Security, O=IBM, C=US**

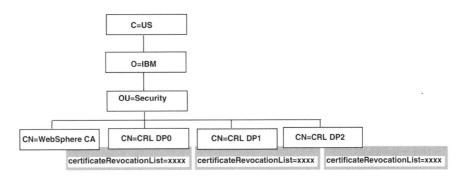

**FIGURE 5.5**
An example of three CRLs stored at distribution points, all of which are in the form of a directory

All of the CRLs located at these points are issued by a CA with the following name

**CN=WebSphere CA,OU=Security, O=IBM,C=US**

In this example the CRLs are physically stored under their respective directory entries indicated by the DP names. In each entry the CRL is stored as a value for the **certificateRevocationList** attribute defined by the standard PKIX LDAP schema (we discuss the LDAP schemas for PKI in Chapter 8).

## Certificate Policies

This noncritical extension can be used to encode policy information that governs the conditions under which a certificate is issued as well as policies applicable to the certificate use. Each of these policies is associated with an OID along with optional qualifiers. Validating applications are required to be able to interpret this extension and adhere to it when it is marked critical. The following is the ASN.1 definitions relating to this extension.

```
id-ce-certificatePolicies OBJECT IDENTIFIER ::= { id-ce 32 }
certificatePolicies ::= SEQUENCE SIZE (1..MAX) OF PolicyInformation

PolicyInformation ::= SEQUENCE {
     policyIdentifier   CertPolicyId,
     policyQualifiers   SEQUENCE SIZE (1..MAX) OF
                        PolicyQualifierInfo OPTIONAL
}
CertPolicyId ::= OBJECT IDENTIFIER
```

The PKIX certificate and CRL profile standard recommend simply designating a policy through an OID and avoid using qualifiers wherever possible. A policy qualifier has the following ASN.1 syntax.

```
PolicyQualifierInfo ::= SEQUENCE {
     policyQualifierId   PolicyQualifierId,
     qualifier           ANY DEFINED BY policyQualifierId
}
```

The PKIX standard has designated two standard qualifiers. The first is the Certification Practice Statement (CPS) published by the CA and defined by the following OID.

```
  id-qt        OBJECT IDENTIFIER ::= { id-pkix  2 }
  id-qt-cps    OBJECT IDENTIFIER ::= { id-qt  1 }
```

The CPS qualifier takes the form of a **URI** used to locate the policy.

The second qualifier that is defined is the user notice for display to a relying party while the certificate is being used.

**id-qt-unotice  OBJECT IDENTIFIER ::=  { id-qt  2 }**

The defined policy qualifiers are specified by the following ASN.1 definitions.

**Qualifier ::= CHOICE {**
**    cPSuri          CPSuri,**
**    userNotice      UserNotice**
**}**

where

**CPSuri ::= IA5String**
**UserNotice ::= SEQUENCE {**
**    noticeRef       NoticeReference OPTIONAL,**
**    explicitText    DisplayText OPTIONAL**
**}**

and

**NoticeReference ::= SEQUENCE {**
**    organization    DisplayText,**
**    noticeNumbers SEQUENCE OF INTEGER**
**}**

**DisplayText ::= CHOICE {**
**    visibleString   VisibleString (SIZE (1..200)),**
**    bmpString       BMPString    (SIZE (1..200)),**
**    utf8String      UTF8String   (SIZE (1..200))**
**}**

## Policy Mapping

This extension applies to CA certificates only. It is intended for mapping CA policies adopted by an issuing authority to those that govern the environment of the subject authority in which this extension is present. The mapping is implied by the value of the extension which consists of a pair of OIDs. The first identifies the issuer's policy while the second identifies the corresponding subject policy. The policy mapping extension must be non-critical. It is defined as follows:

```
id-ce-policyMappings OBJECT IDENTIFIER ::= { id-ce  33 }
PolicyMappings ::= SEQUENCE SIZE (1..MAX) OF SEQUENCE {
    issuerDomainPolicy      CertPolicyId,
    subjectDomainPolicy     CertPolicyId
}
```

## Policy Constraints

The policy constraint extension when encoded in a CA certificate may constrain the validation of a trust path involving the underlying certificate in two ways.

- It can be used to prohibit policy mapping
- It can require that each certificate in the trust path have a particular policy identifier

This extension may be or may not be critical.

```
id-ce-policyConstraints OBJECT IDENTIFIER ::=  { id-ce 36 }

PolicyConstraints ::= SEQUENCE {
    requireExplicitPolicy    [0] SkipCerts OPTIONAL,
    inhibitPolicyMapping     [1] SkipCerts OPTIONAL
}


SkipCerts ::= INTEGER (0..MAX)
```

The **requireExplicitPolicy** field is an integer that indicates the length of s subpath in the trust path where acceptable policies are required to be applicable. Such policies are determined from the certificate policies extension. The **inhibitPolicyMapping** field is an integer indicating the length of a subpath after which policy mapping is no longer permitted. A value of **1** indicates that policy mapping may be applicable to the certificate issued by the subject of the current certificate but is not applicable to the chain afterward.

## Private Internet Extensions

A number of extensions that we have so far discussed lend themselves well to applications written to the Internet paradigm of computing; in particular those that make use of the **GeneralName** data type. Nevertheless, the PKIX working group has chosen to introduce Internet specific X.509 extensions grouped under the **id-pkix** namespace and directly emanating from the **id-pe** (for private extensions) OID defined here.

**id-pe  OBJECT IDENTIFIER ::= { id-pkix 1 }, -- {1.3.6.1.5.5.7.1}**

One currently defined Internet private extension is the Authority Informa-tion Access (AIA).

- **AIA**. This is a noncritical extension used to specify the way to access additional CA information such as the online validation services that the CA authorizes, or some other type of the CA policy information. This extension is specified by the following ASN.1 definitions.

  **AuthorityInfoAccessSyntax ::= SEQUENCE SIZE (1..MAX) OF**
  **AccessDescription AccessDescription ::= SEQUENCE {**
          **accessMethod    OBJECT IDENTIFIER,**
          **accessLocation    GeneralName**
  **}**

- Object identifiers used in the **accessMethod** field emanate from the arc:

  **id-ad OBJECT IDENTIFIER ::= { id-pkix  48 }**

The AIA extension consists of a sequence of one or more **AccessDescrip-tion** type of elements. Each element characterizes a particular CA access information paramterized using two components:

- **accessMethod**
- **accessLocation**

  The first identifies the type of information being exposed by the CA for access by other entities (note that the use of the term **accessMethod** is slightly confusing here). The second parameter determines the location of the information exposed as evidenced by the use of the use of the **GeneralName** data type. Note here that the syntax does not allow for the specification of multiple locations of one particular type of access information. The following CA issuers information identifier, **id-ad-calssuers**, is an example of a currently defined AIA extension.

**id-ad-calssuers OBJECT IDENTIFIER ::= { id-ad  2 }**

The **id-ad-calssuers** OID is used to list the CAs that are above the one that issued the certificate containing this extension. This type of infor-mation is useful in computing a certification path.

# About the X.509 Certificate Extensions

Before we leave the subject of X.509 certificate extensions, it is worth noting that the format of an X.509 extension in its generic form can be used to encode any type of attribute possible. This generalization is based upon three parameters: the type of the extension in the form of an OID, its importance level (through the critical flag), and the syntactic form of the value itself being an opaque octet string. The extension's value, therefore, remains valid irrespective of the type of information it contains provided it is wrapped within an **OCTET STRING**. The semantics of the extension remains subject to the OID used. Provided that an extension is not marked critical, the PKIX model mandates that users to whom the extension is not recognizable overlook it and go on.

By being part of the digitally signed information, the extensions field is automatically attributed a high level of trust. It is apparent that some environments may resort to using private extensions of their own in order to build a higher level of trust in the security attributes of the certificate subject. Such an approach can be used to leverage proven security mechanisms that existed in those environments for so long and that are not designed to easily integrate with the PKI model. The latest Internet and Web technologies on the other hand are designed with PKI integration capabilities. Examples include web servers commonly referred to as HTTP daemons, and more recently Web Application Servers (WAS).

Use of private extensions can be the bridge between a Web server security in the form of a PKI-based SSL protocol, for instance, and a legacy application residing in back-end systems. One method of building a security bridge between the two components is by way of encoding a private extension in the user certificate (see Figure 5.6). A concrete example would be the use of a private extension to map a certificate subject onto his/her identities as represented in the back-end user registries such as that of an IBM mainframe registry (RACF). Security attributes attached to a user's certificate in this fashion may, however, require stringent validation and verification processes before they are encoded in a certificate. Generally, a user would be required to securely prove that he/she is in possession of the attribute being requested in an extension.

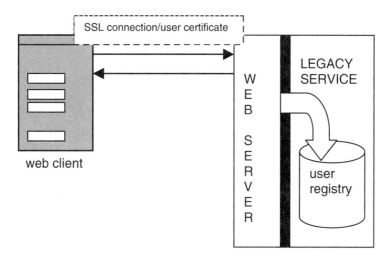

**FIGURE 5.6**
X.509 certificate extensions cn be used to bridge between a PKI-based security mechanism and a legacy security system

# X.509 v2 CRL Extensions

Recall that X.509 extensions whether relating to certificates or CRLs all adhere to the same generic syntax we presented earlier. A CRL extension that is marked critical must be rejected by a validating entity when it cannot interpret it. A noncritical extension may be ignored. As they are in certificates, CRL extensions are a means by which attributes beyond the statically defined fields can be associated with a particular CRL.

## Authority Key Identifier

The syntax as well as the semantics of this extension are the same as those we discussed under the CA and subject key identifier extensions. AKI provides a means of distinguishing, among potentially multiple keys, the public key corresponding to the private key used by the CA to sign a CRL. A CA may have multiple keys for reasons we discussed earlier.

Implementations conforming to the PKIX standard are required to include this extension in all CRLs issued.

# CRL Number

The CRL number extension is used to assign monotonically increasing numbers to CRLs. Although this extension is noncritical it can be useful in determining CRLs that supersede earlier ones. The OID and the value of this extension are:

**id-ce-cRLNumber OBJECT IDENTIFIER ::= { id-ce 20 }**
**cRLNumber ::= INTEGER (0..MAX)**

The CRL number is also used in the Delta CRL indicator extension that we discuss shortly.

# Issuer Alternative Names

The issuer alternative names extension is used to designate alternate names to the CA issuing the CRL in the same way that we discussed earlier for the alternative names of a certificate issuer extension. Internet-related names are the ones most recommended. They include an e-mail address in the form mandated by RFC 822, a DNS name, an IP address, and a URI. It is recommended that this extension not be marked critical.

# Delta CRL Indicator

A Delta CRL represents the difference in the revocation information between a current CRL and a previously issued one. The difference here relates to the revoked certificates. Thus, only certificates that have been revoked since the last full CRL was issued are contained in the Delta CRL. Note the reference here to a previous full CRL as the base for the Delta. The full CRL must be issued along with each Delta CRL.

The issuance of Delta CRLs over regular time intervals yields revocation information that is easier to manage and process. It can be efficient for validating applications to deal with multiple disjoint revocation information. The division of such information enables for concurrent processing. Figure 5.7 illustrates the relationship between full and Delta CRLs.

When present the Delta CRL extension must be marked critical. The following are the ASN.1 definitions relating to this extension.

**id-ce-deltaCRLIndicator OBJECT IDENTIFIER ::= { id-ce  27 }**

**deltaCRLIndicator ::= BaseCRLNumber**

**BaseCRLNumber  ::= CRLNumber**

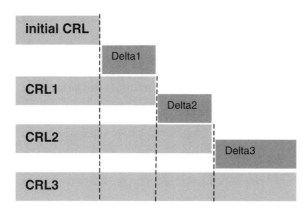

**FIGURE 5.7**
The relationship between CRLs and Delta CRLs

**BaseCRLNumber** refers to the full CRL with which the difference is represented by the current Delta. In the PKIX standard the value of the **cRLNumber** field in the full CRL and in the corresponding Delta CRL must be identical. Generally, it simply matters to number CRLs and Delta CRLs in a monotonically increasing fashion and that the **BaseCRLNumber** is unambiguously resolved to a unique CRL.

## Issuing Distribution Point

The issuing distribution point extension is a way for the issuing authority to qualify the CRL with a number of attributes:

- A flag indicating whether the CRL contains revocation information relating to user certificates only as opposed to CA certificates.
- A flag indicating whether the CRL contains CA revocation information. A CRL with such revocation information is referred to as the Authority Revocation List (ARL).
- The distribution point name indicating the location where the CRL will be made available.
- The revocation reasons, if any. This information forms the basis for the CRL creation.
- A flag asserting whether or not the issuer of the CRL is the same authority which had issued the revoked certificates (**indirectCRL**).

These attributes are reflected by the following ASN.1 definitions for the issuing distribution point extension.

```
id-ce-issuingDistributionPoint OBJECT IDENTIFIER ::= { id-ce 28 }
issuingDistributionPoint ::= SEQUENCE {
    distributionPoint        [0] DistributionPointName OPTIONAL,
    onlyContainsUserCerts [1] BOOLEAN DEFAULT FALSE,
    onlyContainsCACerts   [2] BOOLEAN DEFAULT FALSE,
    onlySomeReasons       [3] ReasonFlags OPTIONAL,
    indirectCRL              [4] BOOLEAN DEFAULT FALSE
}
```

The format of the **DistributionPointName** was defined earlier under the certificate extensions section. Omitting the **onlySomeReasons** field means the underlying distribution point shall contain revocation information that includes all possible revocation reasons. This extension must be marked critical.

### Relationship to the CRL Distribution Points Extension

The commonality between the CRL extension of the issuing distribution point name and the certificate extension of the CRL distribution points is represented by the name of the distribution point. This name should be identical across the two extensions. The distribution point name of the issuing distribution point extension found in the CRL is intended for use by an agent of the public key infrastructure concerned with publishing CRLs. Such an agent, that may well be the RA of the infrastructure (see Chapter 6), relies on the presence of the issuing distribution point name in order to publish a CRL that the CA issues. This relationship is illustrated in Figure 5.8.

## CRL Entry Extensions

Two extension fields are present in the structure of a CRL v2. The syntactic difference between the two is the scope in which they appear. The first has the CRL scope while the second has the scope of each revoked certificate entry. The **crlEntryExtensions** field is intended to associate additional attributes with each revoked certificate. In the following we discuss the standard CRL entry extensions all of which are mandated to be noncritical extensions.

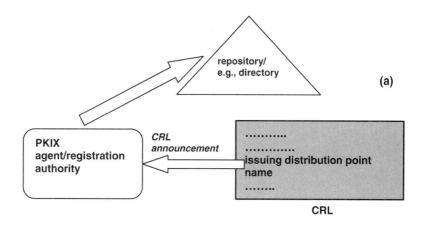

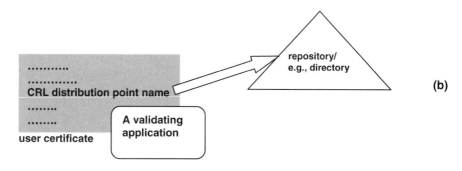

**FIGURE 5.8**
(a) Using the CRL issuing distribution point name to publish a CRL during the issuance of a CRL, and (b) the use of the distribution name from the CRL distribution point in a certificate extension during a validation process

# Reason Code

The reason code extension is used to identify one particular reason for the revocation of the underlying certificate. It is associated with the following object identifier:

**id-ce-cRLReason OBJECT IDENTIFIER ::= { id-ce   21 }**

Its value is defined by:

```
CRLReason ::= ENUMERATED {
    unspecified              (0),
    keyCompromise            (1),
    cACompromise             (2),
    affiliationChanged       (3),
    superseded               (4),
    cessationOfOperation     (5),
    certificateHold          (6),
    removeFromCRL            (8)
}
```

It is recommended that the reason code in a CRL entry extension be absent instead of using the **unspecified** value. That literally recommends against using the **unspecified** value. While **certificateHold** indicates a certificate suspension, **removeFromCRL** is an explicit resumption of the certificate validity. Note that the revocation reason included in this extension should be consistent with the reason flags that may be present in the issuing distribution extension.

# Invalidity Date

The invalidity date extension indicates the date on which it is known that the certificate became invalid. The extension refers to a time that generally precedes the revocation date. It is used to track the time at which the certificate was known or suspected to be invalid.

This extension has the following object identifier and value, respectively.

```
id-ce-invalidityDate OBJECT IDENTIFIER ::= { id-ce 24 }
invalidityDate ::=  GeneralizedTime
```

# Certificate Issuer

This CRL entry extension identifies the certificate issuer associated with an entry in an indirect CRL. Recall that an indirect CRL is one with the **indirectCRL** field in the Issuing Distribution Point extension is set to **TRUE**. The rules that govern the relationship between this extension and the **indirect-CRL** flag are summarized below:

- If this extension is not present on the first entry in an indirect CRL, the certificate issuer defaults to the CRL issuer.

- On subsequent entries in an indirect CRL, if this extension is not present, the certificate issuer for the entry is the same as that for the preceding entry.
- The presence of this extension in any entry takes precedence and overrides any value known for the issuer from previous entries.

The certificate issuer extension is defined as follows:

**id-ce-certificateIssuer   OBJECT IDENTIFIER ::= { id-ce  29 }**
**certificateIssuer ::=    GeneralNames**

This extension is evidently important to the certificate validation procedures. Its inclusion within indirect CRLs is therefore recommended.

# Hold Instruction Code

The hold instruction code indicates, through an object identifier, the action to be taken after encountering a certificate that has been placed on hold. It is identified by:

**id-ce-holdInstructionCode OBJECT IDENTIFIER ::= { id-ce  23 }**

The value of this extension simply consists of an object identifier.

**holdInstructionCode ::= OBJECT IDENTIFIER**

The arc of OIDs specifically defined for hold instruction codes is:

**holdInstruction ::= { iso(1) member-body(2) us(840) x9-57(10040) 2 }**

The following are the instruction codes that are mandated by the PKIX standard.

- **id-holdinstruction-none   OBJECT IDENTIFIER ::= {holdInstruction 1}**
- **id-holdinstruction-callissuer ::= {holdInstruction 2}**

  The PKIX standard mandates that a validating entity in this case call the certificate issuer. However there is no qualification of how this might be done. It is likely that the interaction with the CA here is to be performed via an out-of-band means and furthermore it may involve the intervention of a human.

- **id-holdinstruction-reject OBJECT IDENTIFIER ::= {holdInstruction 3}**

  The certificate must be rejected in this case.

# Trust Establishment in PKIX

**6**

Various PKI trust models and topologies can be adopted. Deciding on one model can depend on many factors, most important of which are the security policies enforced by a particular environment and the structure of an organization as well as its relationships with other organizations. PKI-based trust establishment can be performed in many different ways. What we discuss in this chapter are recommendations as to what may yield a reliable PKI environment. We begin by reviewing the trust models found in PKI and we conclude with the PKIX recommendations for the certificate validation procedures. ■

## Introduction

In broad terms trusting a particular entity means a-priori knowledge of the entity's expected behavior. In a trusted computing system the behaviors of any of the participating entities are expected to not affect the security properties of that system in a way inconsistent with policies in place. In a sense those policies remain invariant with respect to the computational transformations resulting from the services that the system offers. In the field of cryptography trust can be measured by a number of factors such as the strength of a particular cryptographic algorithm, the size of a key space, or the methods by which private keys are managed and secret keys are distributed.

In a public key infrastructure the term trust is generally intended to measure the level of assurance in the legitimacy of a public key certificate. Ultimately this trust property is founded on the strength of the infrastructure against a compromise in the signing key of the CA. Formulating this in terms of expectations and behavior means that the issuing CA is expected to use a tamperproof key store or one that exhibits a high level of security. Additionally the public key certificate of the trusted CA is expected to have been distributed to any reliant party in a manner that yields a high level of assurance.

Establishing the trust property thereafter is achieved by way of computing a certificate trust path and subsequently validating it in accordance with the trust structure that a particular enterprise adopts. In the next sections we discuss common trust topologies.

# Hierarchical Trust

A hierarchical topology is one that maps the trust layout of an organization top down into a tree structure [HOUS99]. At the top of the tree is the root certificate authority. Extending branches may lead to leaf nodes that represent end entities in the organization or may lead to other sub-authorities. The rational for the partitioning may stem from the need to manage a large enterprise into sub-organizations, each with its own managing CA. Figure 6.1 illustrates a general hierarchy structure. Generally there is no requirement that one CA certify end entities only or other CAs only. A particular CA may issue certificates to end entities as well as to certificate authorities. But for all practical purposes, however, the role of each CA may be best managed by requiring that it certify subordinate CAs only or end entities only. Such a separation enforces the hierarchy structure of an enterprise and point out the controlling elements of trust.

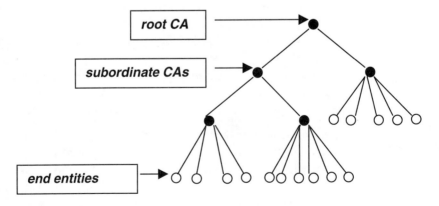

**FIGURE 6.1**
A hierarchical trust topology with one root governing a two- and three-level hierarchy

The hierarchical trust topology allows for the delegation of trust down to subordinate authorities. The root, high trust, authority becomes concerned with the trust delegation task down to a smaller number of subordinate authorities. The fact that the top CA is concerned with the dissemination of trust to a small number of entities allows for managing the strict controls and policies that need to apply at this highest level. One such policy may require the offline distribution of the root CA certificate in a highly secured fashion to the immediate subordinate CAs that it manages. There is a fundamental reason behind the secure distribution of the top certificate—the process of building a trust chain begins at the root CA.

Building a trust chain consists of backtracking the path from an end entity certificate all the way to the root trusted CA. This backtracking process entails a number of validation steps, two of which are fundamental. The first is the determination of the chain by starting at the leaf end-entity certificate, associating an issuer name at this level with a subject name in a certificate of an authority at the immediate upper level until the root is reached. Figure 6.2 illustrates this process of computing a trust path. For each subject name determined as such the corresponding CA certificate is retrieved, perhaps from a repository such as a directory service or one referred to through some URI.

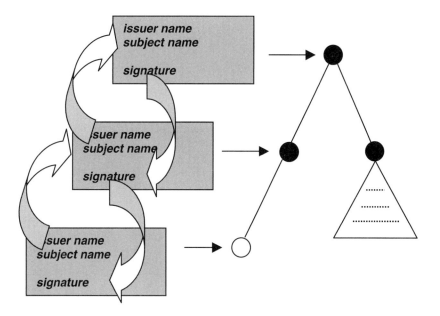

**FIGURE 6.2**
Computing a trust path in a hierarchical trust model

The second step consists of validating the series of cryptographic signatures in the previously computed trust path. This process begins with the certificate of the root trusted CA and proceeds until it reaches the leaf end-entity certificate. We discuss further details of the validation procedure later in this chapter.

As illustrated in Figure 6.2, the determination of the path via the backtracking of issuer and subject names is computed in a bottom-up fashion starting with the end-entity certificate. By contrast, the signature validation process is performed in a top-down fashion beginning with the certificate of the trusted authority.

Signature validation is the process in which the fundamental trust of a certificate is built. It is all based on the basic assumption that the public key of the root CA is trusted. Recall that assurance in this assumption is based upon the secure distribution of the root CA certificate. This distribution process defines what can be termed as the "bootstrap" of trust.

The high assurance public key of the root is used to validate the signature value in the CA certificate immediately below it in the hierarchy as determined by the path. Once this is validated, the immediate subordinate CA implicitly inherits the highly assured trust property and becomes the trust root. The procedure continues recursively until the signature in the leaf end-entity certificate is validated. A special case of this path validation scheme is one in which there is only one level of hierarchy, and thus the self-signed root CA certificate is used to directly validate the signature in the end-entity certificate.

The fundamental element of trust in a certificate chain rests in the secure distribution of the root CA certificate to all of the entities below it in the hierarchy. As such the dissemination of the root CA certificate may involve an offline distribution method. For instance the certificate can be mailed to the respective human entities in a nonvolatile storage medium such as a diskette. Upon receipt, each entity computes a digest of the certificate using SHA-1 or MD5 and then calls the human trusted with the administration of the CA to confirm the digest value.

The notion of a single point of trust does not necessarily concern the root CA only. Rather it can be applied down the tree hierarchy in a delegated fashion. The property that makes this delegation stand is that the recursive signature validation scheme as described, can also be started at some highly trusted intermediate CA. Any compromise in the signing keys above this intermediate CA will ultimately be detected once validation reaches the trusted intermediate CA. The trust path, therefore, requires the existence of at least a single high assurance authority along the path irrespective of its position in the tree hierarchy.

A delegation scheme of this type lends it self well to situations in which end users of some global enterprise only need to be aware of "regional" certificate authorities that directly manage their portion of the business, but need not be concerned with the corporate CA.

## Advantages of the Hierarchical Scheme

The main advantage of setting up a multilevel trust hierarchy is to bridge multiple organizations, public key infrastructures within, say, a large organization without having to reissue the public key credentials deployed within each of the organizations. Let us assume that an enterprise that has grown due to a merger decides to join its existing and distinct public key infrastructures into a single hierarchy so that services in one organization can be accessible to the members of the other organization and vice versa.

The hierarchical scheme of trust can provide a solution in this case by having each of the disjointed CAs become subordinate to the root CA, one that is perhaps designated and managed at the corporate level. Figure 6.3 illustrates a simple hierarchy consisting of two intermediate CAs, and joining two different organizations.

The procedural steps required to effect this merge may consist of the following

- Have each subordinate CA revoke its existing self-signed certificate and publish it in a certificate revocation list, actually an ARL. This will ensure that a trust path should always lead to the new root CA.

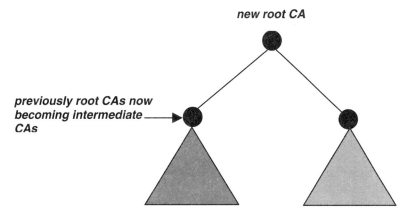

**FIGURE 6.3**
Joining two organizations using the hierarchical trust model

- Have each subordinate CA acquire a new certificate from the new root CA. In order to avoid a CA key update process, each CA may use its current public key when requesting the new certificate.
- Distribute the new root CA certificate in a secure fashion to all of the end entities in the merged organizations including the two subordinate CAs and have each entity replace this certificate for the old trusted root.

The net effect of this join is the dissemination of trust across the two previously disparate organizations via the new root CA that represents the trust anchor for the entire enterprise. Note that if so desired one can split the two organizations by reversing each  of the steps in the trust join operation as described. First each CA requests revocation of its own certificate from the root CA. Each subordinate CA then uses its current public key to issue a self-signed certificate for itself and push it down to each of the entities it certifies through a highly assured channel.

Joining existing public key infrastructures by building a single multilevel hierarchy results in a unified trust model. In this model a single authority can represent the trust in the entire organization. Similarly, the affected trust join operation enables the organization to continue delegating to each subordinate CA the PKI management tasks for it own domain of operation.

The use of multilevel hierarchies, however, extends a certificate trust path and thus may affect performance of the certificate validation process. In order to mitigate the extent of  this problem, a PKI deployment as such may resort to computing and then pushing the trust paths to each end entity's local environment ahead of any validation processing.

# Cross-Certification

The proliferation of PKIs, particularly in the Internet space, ultimately leads to the need for extending the benefits provided by public key certification across the boundaries of certification domains. Such domains may consist of disparate organizations and departments within a single enterprise, or, further yet, spanning multiple enterprises. In many cases the requirement for automated interactions between disparate organizations is what drives the need to maintain the benefits of PKI-based security in applications that bring about those interactions. The basic issue here is that of joining independently deployed PKIs with a minimum disruption and a transparency to end users. Most importantly, in joining disparate PKIs it is sometimes desirable to maintain the independence characteristic that each domain enjoys whereby each certification authority remains the sole authority for its own domain of operations.

Functionally, the hierarchical scheme that we previously discussed can be sufficient for bridging two certification domains. The result of which is tightly linked organizations, virtually becoming a single domain. The drawback is that end entities will not be completely shielded from the merge operation. Cross-domain certification, on the other hand, achieves similar trust semantics in joining disparate PKIs, yet it maintains a transparency of the process with respect to end entities.

Cross-certification is a method of joining two disparate PKIs without incurring any effect on the end entities and without subordination of either infrastructure to any other authority. It is a peer-to-peer contract between two CAs to honor certificates exchanged, through security protocols, upon service requests crossing each other's domain. Each end entity member in the communities joined via a cross-certification process remains in possession of the certificate of his/her respective trusted root CA prior to the merge taking place. This is contrary to the hierarchical scheme in which end entities are to acquire the certificate for the new root CA. The trust model remains invariable in the cross-certification case while it takes a different form in the hierarchical case.

A CA *A* that issues a cross-certificate to authority *B* underscores the fact that end-entity certificates issued by *B* to its own community members are now trusted for use within the domain certified by authority *A*. Similarly authority *B* may issue a cross-certificate for authority *A*, and thus domains *A* and *B* are said to be mutually cross-certified, also referred to as a two-way cross-certification. In essence a two-way cross certification is equivalent to joining two domains under a single trusted root CA, but without a direct impact on end users.

It is worth noting that structurally a cross-certificate is simply an X.509 v3 certificate with a base constraint extension indicating that it is a CA certificate and in which the subject and issuer names represent two different CAs. It certifies the public key of an already operating subject CA as a signature key used for issuing certificates.

The result of a cross-certification is the publication of an ASN.1 object, described next, in a repository that maintains certificates for the CA being cross-certified. We discuss the attributes used by one particular such repository, based on LDAP, in order to store certificate information, including cross-certificates, in Chapter 8.

```
CertificatePair  ::= SEQUENCE {
        forward        [0] Certificate  OPTIONAL,
        reverse        [1] Certificate  OPTIONAL
}
```

The forward element in the sequence contains the cross-certificate issued to
the CA associated with the certificate pair attribute (this CA). While the
reverse element contains a certificate that this CA has issued to another CA
[HOUS99]. The simultaneous presence of the two elements indicates a two-
way cross-certification. In this case the subject name in the forward certificate is the issuer name in the reverse certificate, while the issuer name in the
forward certificate is the subject name in the reverse certificate. At least one
element of the **CertificatePair** sequence shall be present. Figure 6.4 illustrates the naming relationship between cross-certificates and CA certificates
in a mutual cross-certification scenario.

The cross-certification scheme is essentially a one-way operation; that is,
each operation results in the creation of either a forward or a reverse element
but not both. It is worth noting that for a two-way cross-certification (result
of two cross-certification operations) it would be desirable to maintain a single **CertificatePair** sequence with the forward and the reverse elements
instead of generating two sequences each with one element (a forward or a
reverse certificate).

## Cross-Certification Grid

Given a network of CAs, the cross-certification process can be modeled as a
direct graph whose nodes represent the participating CAs while the edges

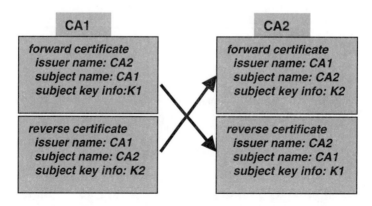

**FIGURE 6.4**
Certificate relationships in a two-way cross-certification case

represent the direction of the certification. A directed edge from *A* to *B* indicate a one-way cross-certification of authority *B* by authority *A*. Figure 6.5 illustrates a cross-certification grid comprised of five CAs.

Note that because the cross-certification in one direction is a transitive relationship, CA2 becomes implicitly engaged in a two-way cross-certification with CA5. CA2 is explicitly cross-certified by CA5. Meanwhile CA2 cross-certifies CA1 which in turn cross-certifies CA3 and hence CA2 indirectly cross-certifies CA3. In turn, CA3 cross-certifies CA5 and thus CA2 implicitly cross-certifies CA5. In that sense the respective communities of CA2, CA1, CA3, and CA5 are now entitled to interact across the domains represented by these CAs. For a purist, such communities are defined by the strongly connected component in the directed graph representing the cross-certification network of trust.

## Hub-Based Cross-Certification

Because of the transitivity property exhibited by the cross-certification operation in each direction, a common hub-like CA can be used to bridge a net-

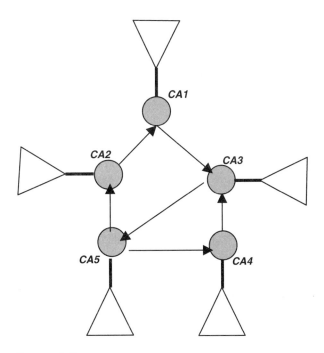

**FIGURE 6.5**
An example of a cross-certification network

work of CAs, thereby establishing a complete cross-certification grid (one in which each CA is cross-certified with each other CA in the network). In this trust topology every CA is mutually cross-certified with the hub CA only. Figure 6.6 illustrates this topology. Note that the advantage here is that the number of cross certifications performed in this case is linear in the order $n$ of the number of CAs involved; while in the previous case it is in the order of $n^2$.

# Hybrid Model

The hybrid model is a trust scheme that combines the hierarchical and the cross-certification methods. A multilevel hierarchy can be the result of a merging of two organizations, while the cross-certification process might be driven by the need to extend the trust to a third-party business partner. The complexity of a hybrid configuration may directly affect the performance of constructing a trust path. Implementations may need to optimize path construction by caching constructed paths for subsequent uses. Figure 6.7 shows a trust path between communicating entities. The path spans two domains in a hybrid scheme of trust.

# Web Trust Model

The web model evolved with the advent of the SSL as a security protocol between the client browser and a target web server. It uses a more relaxed trust model in which a user can pick and choose among the trust anchors

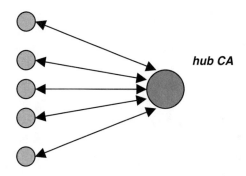

**FIGURE 6.6**
A network of CAs mutually cross-certified through a hub CA

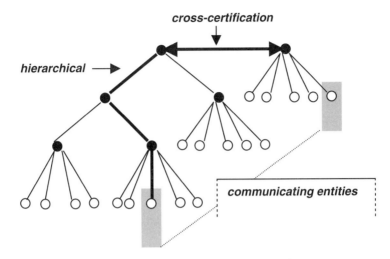

**FIGURE 6.7**
An example of a hybrid trust scheme bridging two entities

that he/she deems worthy of being root CAs. An end entity in the web trust model maintains one or more root CA certificates in its local environment (the browser's key store). Validating a certificate as such consists of finding a trust path to one of the trusted CAs. Generally, these trust paths are shallow and in the most part consist of two certificates, the end entity's and that of the root CA from the browser's key store. The reason for this is to achieve high performance of the web-based applications. Figure 6.8 illustrates a web trust model in which the CAs are completely disjointed.

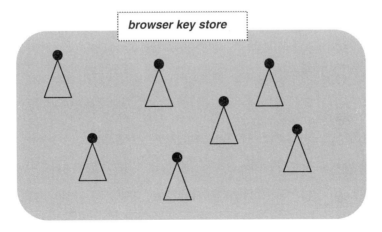

**FIGURE 6.8**
The web trust model: discretional trust of CAs

# Certificate Validation

Validating a certificate is a process that begins with two certificates, one for an end entity and another for a root-trusted CA. The certificate for the end entity's public key is the object in which the validation process attempts to establish trust. The certificate of the root CA represents the trust anchor for the validating entity and is the starting point for the signature validation steps.

The validation process is composed of two main steps:

- Trust path construction
- Trust path verification

## Trust Path Construction

This phase of the validation determines a sequence of certificates that leads from the trusted root CA to the end entity's certificate. The complexity of constructing such a path is directly affected by the topology of the trust network in which the end entity as well as the root CA participate. In the simplest case a trust path may consist of a single-level hierarchy where the root certificate directly leads to the end-entity certificate as shown in Figure 6.9 (a). In a more complicated scenario, however, a trust path may span different domains and several CAs. Figure 6.9 (b) depicts a case where the trust path spans two domains through a combination of hierarchical and cross-certification schemes.

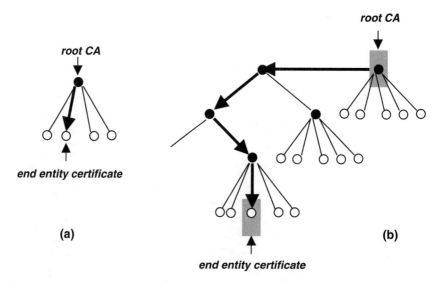

**FIGURE 6.9**

Constructing a trust path. (a) a simple case, and (b) a more involved scenario

Formally, the output from the trust path construction procedure is a sequence of $n$ certificates numbered 1 through $n$, and satisfying the following properties:

- for every certificate $c$ in {1,($n$–1)}, the subject of certificate $c$ is the issuer of certificate $c+1$.
- certificate $c=1$ is the self-signed certificate
- certificate $c=n$ is the end-entity certificate

## Trust Path Validation

Once a trust path is constructed it is ready for the validation process. Here we outline the basic elements that define such a process. First we enumerate the input required. Then we go over the major steps of the validation procedure as outlined in [HOUS99].

# Validation Input

We begin by listing the elements that are generally considered to be the basis for the validation of a trust path. It should be noted, however, that particular organizational policies may require different input information.

- A certification path of length $n$ with the self-signed certificate being certificate $i=1$, and the end entity certificate is $i=n$
- Current date/time
- Time, $t$, for which the validity of the path is to be determined. ($t$ can be the current date/time, or some point in the past.) Perhaps there is no point in evaluating a trust path using a future time since any available revocation information reflects past to current time actions only. Future revocation actions may not be all known
- A set of initial policy identifiers (each comprising a sequence of policy element identifiers). This identifies one or more certificate policies that may constrain the validation process

# Validation Procedure

First we note that failing any of the verifications listed next should result in rejecting the trust path for the certificate being validated. Also note that steps outlined are essential but may not be inclusive.

Beginning at the top of the trust path (the root self-signed certificate number 1), we iterate over each of the subsequent certificates in the path; for each we perform the following validations:

- If this certificate is not for the end entity, verify that it is a CA certificate (as specified in the basic constraints extension). Note that the PKIX certificate and CRL profile specification require the presence of this extension in a CA certificate.

- If a key usage extension is marked critical, ensure that the **keyCert-Sign** bit is set.

- Verify the basic certificate information, including:
  - ✓ Certificate signed using the subject public key from certificate $i$-1. For $i$=1 this step may be omitted because it applies to the root certificate which is assumed trusted through other means.
  - ✓ Certificate validity period includes time $t$.
  - ✓ Use either a CRL distribution point information, or any other appropriate methods, including out-of-band means, in order to obtain the revocation information that applies to this certificate. Verify that the certificate had not been revoked at time $t$ and is not currently on hold status that commenced before time $t$.
  - ✓ Verify that the issuer name of certificate $i$ is the subject name in certificate $i$-1. Note that this property of verifying the subject and issuer names chain correctly should have been already performed by the trust path construction procedure.

- If the name constraint extension is present, update the permitted and excluded subtrees of the name space according to the following:
  - ✓ Set the new permitted subtrees to the intersection of the previous permitted subtrees and the value found in the name constraint of this certificate, if any.
  - ✓ Set the new excluded subtrees to the union of the previous excluded subtrees and the corresponding value that is found in the name constraint of this certificate, if any.

- Verify that the subject name and subject alternative name extension, when present, are consistent with the constrained subtrees that are accumulated so far from prior or a present name constraint extension. The latter defines the naming space of subtrees to within which all subject names in subsequent certificates in the certification path are required to adhere. The initialization of this name space begins at the root certificate.

- Verify that the subject name and subject alternative name extension, when present, are consistent with the excluded name space as defined by any name constraints extensions that are so far encountered along the path. Recall that a certificate whose subject name is consistent with the excluded subtrees is automatically rejected even when it is consistent with the constrained subtrees.
- Recognize and process any critical extension present in the certificate.
- If a policy constraints extension is present in the certificate, update the explicit policy and policy mapping states as follows:
  - ✓ Set the required explicit policy to the lesser of its current value, and the sum of the corresponding value in this certificate augmented with the certificate number in the path, $i$.
  - ✓ Set the inhibit policy mapping state to the lesser of the current value and the sum of the corresponding value in this certificate, if present, augmented with the certificate index, $i$.
- Verify that policy information is so far consistent with the initial policy set.
  - ✓ If the explicit policy is less than or equal to $i$, a policy identifier in the certificate shall be in the initial policy set.
  - ✓ If the policy mapping variable is less than or equal to $i$, the policy identifier may not be mapped.
- Verify that policy information is consistent with the acceptable policy set.
  - ✓ If the certificate policies extension is marked critical, the intersection of the policies extension and the acceptable policy must not be empty.
  - ✓ The acceptable policy set is updated with the resulting intersection.
- Verify that the intersection of the acceptable policy set and the initial policy set is non-null.

## Online Encapsulation of Certificate Validation

Validating a trust path for a certificate can be a complex procedure and certainly may require use of optimization procedures to alleviate any related performance problems. The Internet computing paradigm scales to very high limits. The nature of this high degree of scalability is overall dictated by the unsurpassed number of potential participating clients and available services. With that in perspective, it becomes apparent that offloading all or some of the certificate validation steps from Internet clients and services will have implication on the ease of deployment and acceptance of Internet security protocols that are built on PKI.

Online Certificate Status Protocol, known as OCSP, is the PKIX specification for the encapsulation of timely certificate revocation information [MYER99]. Certificate revocation lists are generally issued at the end of periodical intervals of time. Thus, accurate revocation status for a particular certificate may not be available within a CRL issuance interval. Timely revocation information can certainly be a critical element for the success of business transactions that are based on PKI for their security. Financial applications are an example of such applications.

An OCSP server, by definition, is intended to determine timely certificate revocation statuses instead of simply relying on existing CRL information. In a broader perspective, an OCSP server can be used as a mechanism to hide all of the complexities associated with managing revocation information and returning timely answers to certificate status inquiries. This includes constructing trust paths and validating them.

An OCSP server is a third-party entity trusted for computing a certificate status response. The trust associated with such a server can be due to any of the following scenarios:

- The OCSP service is rendered by the CA issuing the certificate in question

- The OCSP service is provided by a trusted server but other than the CA. Trust here is based upon the public key of the OCSP server being distributed to the requester in a high assurance fashion

- The OCSP service is provided by a CA designated responder (authorized responder). The responder in this case is in possession of a certificate issued directly by the delegating CA indicating that the responder is authorized to service OCSP requests for certificates issued by that CA. We describe this in further details in the section on OCSP topology.

Note, however, that the process of trusting an OCSP responder can be achieved through other out-of-band means.

## OCSP Definitions

OCSP is a basic request/response protocol. It consists of a single request type namely inquiring about the revocation status of a sequence of certificates. In response, a client may receive either of two message types: a certificate status or an error. The certificate status is conveyed by the OCSP server in one of three possible states:

- good
- revoked
- unknown

The *good* status simply means that the certificate has not been revoked. A positive response as such does not automatically imply the validity of the certificate. Response extensions may contain additional information regarding the status of the certificate most important of which is the validity. The *revoked* status indicates that the certificate has been revoked. Note that the certificate in this case might be on hold or permanently revoked.

The *unknown* state means that the OCSP server is unable to determine the revocation status of the certificate.

Each of the status flags can be associated with the following time stamps:

- **thisUpdate**. Indicates the time at which the returned status is asserted. For a *revoked* status this may correspond to the **revocation-Date** field for the certificate as shown by its entry in a corresponding CRL.
- **nextUpdate**. Indicates a future time by which newer information about the certificate status can be available. This might be the time at which the next CRL update takes place. When this value is not set, the client should assume that the newer revocation information is available at any future time.
- **producedAt**. This is the time at which the OCSP responder formed and signed the response message.

## OCSP Topology

OCSP is a simple protocol that consists of two participating entities, one at each end of the protocol. The client, a certificate validating application, plays the role of the initiator. It has at its disposition a single request type which inquire about a certificate status. The OCSP responder, the other end of the protocol, receives a certificate status request, and computes an appropriate response to send to the client. Although other means can be used to configure the OCSP responder and its client, an explicit method for bridging the two entities is through the AIA extension that the certificate may contain. Recall that the AIA extension has the following structure:

```
AuthorityInfoAccessSyntax ::= SEQUENCE SIZE (1..MAX) OF
AccessDescription AccessDescription ::= SEQUENCE {
        accessMethod     OBJECT IDENTIFIER,
        accessLocation   GeneralName
}
```

An authorized OCSP server is indicated by the OID:

**id-ad OBJECT IDENTIFIER ::= { id-pkix  48 }**
**id-ad-ocsp    OBJECT IDENTIFIER ::= { id-ad 1 }**

The network location of the OCSP server is determined by a validating application based upon the **accessLocation** value. In most implementations the location is encoded in the form of the server's URL.

## Source for Timely Revocation Information

An OCSP server may be configured to access certificate revocation information in the form of CRLs stored locally or over a network. Since the main purpose of an OCSP responder is to provide timely revocation information, relying on CRLs may not meet accuracy of a certificate status at any given time. Timely revocation information is generally kept by respective certificate authorities in an Issued Certificate List (ICL). Implementation, therefore, may best provide accurate revocation statuses by granting an OCSP responder a read access to the ICL store.

Additionally, one or more CAs are certainly needed in order to generate and announce revocation information to the OCSP responder. The method used for CRL announcement can be online or offline.

## Authorizing an OCSP Server

If an authorized OCSP server is to be used, the trust in the server must be established by having an authorizing CA issue a signer certificate to the OCSP entity. This certificate is used by an OCSP client to verify the signature of a particular OCSP server on a response message. The OCSP signing delegation is achieved through the extended key usage extension that the delegating CA encodes in a certificate issued to the OCSP responder. The following is the OID used for this particular extended key usage value.

**id-kp-OCSPSigning   OBJECT IDENTIFIER ::= {id-kp 9}**

Recall that the OID arc for the key purposes is:

**id-kp OBJECT IDENTIFIER ::= { id-pkix 3 }**

The client of an OCSP responder is required to identify the issuer of the certificate for which the status is being sought. The OCSP specification recommends using the combination of two parameters:

- The distinguished name of the issuing CA
- The CA's public key

As shown in the next section, it is the hash of these two parameters that the client sends to the OCSP server. The server is therefore required to map these values by first performing the corresponding hashing function. A-priori computation of the digest values for all possible authorizing CAs might be helpful here. Knowledge of the hashing algorithms used is required for this computation.

Figure 6.10 illustrates the overall elements that participate in enabling an OCSP environment.

## The OCSP Protocol Syntax

OCSP is a basic protocol built on two message types, a request and a response. The simplicity of these two messages can be further achieved when omitting various optional fields.

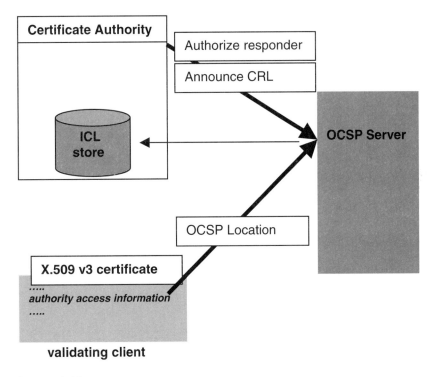

**FIGURE 6.10**
Enabling elements of an authorized OCSP responder

## The Request Message

The client request message is defined by the following ASN.1 structures.

```
OCSPRequest ::= SEQUENCE {
    tbsRequest          TBSRequest,
    optionalSignature [0] EXPLICIT Signature OPTIONAL
}

TBSRequest ::= SEQUENCE {
    version             [0] EXPLICIT Version DEFAULT v1,
    requestorName       [1] EXPLICIT GeneralName OPTIONAL,
    requestList         SEQUENCE OF Request,
    requestExtensions   [2] EXPLICIT Extensions OPTIONAL
}

Signature ::= SEQUENCE {
    signatureAlgorithmAlgorithmIdentifier,
    signature           BIT STRING,
    certs               [0] EXPLICIT SEQUENCE OF Certificate OPTIONAL
}

Version ::= INTEGER { v1(0) }

Request ::= SEQUENCE {
    reqCert                 CertID,
    singleRequestExtensions [0] EXPLICIT Extensions OPTIONAL
}

CertID ::= SEQUENCE {
    hashAlgorithm       AlgorithmIdentifier,
    issuerNameHash      OCTET STRING, -- Hash of Issuer's DN
    issuerKeyHash       OCTET STRING, -- Hash of Issuers public key
    serialNumber        CertificateSerialNumber
}
```

## The Response Message

This response is a sequence of two elements:

- A response status
- An optional response value

The response value is optional so such a response may represent an error code and thus only the response status field becomes relevant.

```
OCSPResponse ::= SEQUENCE {
    responseStatus    OCSPResponseStatus,
    responseBytes     [0] EXPLICIT ResponseBytes OPTIONAL
}
```

```
OCSPResponseStatus ::= ENUMERATED {
    successful (0),              -- response has valid confirmations
    malformedRequest (1),       -- illegal confirmation request
    internalError (2),          -- internal error in issuer
    tryLater (3),               -- try again later.
                                -- (4) is not used
    sigRequired (5),            -- must sign the request
    unauthorized (6)            -- request unauthorized
}
```

In the absence of an error (value of **0** for response status), a response value is encapsulated as a sequence of (OID, value) pairs.

```
ResponseBytes ::= SEQUENCE {
    responseType    OBJECT IDENTIFIER,
    response        OCTET STRING
}
```

For the basic OCSP responder, **responseType** is identified as follows:

```
id-pkix-ocsp   OBJECT IDENTIFIER ::= { id-ad-ocsp }
id-pkix-ocsp-basic OBJECT IDENTIFIER ::= { id-pkix-ocsp 1 }
```

The response value is the DER encoding of **BasicOCSPResponse** defined as follows:

```
BasicOCSPResponse ::= SEQUENCE {
    tbsResponseData     ResponseData,
    signatureAlgorithm  AlgorithmIdentifier,
    signature           BIT STRING,
    certs               [0] EXPLICIT SEQUENCE OF Certificate OPTIONAL
}
```

The value of the signature field is computed over the hash of the DER encoding of **ResponseData**. Note here the requirement for the response messages to be signed by the OCSP responder, while for the requester the signature is optional.

Conforming OCSP clients and servers are required to support DSA signatures. The use of RSA signatures, is recommended.

```
ResponseData ::= SEQUENCE {
    version         [0] EXPLICIT Version DEFAULT v1,
    responderID     ResponderID,
    producedAt      GeneralizedTime,
    responses       SEQUENCE OF SingleResponse,
```

```
        responseExtensions    [1] EXPLICIT Extensions OPTIONAL
}

ResponderID ::= CHOICE {
        byName   [1] Name,
        byKey    [2] KeyHash
}

KeyHash ::= OCTET STRING
```

The hash is based on SHA-1 and is computed over the responder's public key (excluding the tag and length fields). Name as noted in Chapter 4 is defined by RFC2459 as

```
Name ::= CHOICE {-- defined in X.501
                  RDNSequence
}

SingleResponse ::= SEQUENCE {
        certID            CertID,
        certStatus        CertStatus,
        thisUpdate        GeneralizedTime,
        nextUpdate        [0] EXPLICIT GeneralizedTime OPTIONAL,
        singleExtensions  [1] EXPLICIT Extensions OPTIONAL
}

CertStatus ::= CHOICE {
        good      [0] IMPLICIT NULL,
        revoked   [1] IMPLICIT RevokedInfo,
        unknown   [2] IMPLICIT UnknownInfo
}

RevokedInfo ::= SEQUENCE {
        revocationTime    GeneralizedTime,
        revocationReason  [0] EXPLICIT CRLReason OPTIONAL
}

UnknownInfo ::= NULL
```

## Controlling the OCSP Service Level

An OCSP service is intended to answer the basic question of whether or not a particular certificate is a member of any applicable CRL. Albeit, this is a crucial step in the validation of a certificate, it is only one step in a much more elaborate procedure for the validation of a trust path as we outlined earlier. The OCSP specification, however, makes it flexible to specify and determine further levels of service at both ends of the protocol. For instance, a client may request a particular service from the OCSP server; while the responder can inform the client of a level of service used in computing an answer to the inquiry.

The method used to control the level of service on the client side consists of encoding the **AcceptableResponse** extension in the request message. This extension is identified by the following OID.

**id-pkix-ocsp OBJECT IDENTIFIER ::= { id-ad-ocsp }**
**id-pkix-ocsp-response OBJECT IDENTIFIER ::= { id-pkix-ocsp 4 }**

It takes a sequence of OIDs for its value:

**AcceptableResponses ::= SEQUENCE OF OBJECT IDENTIFIER**

The OIDs included represent the service levels requested. The revocation status is the most basic of such services; it is identified by the following:

**id-pkix-ocsp-basic   OBJECT IDENTIFIER ::= { id-pkix-ocsp 1 }**

A number of OCSP related extensions are being defined at the IETF. These extensions apply to various services. One that specifically relates to the certificate trust path is the delegated trust decision extension that allows a client to delegate all aspects of deciding the validity of a certificate trust path.

## Defined OCSP Transports

The OCSP standard defines protocol mappings to only one transport protocol, HTTP. In this mapping, clients can use either the **HTTP GET** or **POST** methods to send requests.

- **GET**. A request that uses the **GET** method is constructed as follows. **GET {url}/{url-encoding of base-64 encoding of the DER encoding of the OCSPRequest}**

  where **{url}** points to the location of a particular OCSP responder. It can be derived from the value of **AuthorityInfoAccess** extension found in the certificate in question or it can be known from other local configuration setups for the OCSP client.

- **POST**. An OCSP request using the POST method is constructed by setting the **Content-Type header to "application/ocsp-request"** value while the body of the message is set to the binary value of the DER encoding of the **OCSPRequest**.

Similarly, an HTTP response from the OCSP service is composed of the appropriate HTTP headers, followed by the binary value of the DER encoding of an **OCSPResponse** data type. The **Content-Type** field in the header has the value "**application/ocsp-response**." The **Content-Length** header specifies the length of the DER encoded response. Other HTTP headers may be present and may be ignored if not understood by the requestor. It is worth noting that although OCSP over direct TCP might be of use, it has not been defined by the specification.

# PKIX Topology and Operational Protocols

This chapter looks at the topology of PKIX from the standpoint of its participating entities and their interactions. For each entity we discuss the pertinent roles and make recommendations for a reliable infrastructure. Active elements such as interacting online agents and passive elements such as local key stores and repositories of the infrastructure are described. We devote the rest of the chapter to the details of the PKIX online management protocol. ∎

## Introduction

A public key infrastructure can be thought of as consisting of several online and offline components. The online elements interact in a synchronous fashion using the request-response computing model in either a client/server mode or a peer-to-peer mode. Synchrony here simply underscores the fact that every request blocks until a response is received. The final service response, however, may be communicated synchronously on the first response or might be delayed in some asynchronous fashion. The side effect from the interactions of the PKI components is the manufacturing of the X.509 constructs in the form of X.509 certificates and CRLs. Subsequently, such interactions also result in managing certificate lifecycle operations such as certificate suspension, resumption or revocation. Certificate and CRL announcements are also events that result from the interactions among the PKI components. Furthermore, certificate validation processes may also induce the activity of the infrastructure components.

Online integration of a public key infrastructure with the PKI-enabled business software in an enterprise can be highly desirable. For instance a PKI integration with the company's human resources management software can seamlessly result in the acquisition of a new employee's public key credentials. Similarly, suspending or removing an employee from the company's user registry can immediately result in that employee's public-key credentials suspended or revoked.

In the next sections we discuss the elements that contribute to the PKI topology followed by the operational protocols of the Internet PKI.

# The Infrastructure Topology

A typical Internet public key infrastructure consists of three main entities: an end entity, a registration authority and the certificate authority.

- **End entity**. The end entity represents the subject of an issued or a requested certificate. An end entity subject can be a human, a particular software application such as a Web server, a daemon agent, a host system, or any other programmable system. Components of the IP security protocol are examples of software and host systems end entities [KENT98b]. An end entity ultimately needs to make use of its private key. Secure access to private keys is essential to establishing trust in public key credentials.

- **Registration authority**. The Registration Authority (RA) acts as the point of contact for the CA. End entities, generally, interact with the CA by sending requests to the RA. The RA may perform a broad range of functions relating to the entitlement of end entities to certificates. It may, for instance, confirm the authentication of end entities using a preregistration procedure. The RA may also validate that a subject is entitled to have the attributes requested in a certificate such as a particular key usage. It may verify that a  subject is indeed in possession of the private key associated with the public key requested for certification. POP is only needed when the private and public key pair is generated by the end entity. The RA also represents the access point for the administrator of the infrastructure to perform interactive workflow tasks such as approval of pending certification or revocation requests.

  The functionality of the RA may be part of the CA implementation. But the presence of the RA as a separate entity is prevalent and for good reasons. For one thing the RA is the component that deals with all the aspects of user enrollment for public key credentials in an enterprise. Only after all of the registration processes are successful can a certificate be requested from the CA. The CA may not always be available online, thereby reducing the window of opportunity for a CA compromise. Overall knowing that the RA is the only component that communicates with the CA adds a level of assurance in the security of the whole infrastructure.

- **Certification Authority.** The CA is ultimately the issuer of certificates. It uses its own private key in order to certify the binding between the subject and the public key in the certificate, and hence the subject private key as well. A trusted CA, referred to in the PKIX specifications as the root CA, is an authority which is directly trusted by an end entity. In practice, it is typical that a trusted CA is also at the top of a hierarchy in which it participates. Directly trusting a CA means that an end entity need not validate the trust chain for that CA certificate when present in a trust path. Figure 7.1 illustrates the relationships between the three main entities of a public key infrastructure. The CA is shielded behind its RA.

## Multiple RA Domains

A number of reasons may lead a large enterprise to split its PKI management space into different domains. One basic reason may be due to the geographic divide of end entities managed by the infrastructure. Another reason may be the need to serve separate domains along the company structure or based upon certificate types. Seeking to divide the burden of administrative tasks may also lead to splitting a large PKI infrastructure into multiple smaller domains. In such an environment multiple enrollment domains of a single infrastructure may look like in Figure 7.2.

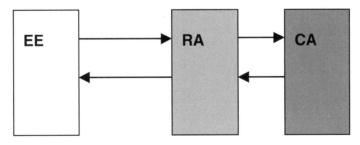

**FIGURE 7.1**
End entity, RA, and CA relationships

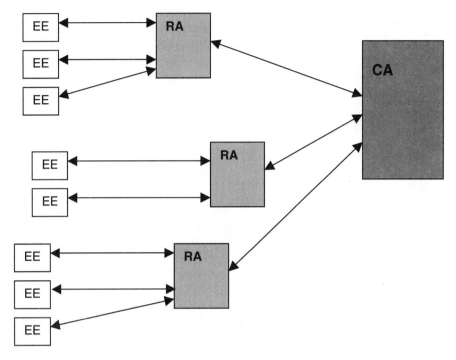

**FIGURE 7.2**
Splitting the PKI management through multiple registration authorities

## RA Enrollment with the CA

The RA may be delegated to perform numerous validation functions. Consequently, it may deny a request for certification even before the request reaches the CA. Because the RA functionality is an integral part of the certification process, the RA needs to enroll with the CA early in the deployment of the infrastructure so that the CA establishes the required assurance that it is indeed interfacing with a legitimate RA. The process of enrolling a registration authority with a CA can be achieved through several methods. One basic approach is to have the CA issue a certificate for the RA and manually install the CA certificate in the RA environment through a trusted human administrator. Digests of both certificates are then computed and compared with each other's stored certificate digests. Subsequent communications between the RA and the CA should be protected using the public key credentials established at the end of the enrollment procedure.

# Other Elements of the Infrastructure

The end entity, RA, and the CA form the core elements of a public key infrastructure. Additionally, a number of other elements participate in the infrastructure by directly contributing to its topology such as a certificate and CRL repository service. Other supporting entities such as a certificate validation service, a workflow engine, or local key store mechanisms can be important to a PKI deployment as well.

## LDAP: The Internet Repository for PKIX

LDAP to an X.500-based directory is the preferred means of maintaining X.509 certificates and CRLs in an Internet PKI deployment [YEON95]. Publishing certificates and CRLs to a directory follows the paradigm of disseminating publicly retrievable information. Such information is intended for PKI-enabled applications and any other relying parties to directly retrieve certificates and establish trust chains. The selection of LDAP is driven by the overwhelming trend that it is the Internet choice for accessing information rich X.500-based repositories.

X.500 defines the directory services model in the OSI world. It encompasses a hierarchical namespace and a query and update protocol [CCIT88, ISOI88]. The latter is known as the Directory Access Protocol (DAP). DAP maps onto the OSI network protocol stack that front-ends a very rich data model and presents a set of operations enabling the deployment of global and regional directory structures. The complexity of X.500 prevented its deployment on smaller platforms and made it difficult to implement a full-blown DAP client that can fit into most available systems. In the end this complexity gave raise to the LDAP protocol. LDAP overall structure and namespace remain essentially those of X.500. The major difference is that LDAP is designed to run directly over the TCP/IP stack, but lacks some of the more esoteric DAP functions. Nevertheless, LDAP has proven to be suitable for most if not all of the directory services sought by applications. The appeal of an X.500-based directory is that it is essentially a directory web in much the same way that HTTP and markup languages characterize the World Wide Web. Anyone with an X.500 or LDAP client may peruse a web of directories just as they can use a web browser to peruse the global Web.

A reliable PKI deployment may opt to limit the interactions with the CA to the RA only, the entity in which the CA has established trust through some enrollment procedure. Thus, the directory service would preferably be connected to the RA, which then performs certificate and CRL publication in response to the CA notifications of certificate and CRL announcements.

## Structural Integrity of the LDAP Repository: Schema Definition

The schema definition is what maintains the structural properties of an LDAP repository intact. The schema represents the set of rules describing what kind of data can be stored in the Directory Information Tree (DIT) and as such helps maintain data consistency and adds a semantics dimension to it. The Object class attribute of each entry determines the type of information that can be stored in that entry.

PKIX objects such as certificates and CRLs are associated with standard Object classes used specifically for storing such objects. We elaborate on the LDAP schema that is applicable to PKIX in the next chapter.

## Issued Certificates Repository

A reliable CA repository (an ICL) for keeping track of all of the certificates that it has issued as well as the revocation states of those certificates is an essential part of a public key infrastructure. Because of its importance throughout the CA lifetime of operations, measures need to be put in place to make this repository a recoverable entity. Recovery here may include periodic backups of the entire repository as well as immediate replication upon the store operations.

The need for an ICL may be dictated by a number of other operational and policy factors. For instance one company's policy might be such that an employee can be issued multiple certificates only for functionally meaningful reasons. The enforcement of such a policy can be based on the usage of the certified key, or the applications in which the certificate is intended for use. The ICL thus provides the basis for enforcing these policies. Similarly, another policy may require the revocation of an old certificate prior to issuing a new one for the same subject. The key to enforcing a policy as such is the requirement that the CA maintain a repository of all the certificates it issues during its entire time of operation. Additionally, the presence of an ICL can be handy for recovering issued certificates as well as for servicing immediate online inquiries about a certificate revocation status. It is worth noting that access to the ICL is generally limited to the core entities of a PKI infrastructure, namely the CA and the RA.

The CA repository, in conjunction with certificate enrollment policies that an enterprise may wish to enforce, yields a controllable way for granting certificates. It should be noted here that a reliable PKIX is one in which certificates are always issued in a controllable manner analogous to the practice of creating users in a legacy authentication registry.

## Local Key Store

While a PKI provides a reliable solution to the key distribution problem, a PKI user remains in control of his/her private key material. A breach in the private key leads to the total compromise in the security of any communication channel that is governed by the certificate associated with that private key.

The process of managing the private key, generally, evolves around the method used to maintain the key material in some encrypted form or isolated in a tamperproof hardware device. Perhaps the simplest of such methods is the wrapping provided by the PKCS#8 specification from RSA, Inc. Here the private key is encrypted using a password-derived key. A more thorough solution that is similar in concept is provided by the PKCS#12 specification, also from RSA, Inc., and which has become widely used as an off-line means of transporting PKI credentials of a user including certificates and private keys. The cryptographic wrapping of private keys that is employed in PKCS#12 can also be based on a secret key derived from a password, while it is generalized to include public key as well.

One method that brings a higher level of assurance and reliability to PKI-based applications is the PKCS#11 [RSA99a] specification along with its related PKCS#15 [RSA00a] for managing and manipulating private keys and public key credentials. The concept adopted in PKCS#11 is the isolation of any manipulations that an application might perform on private keys and credentials to within the confines of a single component (usually in the form of a shared dynamic library). The latter provides a set of cryptographic operations and interacts directly with a storage medium, the credentials token, widely implemented as a hardware device. Software implementations of the token are also available. We discuss this topic in more details in Chapter 9. Figure 7.3 illustrates the layered view of accessing a credentials token through the cryptoki interfaces.

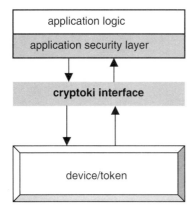

**FIGURE 7.3**

Isolating the manipulation of PKI credentials from applications using the cryptoki

## Protecting the CA Signing Key

The CA private key deserves being the object in need of the most protection possible within a public key infrastructure. After all, the assurance in the certification process is entirely dependent upon the security of this key. Indeed, once a CA signing key is compromised the whole infrastructure including any relying entities and applications are breached. A compromised CA key can lead to all sorts of attacks. Issued and published certificates can be modified, others can be illegitimately revoked. Most dangerous is that certificates can be issued under the auspices of the compromised CA to subjects that are not entitled to certificates. It is prudent to treat the CA signing key with particular care. Software solutions can provide an increasing degree of security to the signing key through encryption. However, because the key must be exposed to generate signatures, it becomes vulnerable to interception and capture.

One approach that affords the CA key a high level of security is the use of tamper-resistant hardware in the form of PCI-based cards to store cryptographic keys. One reliable product in this category is the IBM 4758 coprocessor card that is delivered with a high level of assurance and manufacturing certification. This cryptographic coprocessor provides a simple access interface using the IBM Common Cryptographic Architecture (CCA) APIs as well as the RSA Laboratories PKCS #11 interfaces (cryptoki). It relies on a key-encrypting key, the master key, stored in a tamper-resistant circuitry that withstands physical attacks.

The master key is used to encrypt other sensitive data such as the CA private key using the Triple-DES (DES3) algorithm. The IBM 4758 provides a whole set of cryptographic operations such as random number and key generation, hashing, encryption, generating MACs as well as signing and verifying signatures. These operations are based on common cryptographic algorithms such as SHA-1, MD5, DES, DES3, RSA, and DSA. Figure 7.4 illustrates a high-level layout of the IBM 4758 cryptographic coprocessor. In addition to the cryptographic hardware engine, the card includes a small general-purpose processor. The access control module serves as an authentication mechanism used to log on users to the coprocessor as well as performing access authorization checks based upon the different roles a user might assume. Enforcing access policies as such is achieved by the hardware and protected software. The coprocessor manages DES and Public Key Algorithm (PKA) keys separately.

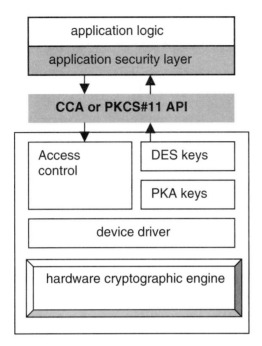

**FIGURE 7.4**

A high-level component layout of the IBM 4758 cryptographic coprocessor

## Workflow Engine

For all practical purposes, a workflow process can be an essential part of a reliable PKI deployment. For one thing certification requests may require approvals so that certificates are granted to users on a discretionary basis. Furthermore workflow processes may be required in order to allow for the human validation of particular certificate attributes that a user is requesting. A basic workflow engine may consist of queuing requests in a pending state and sending notifications to appropriate human approvers. An approver would later interject into the workflow component to approve or reject requests pending his/her approval. Figure 7.5 illustrates an example of a possible layout of a workflow engine in a PKI deployment.

## OCSP Server

The presence of an OCSP server in the infrastructure plays an important role in the deployment of PKI-based applications [MYER99]. As we discussed at length in the previous chapter, an OCSP server may encapsulate parts or all of the certificate validation procedure, thereby relieving applications from

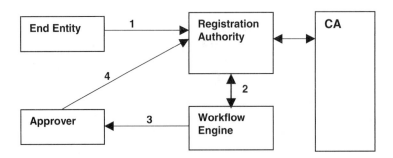

**FIGURE 7.5**
An example of integrating a PKI with a workflow engine

being concerned with the details of this procedure. By centralizing the certificate revocation status in one location, an OCSP server enhances the manageability of an enterprise in which it is deployed. In Figure 7.6 the arrow from the RA to the OCSP server represents the delegation that the CA grants the OCSP server through the RA.

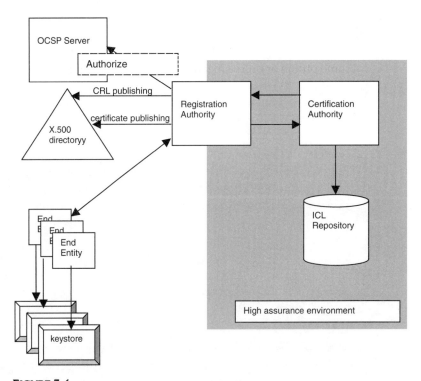

**FIGURE 7.6**
PKIX participating elements

The delegating CA issues a certificate for the responder with a particular extended key usage encoded in it representing the proof of delegation. Certificates issued by the delegating CA include the authority information access extension. This extension is then used by a relying party in order to determine the location of the particular OCSP responder where the revocation information for the certificate at hand is maintained.

# Overview of the PKI Management Operations

Now we discuss PKI operations that support certificate lifecycle management functions. Online protocols involving PKI entities are the vehicle through which most such operations are accomplished. Nevertheless, there is nothing that precludes the use of offline methods for all or parts of the protocols in order to achieve similar operational behaviors.

## Bootstrapping the CA and the RA

This is the initial step in which the CA either inserts itself into an existing PKI hierarchy or establishes itself as the root CA (the top of its own hierarchy). In the first case the CA requests a certificate from the upper authority through some offline or online means. In the second case it generates a self-signed certificate in which it is simultaneously the subject and the issuer. Additionally, the RA authenticates itself to the CA perhaps using a preregistration mechanism. The RA also acquires the CA certificate and inserts it in its own key store. The RA then requests a certificate for itself from the CA. Both online and out-of-bands means can be used in combination for these operations. The mutual assurance in the CA and in the RA certificates can be enforced by way of exchanging certificate digests (fingerprints) using two transport mechanisms, one online and another one out-of-band, for example.

The bootstrapping step results in establishing the core entities of a PKI, namely the CA and the RA through their PKI credentials. Additionally, an empty CRL and an empty ARL are generated by the CA and published accordingly.

## End Entity Initialization

An end-entity initialization consists of importing the root CA certificate as well as the RA certificate. In the Web computing model the RA certificate may really be the certificate of the Webserver or that of the WAS supporting the RA service. These two certificates are stored in the local key store of the end entity. The distribution of the root CA certificate can be accomplished via a directory lookup. However, some validation scheme, usually out-of-band, needs to be in place in order to establish the level of trust necessary in the root CA certificate. To facilitate this important verification procedure, the PKIX specification defines a data type for conveying the hash value of a certificate as follows:

```
OOBCertHash ::= SEQUENCE {
    hashAlg   [0] AlgorithmIdentifier   OPTIONAL,
    certId    [1] CertId                 OPTIONAL,
    hashVal   BIT STRING -- calculated over the self-signed certificate

}
```

**OOBCertHash** (out-of-band certificate hash) is the structure that conveys the hash value of the certificate identified by **certId** whose value is a combination of the identity of the certificate issuer and the serial number of the certificate as follows:

```
CertId ::= SEQUENCE {
    issuer          GeneralName,
    serialNumber    INTEGER
}
```

As we mentioned earlier the root CA certificate and the hash value (fingerprint) as represented in the **OOBCertHash** structure are communicated to the end entity through separate means. Following a guideline as such enhances the security of the procedure thus adding to the assurance in the infrastructure. In the event an authenticated preregistration process is put in place, the end entity is told about its secret preregistration key prior to sending any request to the RA.

## Entity Initial Registration

The initial registration of an end entity, also known as the preregistration step, guarantees that only legitimate users of an enterprise are entitled to digital certificates. It seeks to establish the authentication of users new to the infrastructure as a pre-requisite for the initial certification process. While there can certainly be several ways of achieving end-entity preregistration, the PKIX standard recommends the use of a secret key scheme. Here the RA or the CA and the end entity share a common secret (a password or a passphrase) referred to as the initial authentication key (IAK). The IAK is used to provide message origin authenticity on the initial certificate request. In addi-

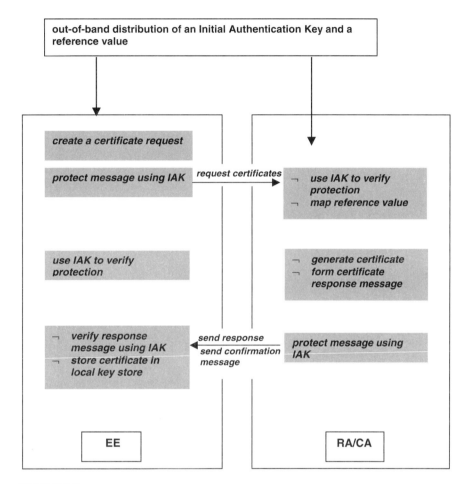

**FIGURE 7.7**
The basis end-entity authentication scheme using a preregistration method

tion to the shared secret, this scheme uses a reference value for keeping track of the preregistration transaction. This initial registration scheme is illustrated in Figure 7.7. Note that while an enterprise may opt to use any suitable preregistration method for its entities, the basic authentication scheme described is required for cross-PKI protocol interoperation.

## Certification Operations

Various certificate request operations can be initiated by the PKIX entities. The following is a brief outline of each of these operations.

- End entity request for certification.
- End entity key pair update. Public key pairs may need to be updated on a regular basis to avoid security breaches, or for any other reasons.
- Certificate renewal. This takes place before or upon a certificate expiry date. Certificate renewal may or may not use the old public key pair.
- CA cross-certification request. This involves one CA requesting a certificate from another CA. The goal is to extend the domain of trust of one CA to the entities served by the CA. Each cross-certification request, as we discussed earlier, represents a one-way certification. Mutual cross-certification is the result of two such operations.
- CA cross-certificate renewal.
- CA key pair update. This operation results in the CA rolling over to using a new public key pair. We discuss this operation in further details in "The Root CA Key Update" later in this chapter.

## Key Recovery

Key recovery operation consists of two independent but sequential steps:

- The archival or safeguarding of a private key material by the infrastructure
- The recovery of an archived private key as warranted

Generally, private key recovery is a sensitive operation which may require an out-of-band procedure in order to enhance the assurance required in proving the end entity's possession of the key being recovered. The private key recovery procedure can be generalized to the PKI credentials recovery procedure where the accompanying public key certificate is recovered as well.

## Revocation Operations

The revocation operation is as important as the certification process. It results in the CA attesting that a certificate is no longer valid for use. As such, it requires the infrastructure's control over who can initiate the revocation action in a way equivalent to the preregistration procedure that precedes certification. Generally, it is permissible for users to take revocation actions against their own certificates. An authorized infrastructure administrator can certainly initiate certificate revocation operations.

## Certificate and CRL Publishing

The PKI infrastructure should include a certificate and CRL publishing mechanism so that reliant parties and end entities can learn about issued certificates and recent CRLs. In most PKIX implementations, the RA acts as the agent that publishes certificates and CRLs. We discuss further details of certificates and CRL repositories in Chapter 8.

## Proof of Possession of Private Key

Public key certification is a process that digitally attests to the binding between a subject as identified by a name along with a set of other attributes and a public key material. Since the public key and its corresponding private key value uniquely correspond to one another, making them inseparable, the certification of a public key indirectly certifies the binding of the private key to the underlying subject as well. Prior to certifying such binding the Internet PKI requires the end entity to demonstrate that it possesses the private key corresponding to the public key being certified. Verifying that the end entity is in possession of the private key and therefore the resulting PKI credentials are usable adds a sense of purpose to the infrastructure. With a secure POP method in place, eavesdropping entities cannot simply replay certification requests.

Establishing POP can be accomplished through various out-of-band means. Online methods, however, are already embedded in the PKIX operational protocols. Depending upon the type of key requested for certification, the following methods are recommended for achieving in-band POP.

- **Signature keys**. The end entity simply signs a value and sends to the RA/CA as part of a certification request. In the PKIX protocol section we discuss the details of the data structure signed by the end entity and verified by the RA/CA.

- **Encryption keys**. There are two common ways for achieving POP for encryption keys:
  - The end entity provides the private key material to the RA/CA encrypted in the certification request. Encryption of the private key uses a shared secret a-priori known between the end entity and the RA/CA.
  - The end entity is required to decrypt a value sent from the RA/CA in order to prove possession of the private key. This method can be achieved either directly or indirectly. The PKIX specification recommends using the indirect method. The latter consists of having the infrastructure return the issued certificate in an encrypted form and have the end entity decrypt it. Encryption is performed using a randomly generated symmetric key which is then encrypted using the public key of the subject end entity and sent along with the encrypted certificate in the response message. Subsequently, the end

entity uses its private key to decrypt the symmetric key. In turn, this key is used to decrypt the certificate. Before the certificate is published, the RA should wait for a confirmation message that the subject end entity sends upon the decryption of the certificate. The confirmation message as such contains an indication as to the successful decryption of the certificate in the form of a hash value computed over the plain certificate. The indirect method  relies on existing PKIX protocol messages for certification request. It is performed using the certification response and certificate confirmation messages only and does not require additional messages.

- **Key agreement keys**. In this case, the end entity and one of the infrastructure core components (either the RA or the CA, but generally the RA) must establish a shared secret key based upon the key exchange parameters of the certified public key. By successfully establishing a shared secret key as such, the end entity proves possession of the private key.

## Root CA Key Update

Periodically, a public key infrastructure may need to update its root CA public key pair. That means a new self-signed certificate is to be issued by the CA for a new public key value. In addition to updating the local CA key store with the new private key and its associated certificate, the implication of this update applies to the following elements:

- The set of existing certificates in the domain of the underlying CA
- The local key store (PSE environment) of each end entity in the infrastructure

For the first item the effect relates to the validation of the certificates issued prior to the key update. The intent is to maintain the validity of these certificates until they expire or are explicitly revoked. Certainly new certificates signed with the new CA key can be reissued to all end entities, but in reality that may not be a practical choice, especially when dealing with a large number of existing end entities.

The second implication is due to the fact that the user's local security environment contains the old certificate of the CA, and thus it should be updated with the new one. Furthermore, such a PSE updated with the new CA certificate alone is not sufficient for the validation of certificates issued with the old CA key. Toward resolving this issue the PKIX specification mandates that the CA signs its certificate for the new public key with its old private key, while it issues a certificate for the old public signed with its new private key. This process results in four certificates for the CA (see Figure 7.8).

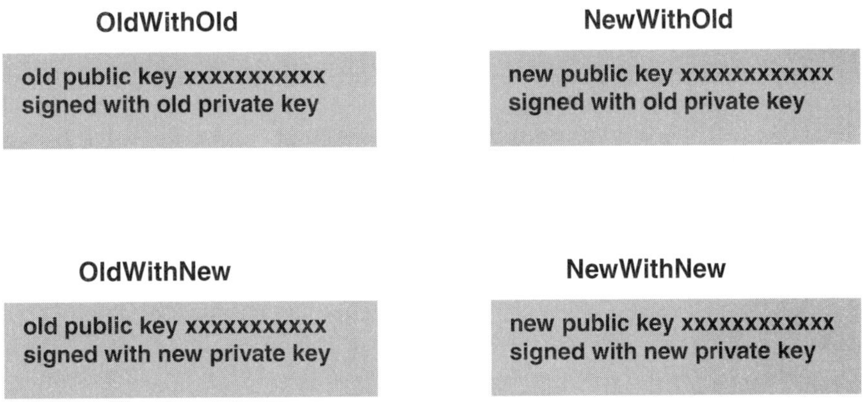

**OldWithOld**

old public key xxxxxxxxxx
signed with old private key

**NewWithOld**

new public key xxxxxxxxxxx
signed with old private key

**OldWithNew**

old public key xxxxxxxxxx
signed with new private key

**NewWithNew**

new public key xxxxxxxxxxx
signed with new private key

**FIGURE 7.8**
Tying the new CA key with the old key during CA key update

## CA Key Update: Certificate Validation Scenarios

We assume that a reliant party such as an application server is about to validate a client certificate and that the issuing root CA has undergone a recent key update. The PSE of the end entity which is the application server is assumed to contain only the old certificate of the root CA.

We assume that the end entity has not yet acquired the new root CA certificate (NewWithNew) but has access to a public repository in which the certificates resulting from the CA key update as shown in Figure 7.8 are published. In this case we distinguish the following validation scenarios with respect to the certificate being validated.

- **Certificate signed with old CA key**. Here the validation procedure simply uses the CA's old certificate to verify the signature of the issuer.
- **Certificate signed using the new CA key**. The end entity uses the NewWithOld Certificate to establish trust in the new key and then uses the new key to validate the signature on the certificate.

In a second scenario we assume that the CA's NewWithNew certificate is securely distributed to a validating entity which became part of the infrastructure after the CA key update had occurred. As in the first scenario we distinguish the following two cases:

- **Certificate signed using the new CA key**. The CA new certificate from the end entity's PSE is used to verify the signature on the certificate.

- **Certificate signed with the old CA key**. We look up the OldWithNew certificate from the public repository that we use to establish trust in the old CA key. We then verify the signature on the certificate.

Note that for an end entity that has securely acquired the old and the new certificates, the validation step will no longer require using the OldWith-New or NewWithOld certificates. In essence these two certificates bridge the old CA key to the new one and vice versa. They are needed only in the described scenarios.

# Certificate Management Protocol (CMP)

CMP is mandated by the PKIX specification for PKI operations within a particular infrastructure as well as an interoperation protocol across disparate infrastructures [ADAM99]. CMP is based on the Certificate Request Message Format (CRMF) specification [MYER99b] now in Version 2. CMP is independent of the underlying transport and provides for its own cryptographic message protection. It does not require separate messages for setting up a client-server security context. Rather, the cryptographic enveloping of its messages is what defines the security contexts of the interacting entities, the end entity, RA, and the CA.

CMP provides for a polling mechanism whereby requests can be serviced in a synchronous fashion or can be asynchronously fulfilled. The choice may depend on workloads, workflow policies, or other criteria that an enterprise may adopt. Figure 7.9 illustrates the overall structure of a CMP message as described by the following ASN.1 definitions.

```
PKIMessage ::= SEQUENCE {
        header    PKIHeader,
        body      PKIBody,
        protection [0] PKIProtection OPTIONAL,
        extraCerts [1] SEQUENCE SIZE (1..MAX) OF Certificate OPTIONAL
    }
```

**PKIMessages ::= SEQUENCE SIZE (1..MAX) OF PKIMessage**

| Header | Body | Protection value (optional) | Additional certificates (optional) |
|--------|------|-----------------------------|------------------------------------|
|        |      |                             |                                    |

**FIGURE 7.9**
The high-level structure of a PKIX message

The data type defined by **PKIMessages** allows an entity to send several requests in one single message. It can for instance be used by a batch application in order to request bulk certificates for users.

## The Message Header

The presence of this field is required in every PKI message. Most notably, this header field indicates the version level of the protocol, and contains addressing information as to the source and the recipient of the message. It also includes a transaction identifier so that a response can be mapped to its corresponding request. The following ASN.1 definition describes the PKI message header field.

```
PKIHeader ::= SEQUENCE {
    pvno          INTEGER    { CMP1999(1), CMP2000(2) },
    sender        GeneralName,
    recipient     GeneralName,
    messageTime   [0] GeneralizedTime      OPTIONAL,
    protectionAlg [1] AlgorithmIdentifier   OPTIONAL,
    senderKID     [2] KeyIdentifier         OPTIONAL,
    recipKID      [3] KeyIdentifier         OPTIONAL,
    transactionID [4] OCTET STRING          OPTIONAL,
    senderNonce   [5] OCTET STRING          OPTIONAL,
    recipNonce    [6] OCTET STRING          OPTIONAL,
    freeText      [7] PKIFreeText           OPTIONAL,
    generalInfo   [8] SEQUENCE SIZE (1..MAX) OF InfoTypeAndValue    OPTIONAL
}
```

- **pvno**. This flag is for the protocol version number. It is set to **1** to indicate CMP V1 or is set to **2** for CMP V2. For some unknown reason the earlier version of the protocol which is presumably V1, the version field was never part of the PKI message.

- **sender**. This field identifies the sender. For generality, the **GeneralName** type, which you may be familiar with now, is used. Thus, a sender value can be the DN of the sending entity, its URI, IP address, or its e-mail address. Generally, the IP address of the sender is used.

- **recipient**. Identifies the recipient of the message. It is of the same form as that of the  sender and is generally encoded as the IP address of the recipient.

- **messageTime**. This field contains the time, represented in a universal form, at which the message was generated by the sender. This can be useful for auditing purposes for example.

- **protectionAlg**. Identifies the type of algorithm used to compute the optional protection field of the PKI message. This identifier, by definition, will also include any possible parameters that the algorithm uses.

Evidently the presence of this field is contingent upon whether or not message protection is in use. When it is, this field must be present.

- **senderKID**. This field is used to identify a key that the sender used to protect the message.
- **recipKID**. This field is generally used only when message protection uses Diffe-Hellman keys.
- **transactionID**. For transactions that require more than one request/ response exchange, this field is used by the recipient to correlate those exchanges correctly. The use of this field is driven by the client and is initially set by the requester. The recipient mirrors the same **transactionID** on the response message and may choose to maintain state for that transaction in its run time as well. In the absence of this field, a recipient must populate it in the response message with its own generated **transactionID** value. Subsequent exchanges must all use the same **transactionID**. A client should not have more than one request with the same **transactionID** in progress at any time with a particular PKI service. Maintaining such a property allows both the client and the server to relate a request to its respective response. Typically, servers require the uniqueness of the **{sender, transactionID}** tuple. In the event of a collision, the server must respond with an error message of type **ErrorMsgContent** and with a **PKIFailureInfo** of **transactionIdInUse**.
- **senderNonce**. This field would typically contain an arbitrary data item generated by the sender for each new message. It is required that the server echo back the same nonce value in the response message. Its use is intended to protect from a replay attack against the PKI message. Such an attack may be attempted by a network eavesdropper that intercepts the sender's message. The intercepted message is then reused with the target recipient. In this scenario the recipient would detect replay by having received the same nonce value more than once. Note however that the nonce can be useful against a replay attack only when it is sent protected using a cryptographic envelope. A nonce which is sent in a clear form can always be replaced by the eavesdropper, and evading the server's detection. The PKIX specification recommends the use of 128-bit of pseudorandom data for the **senderNonce**. The server should keep track of previously received values in order to detect a replay.
- **recipNonce**. Used to echo the **senderNonce** back to the requester.
- **freeText**. This field is added simply for the convenience of exchanging human-readable information. For example information in the native

language of the sender or the recipient that the certificate management protocol makes available to a presentation level application.

- **generalInfo**. This field enables additional information that can be sent over a CMP message. Such information may or may not have a standard format. The **generalInfo** data type consists of a sequence of key and value pairs. Each key is an **OBJECT IDENTIFIER** as shown in the following ASN.1 defintion:

```
InfoTypeAndValue ::= SEQUENCE {
     infoType        OBJECT IDENTIFIER,
     infoValue       ANY DEFINED BY infoType  OPTIONAL
}
```

Two standard uses of this field are:

- **ImplicitConfirm**. This feature is used by the end entity to inform the RA/CA that it does not intend on send an explicit confirmation message upon receiving the issued certificate. It has the following key and value syntax, respectively:

```
implicitConfirm        ::= {id-it 13}
implicitConfirmValue ::=  NULL
where {id-it} = {id-pkix 4} = {1 3 6 1 5 5 7 4}.
```

The RA/CA must send back the same extension in the **generalInfo** field to indicate that it allows for the end entity to bypass the confirmation process. Otherwise, the RA/CA would expect a confirmation message from the end entity.

- **ConfirmWaitTime**. This adaptation of the **generalInfo** field is used by the RA/CA to inform the end entity how long it intends to wait on a certificate confirmation message before it revokes the certificate. Evidently, the **ConfirmWaitTime** extension is used only when the RA/CA policy requires confirmation of a certificate receipt before considering a certificate request complete. The (identifier, value) pair for this extensions is defined as follows:

```
confirmWaitTime      ::= {id-it  14} = {1 3 6 1 5 5 7 14}
confirmWaitTimeValue ::= GeneralizedTime
```

Note the use of the **GeneralizedTime** type in order to allow for a possible time zone difference between an end entity and the RA/CA.

## The Message Body

This field contains the payload of the message. Defined as a set of alternatives through the ASN.1 keyword of **CHOICE**, it includes all possible message types that two communicating entities may exchange. We list the ASN.1 definition of a CMP-based PKI message body. The current level of the PKIX specification allows for 25 message types. We discuss each message separately in the following pages.

```
PKIBody ::= CHOICE {
    ir          [0] CertReqMessages,        --Initialization Request
    ip          [1] CertRepMessage,         --Initialization Response
    cr          [2] CertReqMessages,        --Certification Request
    cp          [3] CertRepMessage,         --Certification Response
    p10cr       [4] CertificationRequest,   --PKCS #10 Cert. Req.
    popdecc     [5] POPODecKeyChallContent,--pop Challenge
    popdecr     [6] POPODecKeyRespContent,--pop Response
    kur         [7] CertReqMessages,        --Key Update Request
    kup         [8] CertRepMessage,         --Key Update Response
    krr         [9] CertReqMessages,        --Key Recovery Request
    krp         [10] KeyRecRepContent,      --Key Recovery Response
    rr          [11] RevReqContent,         --Revocation Request
    rp          [12] RevRepContent,         --Revocation Response
    ccr         [13] CertReqMessages,       --Cross-Cert. Request
    ccp         [14] CertRepMessage,        --Cross-Cert. Response
    ckuann      [15] CAKeyUpdAnnContent,    --CA Key Update Ann.
    cann        [16] CertAnnContent,        --Certificate Ann.
    rann        [17] RevAnnContent,         --Revocation Announcement
    crlann      [18] CRLAnnContent,         --CRL Announcement
    pkiconf     [19] PKIConfirmContent,     --Confirmation
    nested      [20] NestedMessageContent, --Nested Message
    genm        [21] GenMsgContent,         --General Message
    genp        [22] GenRepContent,         --General Response
    error       [23] ErrorMsgContent,       --Error Message
    certConf    [24] CertConfirmContent     --Certificate confirm
}
```

Note that only a handful of CMP message types are exchanged among PKIX entities most of the time. These messages are the initialization request, initialization response, certification request, certification response, and the confirmation messages.

### Certificate Request Message Syntax

The **CertReMessage** structure of a PKI message body is composed of a required field and two optional constructs. The required value is a **CertRequest** data type representing the request content. The optional fields consist of the POP and a set of registration attributes. The ASN.1 definitions of **Cer-tReqMessages** and **CertReqMessage** types follow:

```
CertReqMessages ::= SEQUENCE SIZE (1..MAX) OF CertReqMsg
CertReqMsg ::= SEQUENCE {
   certReq   CertRequest,
   pop       ProofOfPossession  OPTIONAL, -- content depends upon key type
   regInfo   SEQUENCE SIZE(1..MAX) of AttributeTypeAndValue OPTIONAL
}
```

## *The CertRequest Data Type*
The **CertRequest** data type consists of two required constructs (a request identifier and a certificate template) and as one optional object in the form of a sequence of control information.

```
CertRequest ::= SEQUENCE {
   certReqId     INTEGER,
   certTemplate CertTemplate,
   controls      Controls OPTIONAL -- attributes affecting certificate issuance
}
```

The **certReqId** element of the sequence is used for matching a response to its corresponding request.

## *Certificate Template*
The **certTemplate** element of **CertRequest** is used to communicate the binding information that the client is seeking to certify from the infrastructure. Most notable elements in this template are the name of the client, that of the issuer CA, and the public key material for which certification is being requested. Note that except for the public key value, information in this template may be subject to modification by the infrastructure (RA/CA) depending upon locally adopted policies in an infrastructure. The period for which a certificate will remain valid is usually decided at the infrastructure or at least should fall within some time interval that is preset by the infrastructure. The **certTemplate** field has the following ASN.1 structure.

```
CertTemplate ::= SEQUENCE {
   version        [0] Version             OPTIONAL,
   serialNumber   [1] INTEGER             OPTIONAL,
   signingAlg     [2] AlgorithmIdentifier OPTIONAL,
   issuer         [3] Name                OPTIONAL,
   validity       [4] OptionalValidity    OPTIONAL,
   subject        [5] Name                OPTIONAL,
   publicKey      [6] SubjectPublicKeyInfo OPTIONAL,
   issuerUID      [7] UniqueIdentifier    OPTIONAL,
   subjectUID     [8] UniqueIdentifier    OPTIONAL,
```

```
    extensions        [9] Extensions              OPTIONAL
}
```

where:

```
OptionalValidity ::= SEQUENCE {
    notBefore    [0] Time   OPTIONAL,
    notAfter     [1] Time   OPTIONAL  --at least one must be present
}

Time ::= CHOICE {
    utcTime            UTCTime,
    generalTime        GeneralizedTime
}
```

## Certificate Request Controls

The **Controls** element of a **CertRequest** object is used to communicate one or more control values that may affect the infrastructure's processing of the request but will not become part of the issued certificate. Control information is represented by a sequence of (identifier, value) pairs.

**Controls  ::= SEQUENCE SIZE(1..MAX) OF AttributeTypeAndValue**

The set of controls defined by the PKIX specification include:

- **Registration token control**. This attribute contains authentication information, perhaps based on a secret value, intended for the infrastructure to verify the identity of the subject identified in the certificate template. This control information can be useful during the initial request to the infrastructure following a preregistration step in which the secret value is established between the end entity and the RA for instance. This control field is identified by:

  **id-pkip  OBJECT IDENTIFIER :: { id-pkix    pkip(5) }**
  **id-regCtrl  OBJECT IDENTIFIER ::= { id-pkip   regCtrl(1) }**

- **Authenticator control**. This information is used to establish the identity of the subject. However, verification of the identity in this case is based upon a non-cryptographic method such as knowledge of the mother's maiden name, city of birth, and so forth. This control is identified by:

  **id-regCtrl-authenticator    OBJECT IDENTIFIER ::= { id-regCtrl  2 }**

- **Publication information control**. This option enables the client to control the infrastructure's publication of the certificate. It has the following syntax:

```
PKIPublicationInfo ::= SEQUENCE {
    action   INTEGER {
                dontPublish (0),
                pleasePublish (1)
        },
    pubInfos  SEQUENCE SIZE (1..MAX) OF SinglePubInfo OPTIONAL
}
```

If the desired action is **dontPublish**, the **pubInfos** field must not be present. **SinglePubInfor** type is defined as follows:

```
SinglePubInfo ::= SEQUENCE {
    pubMethod   INTEGER {
                dontCare   (0),
                x500       (1),
                web        (2),
                ldap       (3)
            },
    pubLocation  GeneralName OPTIONAL
}
```

The following OID indicates the publication control option.

**id-regCtrl-pkiPublicationInfo  OBJECT IDENTIFIER ::= { id-regCtrl 3 }**

- **Archive options control**. This information enables the client to control the archival options for his/her private key. The private key intended for archival can be communicate in three different ways:
  - Where the key pair is generated by the client, the private key is communicated to the infrastructure on a certification request so that it can be archived.
  - A client can communicate not the private key material but the parameters needed for the key to be regenerated by the infrastructure.
  - A client can instruct the infrastructure to generate and archive the private key. The private key is then returned to the client in the certificate response message. The boolean flag of **archiveRemGen-PrivKey** is used in this case.

The three archive options above are described by the following ASN.1 definition.

```
PKIArchiveOptions ::= CHOICE {
    encryptedPrivKey        [0] EncryptedKey,
    keyGenParameters        [1] KeyGenParameters,
    archiveRemGenPrivKey    [2] BOOLEAN
}
```

The end entity that generates its own public key pair may communicate the private key material to the infrastructure in two ways as indicated by the following ASN.1 **CHOICE** in which **EnvelopedData** is generally the preferred method.

```
EncryptedKey ::= CHOICE {
    encryptedValue    EncryptedValue,
    envelopedData     [0] EnvelopedData
}
```

The **EncyptedValue** alternative has the following syntax:

```
EncryptedValue ::= SEQUENCE {
    intendedAlg [0] AlgorithmIdentifier   OPTIONAL,
                -- the intended algorithm for which the value will be used
    symmAlg     [1] AlgorithmIdentifier   OPTIONAL,
                -- the symmetric algorithm used to encrypt the value
    encSymmKey[2] BIT STRING              OPTIONAL,
                -- the (encrypted) symmetric key used to encrypt the value
    keyAlg      [3] AlgorithmIdentifier   OPTIONAL,
                -- algorithm used to encrypt the symmetric key
    valueHint   [4] OCTET STRING          OPTIONAL,
                -- a brief description or identifier of the encValue content
                -- (may be meaningful only to the sending entity, and used only
                -- if EncryptedValue might be re-examined by the sending
                -- entity in the future)
    encValue    BIT STRING
}
```

For the **EnvelopedData** alternative, the private key must be placed in the **encryptedContent** octet string part of the **encryptedContentInfo** structure as defined by the PKCS #7 specification discussed in Chapter 10.

For the key regeneration archive option there is no particular syntax for how the key parameters are specified except for the entire parameters being wrapped inside a string of octets as:

**KeyGenParameters ::= OCTET STRING**

Thus, the interpretation of the opaque key generation parameters can be implementation dependent. For instance the key generation parameters for an RSA-based key may consist of a sequence of two random prime numbers. The sequence is then wrapped inside an outer octet string and communicated to the infrastructure. The key archive control option is identified through:

**id-regCtrl-pkiArchiveOptions   OBJECT IDENTIFIER ::= { id-regCtrl  4 }**

- **OldCertID control**. This control information is used to request that cer-tification be performed in reference to an existing certificate that the client had already obtained. The certificate to be updated is identified via the issuer name and the serial number as follows:

**CertId ::= SEQUENCE {**
    **issuer            GeneralName,**
    **serialNumber   INTEGER**
**}**

This control option can be useful in situations such as:
- An enterprise that is rolling over to a new public key infrastructure
- A certification renewal or update

Note that a reliable public key infrastructure may adopt a policy of replacing the old certificate in the certificate repository with a new one that was issued under an **OldCertID** control option. Doing so avoids the proliferation of public key certificates that are no longer usable.

The **OldCertID** option is identified by:

**id-regCtrl-oldCertID        OBJECT IDENTIFIER ::= { id-regCtrl  5 }**

- **Protocol encryption key control**. This control option is used to spec-ify a key that the CA is to use in encrypting the response message. This option is particularly useful  when the public key pair is generated by the infrastructure. In this case the private key is returned to the requesting entity encrypted using a key specified in the request mes-sage. This control option is identified by:

**id-regCtrl-protocolEncrKey    OBJECT IDENTIFIER ::= { id-regCtrl 6 }**

## The CMP Message Protection Field

CMP message protection provides the following two security services:

- Message origin authentication
- Data integrity

The input to the CMP message protection procedure is the DER encoding of a sequence containing the message header followed by the message payload as defined by the following:

```
ProtectedPart ::= SEQUENCE {
    header  PKIHeader,
    body    PKIBody
}
```

Using asymmetric public keys in order to establish message authenticity generally requires an already certified public key which is likely not to be the case on an initial certification request. We distinguish two scenarios.

- The first applies to the initial certificate enrollment phase.
- The second is applicable to the case where the requesting entity already holds a certified public key.

### Protecting the Initial Enrollment Transaction

During the initial certification request message protection can be performed using a shared secret key distributed using some in-band or out-of-band transport mechanism. The PKIX specification mandates the use of a password-based MAC defined by the following:

```
PasswordBasedMac ::= OBJECT IDENTIFIER --{1 2 840 113533 7 66 13}
PBMParameter ::= SEQUENCE {
    salt            OCTET STRING,
    owf             AlgorithmIdentifier,  -- a one-way hash function (SHA-1
                                             recommended)
    iterationCount INTEGER,               -- number of times the owf is applied
    mac             AlgorithmIdentifier   -- e.g., DES-MAC, Triple-DES-MAC
                                          -- or HMAC [RFC2104, RFC2202])
}
```

The **salt** value is initially appended to the password. The identified hash function is applied to the concatenation of the password and salt **iteration-Count** times. On each iteration the input is set to be the output from the previous iteration. The resulting value, referred to as $BASEKEY$ with a size of $H$ is then used to form the symmetric key for the computation of the MAC value as quoted in the following statements from the PKIX CMP specification:

> If the MAC algorithm requires a $K$-bit key and $K \leq H$, then the most significant $K$ bits of **BASEKEY** are used. If $K > H$, then all of **BASEKEY** is used for the most significant $H$ bits of the key, and **OWF("1" II BASEKEY)** is used for the next most significant $H$ bits of the key, while **OWF("2" II BASEKEY)** is used for the next most significant $H$ bits of the key, and so on, until all $K$ bits have been derived. The notation **"N"** is for the ASCII byte encoding the number N and "I I" represents concatenation.

Although not a requirement, it is recommended that a single transaction, such as one that starts with the initial certification request and continues through the final confirmation message, uses the same parameters for the MAC computation.

## Public Key-Based Protection

This is a scenario in which the end entity already holds a certified public key. We distinguish the following specific cases:

- **Diffie-Hellman key**. Here the sender and the recipient are assumed to already hold Diffie-Hellman certificates containing compatible parameters. The sender generates a symmetric key based upon its private DH key value and the DH public key value of the recipient. The CMP message protection field is then computed as a MAC value keyed with the symmetric key derived through the Diffie-Hellman process. The protection algorithm in this case has the following object identifier:

```
DHBasedMac ::= OBJECT IDENTIFIER --{1 2 840 113533 7 66 30}
DHBMParameter ::= SEQUENCE {
    owf  AlgorithmIdentifier, -- SHA-1 recommended
    mac  AlgorithmIdentifier  -- the MAC AlgId (e.g., DES-MAC,
                                    Triple-DES-MAC or HMAC)
}
```

- Due to its effect on interoperation, we quote the following paragraph from the PKIX specification on how the protection value is computed in this case.

> In the above **protectionAlg, owf** is applied to the result of the Diffie-Hellman computation. The **owf** output (called *BASEKEY* for ease of reference, with a size of *H*) is what is used to form the symmetric key. If the MAC algorithm requires a K-bit key and $K <= H$, then the most significant $K$ bits of *BASEKEY* are used. If $K > H$, then all of *BASEKEY* is used for the most significant $H$ bits of the key, *OWF("1" || BASEKEY)* is used for the next most significant $H$ bits of the key, *OWF("2" || BASEKEY)* is used for the next most significant $H$ bits of the key, and so on, until all K bits have been derived.

- **Signature key**. The sender uses his/her private key from a certified public key pair to sign the CMP message. The protection field, thus, contains the signature value while the protection algorithm field identifies the signature algorithm used.

## CMP Message Types

Current level of CMP (V2.0) allows for 25 message types that define PKIX management operations. A brief description of each message follows. Refer to RFC 2510 for a complete set of interoperability profiles describing details of message contents.

### Initialization Request

The structure of an initialization request is of type **CertRequestMessages** which we previously described. It is intended for use by an entity requesting a certificate for the first time.

### Initialization Response

Contains a **certRepMessage** data type. It is sent by the infrastructure to the client in response to an initial certification request. For each requested certificate, the response contains a **PKIStatusInfo** field indicating the fulfillment status for the request, possibly an issued certificate, as well as an encrypted private key material in case the key generation procedure takes place within the realms of the RA/CA. The following is the ASN.1 structure for the initialization response:

```
CertRepMessage ::= SEQUENCE {
    caPubs      [1] SEQUENCE SIZE (1..MAX) OF Certificate OPTIONAL,
    response    SEQUENCE OF CertResponse
}
```

The optional **caPubs** field may be used by the infrastructure to send the chain of certificates leading up to the root authority directly trusted by the client.

```
CertResponse ::= SEQUENCE {
    certReqId          INTEGER,
    status             PKIStatusInfo,
    certifiedKeyPair   CertifiedKeyPair   OPTIONAL,
    rspInfo            OCTET STRING   OPTIONAL
}
```

The **certReqId** should match a pending certificate request on the client side. A value of **−1** is used to indicate that a request identifier was not specified in the corresponding request message. The **rspInfo** field contains a series of UTF8 name/value pairs.

```
CertifiedKeyPair ::= SEQUENCE {
    certOrEncCert      CertOrEncCert,
    privateKey         [0] EncryptedValue     OPTIONAL,
    publicationInfo    [1] PKIPublicationInfo OPTIONAL
 }
```

```
CertOrEncCert ::= CHOICE {
    certificate        [0] Certificate,
    encryptedCert      [1] EncryptedValue
}
```

## Certification Request
Like for the initial request, this message is encoded as a **certReqMessages** data type. It is intended for use by entities in acquiring additional certificates.

## Certification Response
Similarly a certification response, as for the initialization response message, is sent by the infrastructure to the client in response to a certificate request.

## PKCS #10 Certificate Request
PKCS #10, a specification originating from RSA Inc. and later adopted by IETF RFC 2314, is a syntax describing a certification request [KALI98b]. Here, a certification request is defined by a distinguished name, a public key, and, optionally, a set of attributes, collectively signed by the entity requesting the certification of its public key. The format defined by PKCS #10 is described by the following ASN.1 structure.

```
CertificationRequest ::= SEQUENCE {
    certificationRequestInfo    CertificationRequestInfo,
    signatureAlgorithm          AlgorithmIdentifier{{ SignatureAlgorithms }},
    signature                   BIT STRING
}
```

The **certificationRequestInfo** field encodes a certification request template and defines the input to the signature algorithm identified by the **signature-Algorithm** field. The output from the signing procedure is then encoded in the signature field. In turn, the **CertificationRequestInfo** data type has the following syntax:

```
CertificationRequestInfo ::= SEQUENCE {
    version         INTEGER { v1(0) } (v1,...),
    subject         Name,
    subjectPKInfo   SubjectPublicKeyInfo,
    attributes      [0] Attributes
}
```

Where the **attributes** field is a set of (type, value) pairs, each of which represents a particular attribute.

## A Note About the Use of PKCS #10

A PKCS #10 in itself encapsulates a certificate enrollment request. It is natural to question why a PKCS #10 format is used within yet another certificate request protocol message. The answer is the combination of two factors.

- PKCS #10 alone does not provide a means to authenticate the initiator of the request. Albeit the requester must be in possession of the private key, the signature over the request information does not guarantee that the request is not substituted by an eavesdropper. Tunneling a PKCS #10 format within a CMP request, therefore, enables the establishment of an authenticated session between the initiating entity and the infrastructure.

- The PKCS #10 syntax represents a compact form of a certification request in which a minimal set of attributes is used. It is worth noting here that due to its compacted content a PKCS #10 has been used mainly as a certificate enrollment on its own over Web browsers. In this case a PKCS #10 DER-encoded request is first transformed into its base 64 representation. The result is then provided as a request argument for a target URL under which the infrastructure's RA or CA is running. SSL security protocol has been the mechanism of choice for securing such links, thereby providing various security services such as session authenticity, integrity, and confidentiality.

# POP Challenge

This message is part of the challenge response exchange that takes place in the direct method of establishing POP as we discussed previously. Here the infrastructure, typically the RA, sends the end entity a challenge information for each private key for which a public key certification is requested. The challenge information has the following ASN.1 format:

```
Challenge ::= SEQUENCE {
    owf         AlgorithmIdentifier  OPTIONAL,
    witness     OCTET STRING,
    challenge   OCTET STRING
}
```

**witness** is the result of applying the one-way hash function identified by the **owf** field to a randomly generated integer value. While **challenge** is computed using the public key for which certification is being requested to encrypt the BER encoding of the following structure:

```
Rand ::= SEQUENCE {
    int      INTEGER, -- the randomly-generated INTEGER
    sender   GeneralName -- the sender's name (as included in PKIHeader)
}
```

# POP Response

This is the response to the POP challenge message. The entity being challenged for POP is required to send back the randomly generated integer value that the challenge message carried in an encrypted form. The content of the POP response message is the value of the integer as determined from the encrypted challenge. Each decrypted challenge corresponds to one certification request in the order specified in the request.

**POPODecKeyRespContent ::= SEQUENCE OF INTEGER**

# Key Update Request

This message is intended for use when requesting updates to existing valid certificates. It is also referred to as a certificate update message. Typically a new public key is used for this operation although nothing precludes the use if the old key as well. The syntax of this message is that of **certReqMessages**.

# Key Update Response

This message is sent by the infrastructure to the end entity in response to a key update request. It follows the same syntax as that of the initialization request.

## Key Recovery Request

This message is intended for use in key recovery operations. It has a similar syntax as for the initialization request. The infrastructure should return the archived private key only after establishing POP by the end entity.

## Key Recovery Response

This message content is sent by the infrastructure to the end entity in response to a key recovery request. It has the following syntax.

```
KeyRecRepContent ::= SEQUENCE {
    status         PKIStatusInfo,
    newSigCert     [0] Certificate              OPTIONAL,
    caCerts        [1] SEQUENCE SIZE (1..MAX) OF Certificate     OPTIONAL,
    keyPairHist    [2] SEQUENCE SIZE (1..MAX) OF CertifiedKeyPair OPTIONAL
}
```

## Revocation Request

A revocation request content carries a sequence of certificates to be revoked. Each certificate is identified through a **CertTemplate** data type. Thus, allowing the requester to identify as much as they possibly can about the certificate to be revoked.

```
RevReqContent ::= SEQUENCE OF RevDetails
RevDetails ::= SEQUENCE {
    certDetails       CertTemplate,
    crlEntryDetails  Extensions  OPTIONAL  -- requested crlEntryExtensions

}
```

Because a certificate membership in a CRL is determined by its own serial number, the **certDetails** field should contain the serial number of the certificate being revoked. Otherwise the infrastructure might attempt to identify the certificate using any other attributes that are encoded in the **certDetails** object. Identifying a certificate through attributes other than a serial number, however, can be error prone and may lead to revoking the wrong certificate. Generally, the combination of the certificate issuer and the certificate serial number are sufficient for the identification of a certificate.

## Revocation Response

This message is produced in response to a revocation request. It has the following syntax:

```
RevRepContent ::= SEQUENCE {
   status     SEQUENCE SIZE (1..MAX) OF PKIStatusInfo,
   revCerts   [0] SEQUENCE SIZE (1..MAX) OF CertId OPTIONAL,
   crls       [1] SEQUENCE SIZE (1..MAX) OF CertificateList  OPTIONAL

}
```

The **status** sequence indicates the completion state of the revocation request. The sequence is ordered according to the certificate requested for revocations as represented by **RevReqContent**.

## Cross-Certification Request

This message follows the same syntax as that of a certification request encoded using the **CertReqMessages** data type. The only applicable restriction is for the requesting CA to generate its public key pair.

## Cross-Certification Response

This message is produced in response to a cross-certification request. It follows the same syntax as for the certification response message.

## CA Key Update Announcement

Following a CA key update, the infrastructure may use this type of message to announce the key update event. Depending on implementation, this announcement message may be sent by the CA to the RA only, or it can be sent to the end entities managed by the underlying CA. In the latter case, the content of the message may or may not be sent over CMP. Rather, some other transport mechanism such as electronic mail can be used. Recall that the distribution of the certificate for a trusted CA requires a high level of assurance but in the case of the CA key update this assurance is provable simply from the certificates generated in the process. The following is the ASN.1 definition of the CA key update announcement.

```
CAKeyUpdAnnContent ::= SEQUENCE {
   oldWithNew        Certificate, -- old pub signed with new priv
   newWithOld        Certificate, -- new pub signed with old priv
   newWithNew        Certificate  -- new pub signed with new priv
}
```

## Certificate Announcement

In the absence of a certificate publication method, this message can be used to announce an issued certificate to the member entities of an infrastructure. This announcement has the following syntax.

**CertAnnContent ::= Certificate**

Certificate announcement as such can be unnecessary in environments where the certificates are published to a central repository accessible to the PKI-relying parties such as a LDAP-based directory.

## Revocation Announcement

When a revocation request is not initiated by the subject of the certificate, the infrastructure may choose to notify the concerned subject of such event. The following is the ASN.1 description of this announcement.

```
RevAnnContent ::= SEQUENCE {
    status          PKIStatus,
    certId          CertId,
    willBeRevokedAt GeneralizedTime,
    badSinceDate    GeneralizedTime,
    crlDetails      Extensions  OPTIONAL

}
```

## CRL Announcement

This message is used by the CA to announce the CRL issuance event to the RA or perhaps some other infrastructure agent such as an OCSP server. A CRL announcement message carries the encoding of the following ASN.1 type.

**CRLAnnContent ::= SEQUENCE OF CertificateList**

## PKI Confirmation Content

This represents the final message in the PKI protocol exchange. Generally, confirmation is conveyed by simply sending a message that contains only the PKI header. Nevertheless, the PKIX specification adopts the following primitive syntax as a content for this message.

**PKIConfirmContent ::= NULL**

## Nested Message

This content type serves the purpose of tunneling an entire PKI message within another one. A typical scenario applies to an end entity that sends a protected PKI message to the RA. The latter wraps the end entity's message unchanged into a new PKI message; i.e, the body of the new message is simply the entire end entity's PKI message. The RA then applies its own protection to the new message and sends it to the CA. The syntax of this content type is evidently that of **PKIMessages**.

## General Message

This message is intended to carry a **SEQUENCE OF** (type, value) pairs of attributes. Any data items with well-known object identifiers can be used as attributes. Due to the generic form of an attribute when encoded as an **OCTET STRING** value, this message allows organizations to extend PKIX operations according to the specific needs. The general message content has the following ASN.1 structure.

```
GenMsgContent ::= SEQUENCE OF InfoTypeAndValue
InfoTypeAndValue ::= SEQUENCE {
    infoType      OBJECT IDENTIFIER,
    infoValue     ANY DEFINED BY infoType  OPTIONAL
}
```

Note the **infoValue** field being optional as an OID alone may be sufficient to convey information.

## Error Message

This message content can be generated by any entity in the infrastructure. It is used to convey an error status resulting from an anomaly while processing a PKI transaction. The following structure is used to represent error conditions.

```
ErrorMsgContent ::= SEQUENCE {
    pKIStatusInfo     PKIStatusInfo,
    errorCode         INTEGER        OPTIONAL,
    errorDetails      PKIFreeText    OPTIONAL

}
```

The optional elements of **errorCode** and **errorDetails** are left unspecified. As such they may represent implementation-specific error codes.

```
PKIStatusInfo is defined as
PKIStatusInfo ::= SEQUENCE {
    status          PKIStatus,
    statusString    PKIFreeText   OPTIONAL,
    failInfo        PKIFailureInfo OPTIONAL
}

PKIStatus ::= INTEGER {
```

```
accepted                (0),
grantedWithMods         (1),
rejection               (2),
waiting                 (3),
revocationWarning       (4),
revocationNotification  (5),
keyUpdateWarning        (6)
}
```

The following lists bit string lists the error conditions that may be raised.

```
PKIFailureInfo ::= BIT STRING {
    badAlg                  (0),
    badMessageCheck         (1),
    badRequest              (2),
    badTime                 (3),
    badCertId               (4),
    badDataFormat           (5),
    wrongAuthority          (6),
    incorrectData           (7),
    missingTimeStamp        (8),
    badPOP                  (9),
    certRevoked             (10),
    certConfirmed           (11),
    wrongIntegrity          (12),
    badRecipientNonce       (13),
    timeNotAvailable        (14),
    unacceptedPolicy        (15),
    unacceptedExtension     (16),
    addInfoNotAvailable     (17),
    badSenderNonce          (18),
    badCertTemplate         (19),
    signerNotTrusted        (20),
    transactionIdInUse      (21),
    unsupportedVersion      (22),
    notAuthorized           (23),
    systemUnavail           (24),
    systemFailure           (25),
    duplicateCertReq        (26)

}
```

The standard status codes have the following semantics.

- **0**: —you got exactly what you asked for
- **1**: —you got something like what you asked for; the requester is responsible for ascertaining the differences
- **2**: —you don't get it, more information elsewhere in the message

- **3**: —the request body part has not yet been processed; expect to hear more later (note: proper handling of this status response MAY require a polling mechanism to be available in the underlying transport layer; alternatively, additional polling req/rep **PKIMessages** MAY be defined in a future version of this specification)
- **4**: —this message contains a warning that a revocation is imminent
- **5**: —notification that a revocation has occurred
- **6**: —update already done for the **oldCertId** specified in the key update request message

The **PKIFreeText** type is a sequence of **UTF8String** elements that can be used to carry further language-dependent error information.

## Certificate Confirm

This message is used by an end entity to confirm its acceptance or rejection of a certificate issued to it by the infrastructure. The certificate confirmation status may result in various actions taken by the infrastructure. For instance, an acceptance confirmation might trigger the publication of the certificate to a designated certificate repository. Similarly, a confirmation with a rejection status may lead the CA to remove the certificate from its underlying reposi- tory of issued certificates. This message content is transmitted as the BER encoding of the following ASN.1 structure.

```
CertConfirmContent ::= SEQUENCE of CertStatus
CertStatus ::= SEQUENCE {
    certHash      OCTET STRING,
    certReqId     INTEGER,
    statusInfo    PKIStatusInfo OPTIONAL
}
```

The certificate to which the confirmation applies is identified by the hash value over the certificate. The algorithm used is the same as that used in signing the certificate. The absence of the optional **statusInfo** field, implic- itly indicates that the certificate is accepted. The **certReqId** field is used to match the conformation message with a pending transactional message at the RA or the CA.

Although the PKIX specification allows for an empty **CertConfirmContent** (a zero-length **SEQUENCE**) to indicate that the received certificate is rejected, it is deemed more reliable to explicitly indicate rejection status.

# PKI Certificate and CRL Repositories

PKI constructs, certificates, and certificate revocation lists, are intended to be distributed appropriately so that relying parties such as PKI-based applications are able to retrieve and validate certificates. The distribution process can be performed using out-of-band means. A fully integrated PKI-based application, however, uses embedded location knowledge in order to retrieve certificates and CRL information. Thus, automating the process of consuming and validating certificates. This chapter discusses certificate and CRL distribution methods. ∎

## Introduction

The data constructs that the Internet PKI manufactures, namely an X.509 v3 certificate and the X.509 v2 CRL, have a lifetime that is certainly meant to outlive a one-time use. These data objects, therefore, require life-cycle management operations that, foremost, are based on a persistent storage scheme in which they exist and from which they are retrieved for use by running applications and systems. By storage scheme here it is meant the software components that encapsulate the use of a hardware storage mechanism. A basic example would be a file system, or further yet a database system. A more recent higher abstraction of a data repository system comes in the form of a network-accessible directory. The Internet computing paradigm refers to the collection of data and software agents that define a network resource or a service through the term of a URI. In the Internet realm, PKI data repositories are also identified by URIs accessible through various Internet protocols as specified in the scheme of the corresponding URI.

PKIX constructs draw their identities from two elements:

- the subject name
- the issuer name

Both identities are defined along an ordered hierarchical name space dictated by the following ASN.1 syntax:

**Name ::= CHOICE {**
    **RDNSequence**
**}**
**RDNSequence ::= SEQUENCE OF RelativeDistinguishedName**

The **RDNSequence** data type is what characterizes the hierarchical nature of a PKIX **Name** and forms the structure of an X.500 DN. Each component of the DN sequence, a relative distinguished name (RDN), represents a particular level in that hierarchy. The PKIX naming scheme is adopted from the X.501 standard that came about with the development of the OSI directory service. Naturally, in this directory model, PKIX objects are stored as attributes in the subject and issuer DNs. Before we delve into the directory repository, we briefly discuss basic file repositories intended for use by PKI and that are identified as Internet resources through the protocol schemes of ftp and http.

# FTP

The File Transfer Protocol (FTP) is one of the early application protocols developed to run over TCP/IP networks. It is defined by the IETF RFC 959 described in [POST85]. FTP has become one the most widely available and commonly used Internet tools for sharing files in a transparent way across multiple platforms. File transfers in binary or readable forms can take place between various file and storage systems that may even be using different character encoding schemes and file structures. In the FTP parlance an archive site is a network host that acts as a repository of information.

It has become customary that hosting systems with publicly accessible archives provide the *anonymous* account for users and applications to browse through the archive and transfer files. A user logs on to the hosting system as anonymous and with either a publicly known password or the user's e-mail address as a password instead. Traditionally the anonymous user is only allowed to list specific directory contents and transfer files from those directories. Thus, the user may need prior knowledge of the path names for the particular archive directories.

FTP repositories can be used by PKIs as a cost-effective mechanism for publishing certificates and CRLs. URIs for the FTP locations designated as such are encoded as subject alternative name extensions in the certificates using the IA5String form of a URI. PKI relying parties may be informed of such locations through out-of-band means such as a personal business card. As a safe measure, one needs to verify that the publicly available ftp address is the same as that encoded in the subject alternative name extension of the underlying certificate.

Similarly, a CRL distribution point in a certificate extension can be encoded as an ftp URI from which validating applications can download the corresponding CRL. RFC 2585 defines an ftp extension for transferring certificate and CRL files. The access scheme to a ftp-based repository looks like:

**ftp://ftp.pkistore.com/certificate/JohnDoe.cer**
**ftp://ftp.pkistore.com/crls/crl0101.crl**

Names of files that contain certificates have the suffix **.cer**, while those with suffix **.crl** contain CRLs. Each **.cer** file contains exactly one DER-encoded certificate. Likewise each **.crl** file contains exactly one DER-encoded CRL. Figure 8.1 is an illustration of archiving certificates and CRLs using FTP.

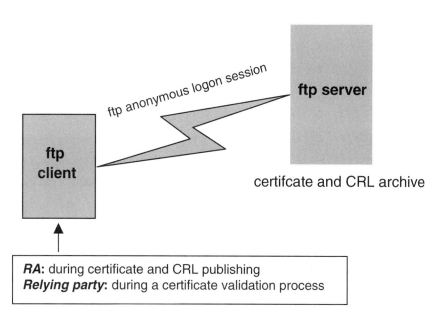

**FIGURE 8.1**
Use of FTP archives for certificates and CRLs

# HTTP

In addition to the ftp extension for handling the transfer of certificates and CRLs, RFC 2585 specifies how an HTTP URI can be used to retrieve certificate and CRL information hosted by an HTTP server [HOUS99b]. A URI as such can also be encoded in the certificate as a subject alternative name extension in the form of an **IA5String** and made available to relying entities through out-of-band means or in-band security protocols. A certificate can be retrieved from its hosting HTTP server by targeting a URL that looks like:

**http://www.pkirepository.com/webstore/JohnDoe.cer**

Similarly, the HTTP URI can encapsulate a repository for CRL information. The certificate CRL distribution points extension in this case can be encoded as an **IA5String** that contains the HTTP URL hosting the CRL information for the certificate. Relying parties would target a URL that looks like:

**http://www.pkirepository.com/webstore/crl0101.crl**

for the download of the CRL.

Like for the ftp URI, the suffuxes of **\*.cer** and **\*.crl** are used as file extensions that each,  contains exactly one certificate or one CRL, respectively.

Certainly HTTP is perhaps the most recognized protocol in the computer software industry. Due to the ubiquitous presence of HTTP clients, the use of web servers for hosting certificate and CRL repositories represents an attractive and cost-effective alternative over other certificate and CRL distribution means. Figure 8.2 illustrates the ease by which a certificate can be retrieved using a web browser.

It is important that when retrieving certificates and CRLs from HTTP-based repositories that one validates the location information handed through any applicable means with that encoded in the certificate.

# Electronic Mail

E-mail is without a doubt the most ubiquitous and massively used of all computer applications today. Early in the IETF history a standard for the format of basic ASCII text email messages was specified in RFC 822 [CROC82].

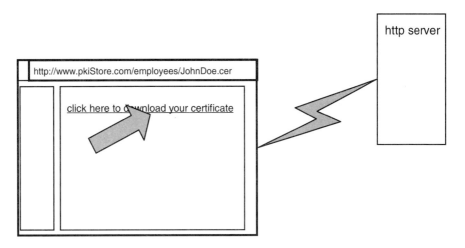

**FIGURE 8.2**
Retrieving a certificate or a CRL from an HTTP-based repository through a browser link

Subsequently, a more generalized e-mail standard, Multipurpose Internet Mail Extensions (MIME), was specified in RFC 1341 [BORE92]. MIME extends the content of an e-mail message to include various data types, thereby offering a richer set of information beyond the simple ASCII text. Such types cover a larger character set range with the inclusion of multibyte characters, as well as different media types such as those representing images and video streams. The MIME specification was carefully designed as an extensible mechanism by way of defining a Content-Type header field, generalized from RFC 1049 [SIRB88], which can be used to specify the type and subtype of data in the body of a message and to fully specify the native representation (encoding) of such data. Content-Types are encoded in the message header field with a syntax that looks like

**type-name/subtype-name**

In particular, an application specific Content-Type with the name of **application** is defined by RFC 1341 for use in transmitting any form of application-specific data .

RFC 822 extends the application MIME type to cover two new subtypes

- **application/pkix-cert**
- **application/pkix-crl**

These new MIME types are used for the distribution of certificates and CRLs via e-mail protocols. For SMTP transports or any other 7-bit transport protocols, Base64 encoding is first applied to the binary representation of the certificate or the CRL before it is sent as an attachment.

While the e-mail distribution method may not be attractive for populating certificate and CRL repositories, it is certainly appealing when pushing certificates to end users.

# DNS

DNS, defined in RFC 1034 [MOCK87a] and RFC 1035 [MOCK87b], has grown to become one of the most successful distributed systems for naming Internet hosts and resources and performing name resolution to corresponding IP addresses. DNS defines a hierarchical tree-structured naming space. Each node of the tree contributes to a particular domain name. The latter consists of an ordered set of labels (symbolic names), each is associated with a particular node. This ordered set begins at a leaf node and follows through a path leading to the root node (one with a null label). Labels are delimited using the dot character '.'. By convention, the labels that compose a domain name are printed or read left to right, from the most specific (farthest from the root) to the least specific (closest to the root). In the example shown in Figure 8.3, the root domain has three subdomains, **EDU**, **MIL**, and **ORG**. The **RPI.EDU** domain has one immediate subdomain **CS.RPI.EDU**.

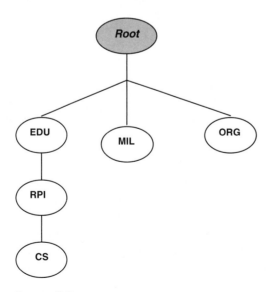

**FIGURE 8.3**
An instance of the DNS naming space

DNS makes use of two other components:

- Name servers which maintain the mapping information about an entire domain tree or a particular sub-tree representing a subset of a domain space. In the latter case a name server also maintains pointers to other name servers that can lead to resolving domain mapping information from any part of the domain tree. A name server is said to be the authority over the subspace it maintains. Authoritative information is organized into units called zones.

- Resolvers are local agents that are directly invoked by application programs. The purpose is to initiate the process of resolving a symbolic domain name into its Internet address. Resolvers are configured to access at least one name server and use that name server's information to answer a query directly, or pursue the query using referrals to other name servers.

Figure 8.4 depicts the layered view that DNS represents. With respect to end users a domain name resolution is an interaction with a local resolver; while to a resolver the interaction may lead to one or more remote name servers. Each name server is an authority over its own particular zone.

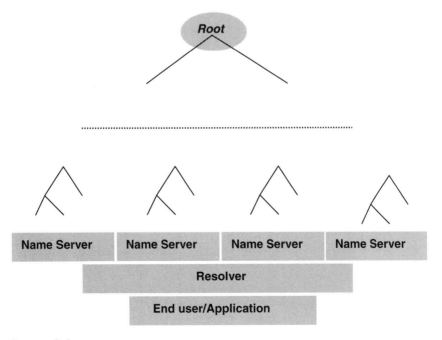

**FIGURE 8.4**
The layered view of resources as presented through DNS

Domain names can be encoded as subject alternative names in certificate extensions. Using a web of DNS revolvers, a domain name encoded in a certificate extension as such can lead to the system hosting certificate and CRL repositories. The appeal of this approach stems from its potential reliance on the effective and widely used DNS mechanism. The ramification of this method on the adoption of PKI in electronic commerce could be far reaching for the simple reason that DNS is already a core component in the Web defined by the Internet.

# LDAP

LDAP is a lightweight front end to the X.500 directory access protocol [HOWE95]. X.500 is the OSI directory service standard which incorporates a number of novel techniques for managing a directory of information. Among these is a Directory Information Tree (DIT) that presents a hierarchical naming model as well as a mechanism for an information model that specifies the kind of information that can be stored in the repository. The X.500 model offers a rich set of directory services and is highly scalable.

X.500, however, requires the use of supporting technologies that are costly to deploy and not so widely used; one downside is its reliance on the OSI protocol stack. The use of such technologies has led to the complexity and the heavy nature of an X.500 directory deployment. LDAP evolved as an alternative to adopting most of the X.500 services yet only at a fraction of the cost. It presents the X.500 information and naming model to clients through a simple protocol that relies on the ubiquitous TCP/IP stack. Some of the differentiating factors between LDAP and the full X.500 include:

- **Transport**. LDAP runs over the ubiquitous Internet protocol of TCP/IP; while the OSI Directory Access protocol (DAP) requires the full OSI multilayer protocol stack.
- **Data representation**. LDAP uses simple string formats to represent directory information; while X.500 uses more complicated and structured constructs.
- **Data encoding**. LDAP adopts a simplified version of the X.500 encoding scheme for its data transport.

## The LDAP Information Model

The LDAP information model is based upon the concept of a directory entry. Aggregate entries define the structure of the directory information tree. Each directory entry can store any type of information provided it is compatible with the structural constraints set for the directory. An entry is a collection of attributes and each attribute is composed of two components: a type in the form of an object identifier and a value. The latter can be of any type possible. Figure 8.5 illustrates the structure of a directory entry as reflected by the following ASN.1 definition.

```
RelativeDistinguishedName ::=  SET OF AttributeTypeAndValue
AttributeTypeAndValue ::= SEQUENCE {

    type     AttributeType,
    value    AttributeValue


}
AttributeType ::= OBJECT IDENTIFIER
AttributeValue ::= ANY DEFINED BY AttributeType
```

Attribute types are referred to through symbolic names that are user oriented and easier to grasp than the numeric OID representations used internally. For instance, the **CN** attribute stands for a common name, the **mail** attribute represents an e-mail address, while the **O** and **OU** attributes represent organizations and organizational units, respectively.

Each entry in the tree has a relatively distinguished name that consists of a set of (attribute, value) pairs separated with the character '+'. In most cases an RDN is composed of a single such pair. Within the scope of an entire DIT, a directory Entry is unambiguously referred to by its distinguished name. This name is formed by concatenating the sequence of entries, starting at the particular entry and leading up to the root of the tree. For instance in Figure 8.6 the entry for Elyes has a DN of

**CN=Elyes, O=Peace Elementary, C=US**

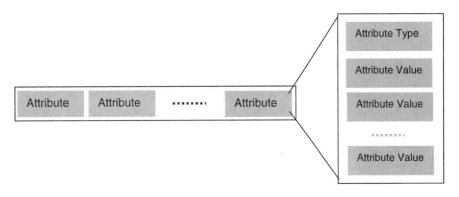

**FIGURE 8.5**
The structure of a directory entry

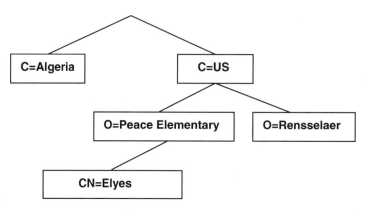

**FIGURE 8.6**
An example of an LDAP directory tree

The hierarchical name space provided by X.500 directories is intended to reflect political, geographical, and organizational boundaries and domains. Entries representing countries generally represent the top of this hierarchy. Deeper levels represent entities such as people or some physical objects such as documents, printers, and so forth.

## LDAP Information Semantics

In order to maintain the consistency of information in a directory tree, LDAP provides control over what attribute types can be stored in an entry, which ones are required, and which are optional. Each entry contains at least one special attribute called **objectclass**, the values of which determine the type of information that can be stored in the entry. In the directory parlance the **objectClass** attribute determines the schema of the directory and identifies the type of directory objects associated with a particular directory entry.

In addition to the constraints imposed on the type of objects stored in an entry of the LDAP directory, an attribute may also be constrained in a number of ways. For instance, an attribute may only have values of a particular data type such as a **String**. Similarly, a value may be specified to behave in a certain way under a particular operation. For example the keyword of **caseIgnoreString** when associated with a String type of attribute implies that case should be ignored during a comparison in which the value of the attribute is involved. This keyword also constrains the value of the attribute to a character string only. Other constraints may include a limitation over the number of values a particular attribute may assume. For instance an attribute that holds a person's unique identifier such as a Social Security number may be constrained to take one a single value.

The structural **objectclass** is the one that determines the type of object stored in an entry, and thus defines the semantics of the entry. While other auxiliary object classes can be added or removed from an LDAP entry, the structural **objectclass** cannot be changed. We devote the rest of this chapter to discussing the LDAP schema as well as attribute definitions reserved for the PKI objects.

## LDAP and PKI

LDAP definitions for PKI objects can be found in separate IETF specifications, RFC 2587 [BOEY99] and RFC 2256 [WAHL97]. The first one defines a minimal schema to support PKIX specific components in LDAPv2. These definitions are notably expressed using a few auxiliary PKIX object classes. The second specification, on the other hand, applies broadly to a generic user schema for use with LDAPv3. RFC 2587 in essence has evolved with PKIX, and although it has been widely implemented by PKI software makers, LDAPv3 schema could become the norm for storing PKI constructs in LDAP repositories.

## PKIX LDAPv2 Schema

As we just noted this schema is specific to PKIX. It defines four object classes with each representing a high level LDAP object as we describe next.

### End Entities

LDAP objects representing PKI end entities can be associated with certificate attributes using the **pkiUser** object class defined as follows:

```
pkiUser  OBJECT-CLASS  ::= {
   SUBCLASS OF   { top}
   KIND          auxiliary
   MAY CONTAIN   {userCertificate}
   ID            joint-iso-ccitt(2) ds(5) objectClass(6) pkiUser(21)
}

userCertificate    ATTRIBUTE ::= {
   WITH SYNTAX             Certificate
   EQUALITY MATCHING RULE  certificateExactMatch
   ID                      joint-iso-ccitt(2) ds(5) attributeType(4)
                           userCertificate(36)
}
```

As stated by its syntax, a **pkiUser** object class is first of all an **auxiliary** class, and hence it represents a flexibility in adding or removing PKIX-related attributes from an LDAP entry. Additionally, the following characteristics are implied by this object class.

- **PkiUSer** derives from **top objectClass**. LDAP objects can be derived from other types of objects through the process of **subclassing** object classes. Subclasses as such further specialize the underlying object. For instance, an **OrganizationPerson** could be is derived from the more generic **Person** object class. This subclassing process results in **OrganizationPerson** having all the attributes that a **Person** object class may have in addition to others of its own that it may introduce. **top** is an abstract object class that is superior to all other object classes. It is identified by the OID of **{2.5.6.0}** and is defined as:

**( 2.5.6.0 NAME 'top' ABSTRACT MUST objectClass )**

The **MUST** keyword implies that all LDAP entries are required to have an **objectClass** attribute.

An entry with a **pkiUser** object class may contain a **userCertificate** attribute. This class is identified by:

**joint-iso-ccitt(2)  ds(5)  objectClass(6)  pkiUser(21) = {2.5.6.21}**

In turn, the **userCertificate** attribute of the **pkiUser** object class is constrained by the following:

- Have the syntax of a **Certificate** object which is that defined by X.509 as defined in RFC 2459. The certificate is encoded in DER format.
- Have an **EQUALITY MATCHING RULE** of **certificateExactMatch** meaning that during a compare operation a user-presented value of such type has to exactly match the value stored in the directory in order to assert a successful match.
- Have an object identifier of

**joint-iso-ccitt(2)  ds(5)  attributeType(4)  userCertificate(36) = {2.5.4.36}**

## Certificate Authorities

A CA can be represented as an LDAP object using the **pkiCA** object class as defined here:

```
pkiCA   OBJECT-CLASS   ::= {
   SUBCLASS OF { top}
   KIND            auxiliary
```

```
MAY CONTAIN  { cACertificate |
               certificateRevocationList |
               authorityRevocationList |
               crossCertificatePair }
   ID   joint-iso-ccitt(2) ds(5) objectClass(6) pkiCA(22)
}
```

**pkiCA**, which is an **auxiliary** class, is characterized by the following:

- As **pkiUser**, it is a subclass of the **top** object class.
- It can be used to store four types of attributes: a CA certificate, a CRL, an ARL, or a cross-certificate pair (as defined by RFC2459).
- It is identified by:

**joint-iso-ccitt(2) ds(5) objectClass(6) pkiCA(22) = {2.5.6.22}**

The **cACertificate** attribute has the same syntax and semantics rules as for **userCertificate** attribute but is distinguished through its own OID as defined in the following:

```
cACertificate  ATTRIBUTE ::= {
   WITH SYNTAX              Certificate
   EQUALITY MATCHING RULE certificateExactMatch
   ID           joint-iso-ccitt(2) ds(5) attributeType(4) cACertificate(37)
}
```

The **crossCertificatePair** attribute is used to store the certificates resulting from a cross-certification process. Recall that the cross-certificate pair may represent certification in either a one-way or two-way direction (mutual cross-certification).

```
CrossCertificatePair  ATTRIBUTE ::={
   WITH SYNTAX              CertificatePair
   EQUALITY MATCHING RULE certificatePairExactMatch
   ID        joint-iso-ccitt(2) ds(5) attributeType(4) crossCertificatePair(40)
}
```

The **certificateRevocationList** attribute is used to store CRL objects. It has the following syntax and semantics:

```
CertificateRevocationList ATTRIBUTE ::={
   WITH SYNTAX              CertificateList
   EQUALITY MATCHING RULE certificateListExactMatch
   ID    joint-iso-ccitt(2) ds(5) attributeType(4) certificateRevocationList(39)
}
```

Similarly, the **authorityRevocationList** attribute is used to store CRL information as it relates to certificate authorities is defined as follows:

```
AuthorityRevocationList  ATTRIBUTE ::={
    WITH SYNTAX              CertificateList
    EQUALITY MATCHING RULE certificateListExactMatch
    ID    joint-iso-ccitt(2)  ds(5)  attributeType(4)  authorityRevocationList(38)
}
```

## CRL Distribution Points

Recall from Chapter 4 that CRL distribution points are a vehicle for specifying the location of certificate revocation information. When CRL distribution points are in effect, CRLs can be distributed across LDAP directories and stored under a special object class called **cRLDistributionPoint** defined as follows:

```
cRLDistributionPoint   OBJECT-CLASS::= {
    SUBCLASS OF  { top }
        KIND            structural
        MUST CONTAIN    { commonName }
        MAY CONTAIN     { certificateRevocationList |
                          authorityRevocationList |
                          deltaRevocationList }
        ID    joint-iso-ccitt(2)  ds(5)  objectClass(6)  cRLDistributionPoint(19)
}
```

The **crlDistributionPoint** attribute must contain a **commonName** attribute defined as:

```
commonName   ATTRIBUTE::={
    SUBTYPE OF     name
    WITH SYNTAX    DirectoryString
    ID        joint-iso-ccitt(2)  ds(5)  attributeType(4)  commonName(3)
}
```

with **deltaRevocationList** defined by:

```
deltaRevocationList      ATTRIBUTE ::= {
    WITH SYNTAX              CertificateList
    EQUALITY MATCHING RULE certificateListExactMatch
    ID        joint-iso-ccitt(2)  ds(5)  attributeType(4)  deltaRevocationList(53)
}
```

## Delta CRLs

Delta CRLs contain partial certificate revocation information representing only updated revocations (see Chapter). LDAPv2 PKIX-related schema distinguishes between full CRLs and delta CRLs in that the latter is assigned its own object class defined below.

```
deltaCRL   OBJECT-CLASS::= {
   SUBCLASS OF { top }
   KIND              auxiliary
   MAY CONTAIN   { deltaRevocationList }
   ID                joint-iso-ccitt(2)  ds(5)  objectClass(6)  deltaCRL(23)
}
```

## User Schema in LDAPv3

The LDAPv3 user schema defines a number of object classes applicable to PKI constructs. These are: **strongAuthenticationuser**, **certificationAuthority**, **certificationAuthority-V2**, and **cRLDistributionPoint**. The following are the ASN.1 descriptions of each of these object classes.

- **End user certificates**
   ( 2.5.6.15 NAME 'strongAuthenticationUser' SUP top AUXILIARY
       MUST userCertificate )

- **Certificate authorities**
   ( 2.5.6.16 NAME 'certificationAuthority' SUP top AUXILIARY
       MUST ( authorityRevocationList $ certificateRevocationList
           $ cACertificate ) MAY crossCertificatePair )

- **Extending the certification authority class**
   ( 2.5.6.16.2 NAME 'certificationAuthority-V2' SUP  certificationAuthority
       AUXILIARY MAY ( deltaRevocationList ) )

- **CRL distribution point**
   ( 2.5.6.19 NAME 'cRLDistributionPoint' SUP top STRUCTURAL
       MUST ( cn ) MAY ( certificateRevocationList $ authorityRevocationList
           $ deltaRevocationList ) )

# PKI Credentials Management

PKI credentials management centers around the means by which private keys and public key certificates are maintained by an entity. These constructs may further be extended to include secret keys and data objects associated with security attributes. This chapter examines a number of standard methods addressing the management of PKI credentials. ■

## Introduction

While a PKI provides the much needed assurance and reliability of a publicly disseminated key material, the associated private key remains under the control of the end entity identified by the subject field in the certificate. Some deployments, however, may resort to trusting private keys to a third-party agent within the organization. A breach in the private key certainly leads to the total compromise of any data security that is based upon the underlying public key certificate. The security of an entity's private key indeed forms the cornerstone of all public key cryptographic services. The security of a private key generally evolves around the way by which the key is maintained in some encrypted form on a particular storage medium or device. Additionally, enforcing an access control policy on the underlying storage components or devices where a private key resides increases the level of assurance in the key. PKI credentials management is not limited to the private key only. Certificates, secret keys, and various security objects generated by or related to public key credentials are also the subject of PKI credentials management.

# PKCS #8

The simplest method of maintaining an encrypted form of a private key is the wrapping provided by the PKCS #8 specification from RSA, Inc. [RSA93a]. Here the key material is encrypted using a secret key encryption algorithm. The password-based encryption specification of PKCS #5 is the encryption method of choice when it comes to finding a user-oriented way for exchanging PKCS #8 encrypted private keys. In PKCS #5 the encryption key is derived from a password [RSA99b].

The encrypted private key information has the following ASN.1 syntax:

```
EncryptedPrivateKeyInfo ::= SEQUENCE {
    encryptionAlgorithm    EncryptionAlgorithmIdentifier,
    encryptedData          EncryptedData
}
EncryptionAlgorithmIdentifier ::= AlgorithmIdentifier

EncryptedData ::= OCTET STRING
```

**EncryptedData** octets are the result of BER-encoding a **PrivateKeyInfo** structure and then encrypting it. Private key information has the following syntax:

```
PrivateKeyInfo ::= SEQUENCE {
    version                Version,
    privateKeyAlgorithm    PrivateKeyAlgorithmIdentifier,
    privateKey             PrivateKey,
    attributes             [0] IMPLICIT Attributes OPTIONAL
}
PrivateKey ::= OCTET STRING
```

The format of the **PrivateKeyInfo** is parameterized through the **AlgorithmIdentifier** field and thus is independent of any cryptographic algorithm. Note also that the same parameterization of the **EncryptedPrivateKeyInfo** enables the use of any cryptographic algorithm to be employed with the PKCS #8 wrapping.

A more thorough solution of wrapping private keys is provided by the PKCS #12 specification which has become a widely adopted offline method of exchanging PKI credentials across users and applications.

# PKCS #12

PKCS #12 provides a much more involved method for the cryptographic wrapping of public key credentials as well as any security objects [RSA99c]. Its generalized syntax enables the protection and transfer of personal identity information across users, applications, and systems. Various confidentiality and integrity modes can be employed in the PKCS #12 wrapping as we discuss next.

## Privacy Modes

This protection mode of PKCS #12 is used to provide the confidentiality service of the personal information being exchanged. The specification allows the use of public key as well as secret key encryption algorithms. In the latter case the secret key may be derived from a password.

### Public-Key Privacy Mode

Here the entity generating the cryptographic wrapper employs the public key of the destination in order to encrypt the personal identity information being transferred. The destination entity uses its own private key to decrypt the exchange content.

### Password-Privacy Mode

In this mode personal information is encrypted using a secret key derived from an input that consists of the user name and a password. The destination is required to have knowledge of the same parameters used at the source in order to decrypt the content. This protection mode simply requires knowledge of a password, as opposed to having access to a private key, in order to unravel protected personal information. Due in part to its user-orientation, this protection mode is widely adopted.

## Integrity Modes

Integrity modes allow for the transfer of personal security objects in their original encoded form, but protects them against tampering by an attacker that substitutes for them. Like for the privacy mode, a public-key integrity mode or one that is based on a password can be used.

### Public-Key Integrity Mode

In this case the source of the transfer uses the private key corresponding to its public key pair to sign the contents of personal information items intended for protection as such. The destination uses the public key of the source in order to verify the integrity and origin authenticity of the information.

### Password Integrity Mode

In the absence of a public key pair for the source, a password-based MAC can be used to protect the exchanged personal information from being substituted or tampered with. The destination is required to have knowledge of the password used by the source.

## The PKCS #12 Format

The cryptographic wrappers that PKCS #12 provides are captured in a single top-level ASN.1 data type called a PFX, the syntax of which is defined below.

```
PFX ::= SEQUENCE {
    version     INTEGER {v3(3)}(v3,...),
    authSafe    ContentInfo,
    macData     MacData OPTIONAL
}

MacData ::= SEQUENCE {
    mac         DigestInfo,
    macSalt     OCTET STRING,
    iterations  INTEGER DEFAULT 1
                -- A much higher value for the iterations count, like 1024,
                   is recommended.
}
```

Currently the PKCS #12 specification is in version 3. **ContentInfo** is the main data type defined and exported by the Cryptographic Message Syntax (CMS) standard of PKCS #7 [KALI98c]. We discuss the details of PKCS #7 in the next chapter. The **macData** field is present only in password integrity mode and contains a MAC value, expressed as a **DigestInfo** data type defined in PKCS #7, followed by MAC salt and an iterations count.

```
MacData ::= SEQUENCE {
    mac        DigestInfo,
    macSalt    OCTET STRING,
    iterations INTEGER DEFAULT 1
               -- A much higher value for the iterations count, like 1024, is
                  recommended.
}
```

## The Payload of a PFX

The content that is wrapped inside a PKCS #12 PFX and which defines the exchanged personal information has a **ContentInfo** type defined in the PKCS #7 specification. We present only the top-level definition of this type in this section, and leave the rest of the details for the next chapter.

```
ContentInfo ::= SEQUENCE {
  contentType    ContentType,
  content        [0] EXPLICIT ANY DEFINED BY contentType OPTIONAL
}
ContentType ::= OBJECT IDENTIFIER
```

Basically a **ContentInfo** is a data payload parameterized by the **content-Type** field. The outer cryptographic wrapper of a PFX uses a content type of **signedData** in public-key integrity mode and **data** in password integrity mode. In the latter case the **macData** field must be present to validate the integrity of a PFX. The top-level PFX, therefore, provides the integrity and the authenticity of the PFX content. Data confidentiality, however, is to be provided by the lower level structures contained within a PFX.

In turn, the content of the **authSafe** field can be either of type **Data** or **signedData**, both which are defined by PKCS #7 and the CMS specification [HOUS99c] (see further details about PKCS #7 and CMS in the next chapter). In the **data** case the content field simply contains the BER encoding of an **AuthenticatedSafe**. While in the **signedData** case the same **Authenticated-Safe** is wrapped within a **ContentInfo** type that captures the signature over the wrapped content. The PKCS #12 specification refers to this as an indirect containment of an **AuthenticatedSafe**. The **AuthenticatedSafe** data type is expressed as a sequence of **ContentInfo**.

```
AuthenticatedSafe ::= SEQUENCE OF ContentInfo
    -- Data if unencrypted
    -- EncryptedData if password-encrypted
    -- EnvelopedData if public key-encrypted
```

**EncryptedData** as well as **EnvelopedData** wrappers apply to the BER encoding of a **SafeContents** value. The latter is defined by:

```
SafeContents ::= SEQUENCE OF SafeBag

SafeBag ::= SEQUENCE {
  bagId        BAG-TYPE.&id ({PKCS12BagSet})
  bagValue     [0] EXPLICIT BAG-TYPE.&Type({PKCS12BagSet}{@bagId}),
  bagAttributesSET OF PKCS12Attribute OPTIONAL
}

PKCS12Attribute ::= SEQUENCE {
  attrId       ATTRIBUTE.&id ({PKCS12AttrSet}),
```

```
  attrValues    SET OF ATTRIBUTE.&Type ({PKCS12AttrSet}{@attrId})
} -- This type is compatible with the X.500 type 'Attribute'

PKCS12AttrSet ATTRIBUTE ::= {
  friendlyName |
  localKeyId,
  ... -- Other attributes are allowed
}
```

Both the **friendlyName** and the **localKeyId** attributes are defined by PKCS #9, which is also an IETF Information RFC 2985 [NYST00]. These attributes provide an optional means of assigning friendly and perhaps meaningful names to keys and other constructs stored in a PKCS #12 format.

```
friendlyName ATTRIBUTE ::= {
  WITH  SYNTAX  BMPString (SIZE(1..pkcs-9-ub-friendlyName))
  EQUALITY MATCHING RULE caseIgnoreMatch
  SINGLE VALUE TRUE
  ID pkcs-9-at-friendlyName
}

localKeyId ATTRIBUTE ::= {
  WITH  SYNTAX  OCTET STRING
  EQUALITY  MATCHING  RULE  octetStringMatch
  SINGLE VALUE TRUE
  ID pkcs-9-at-localKeyId
}
```

Currently there are six types of safe bags defined by the PKCS #12 specification.

```
bagtypes OBJECT IDENTIFIER ::= {pkcs-12  10  1}

BAG-TYPE ::= TYPE-IDENTIFIER

keyBag   BAG-TYPE ::=
  {KeyBag IDENTIFIED BY {bagtypes 1}}
pkcs8ShroudedKeyBag BAG-TYPE ::=
  {PKCS8ShroudedKeyBag IDENTIFIED BY {bagtypes 2}}
certBag BAG-TYPE ::=
  {CertBag IDENTIFIED BY {bagtypes 3}}
crlBag BAG-TYPE ::=
  {CRLBag IDENTIFIED BY {bagtypes 4}}
secretBag BAG-TYPE ::=
  {SecretBag IDENTIFIED BY {bagtypes 5}}
safeContentsBag BAG-TYPE ::=
  {SafeContents IDENTIFIED BY {bagtypes 6}}
```

```
PKCS12BagSet BAG-TYPE ::= {
   keyBag |
   pkcs8ShroudedKeyBag |
   certBag |
   crlBag |
   secretBag |
   safeContentsBag,
   ... -- For future extensions
}
```

It is apparent at this point that there are multiple levels of indirections within a PKCS #12 content. Figure 9.1 illustrates the nesting of various ASN.1 data types in a PKCS #12 encoding.

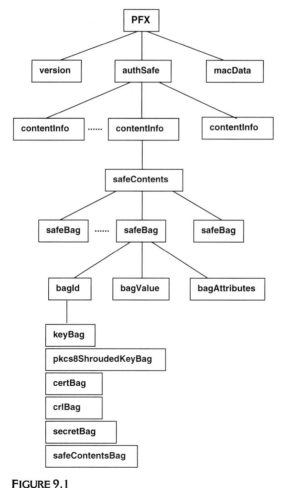

**FIGURE 9.1**

The nested types hierarchy that exists in PKCS #12 contents

# PKCS #11

PKCS #8 and PKCS #12 are essentially intended for use as cryptographic wrappers of PKI credentials with the goal of securing the exchange of the credentials wrapped as such. PKCS #11, on the other hand, provides the security of stored PKI credentials, but adopts a different approach. Its characterizing aspect stems from the fact that it is not simply a secure key store. Rather, PKCS #11 enables access to PKI credentials as well as to the cryptographic functions that operate on those credentials via a standard layer of programming interfaces [RSA99a]. In turn, functions providing the implementation of those interfaces are confined to a single software component (usually in the form of a shared dynamic library).

Functionality of a PKCS #11 library consists of a set of cryptographic operations that can be implemented in software or hardware, and access methods to a storage medium called a credentials token, widely implemented as a hardware device. Software implementations of the token are also available. Existing Internet browsers are good examples of applications that provide software implementations of the PKCS #11 tokens.

As illustrated in Figure 9.2, the PKCS #11 library, commonly known as *cryptoki* (short for cryptographic token interface), provides for a common logical

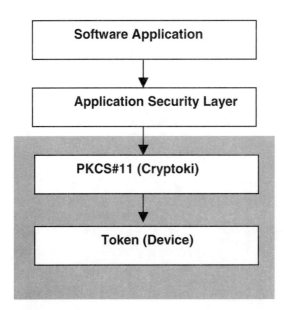

**FIGURE 9.2**
Isolating the manipulation of PKI credentials in PKCS #11

view of a cryptographic token residing on a slot of a computer system. When invoked by a security layer of an application, through a generic set of programming interfaces, the PKCS #11 library interacts with the device driver of the token for cryptographic services that can be based upon private keys and public key certificates maintained in the token.

PKCS #11 seeks not only to maintain a secure storage of a private key through a secret personal identification number (PIN) access, but equally important it provides a portable security layer that isolates users from the details of the hardware tokens in which public key credentials reside.

## Logical Content of a Token

Three types of objects can be stored in a Cryptoki token:

- A **data** object is defined by an application and its interpretation, therefore, may remain specific to that application only.
- A **certificate** object stores a certificate such as an X.509 certificate.
- A **key** object contains a cryptographic key that can be a secret, a private, or a public key.

Each cryptoki object is associated with a standard set of attributes that attach values to the object according to its type. For example, an X.509 certificate can be associated with the key identifier attribute in order for applications to quickly distinguish among multiple public/private key pairs held by the same subject.

A cryptoki object can be a *session* object or a *token* object. Session objects are temporary objects that have a lifetime of the session in which they are created. A session is scoped by the lifetime of a connection between an application and the token. Once a session is closed, session objects are automatically destroyed. Session objects are only visible to the application in which they are created. Token objects, however, have a lifetime that extends beyond a session or a process execution. They remain in the token until explicitly removed by an application with sufficient access permissions.

Objects can be categorized along access requirements. Public objects do not require an application to authenticate to the token; access to private objects requires user authentication. Labeling an object as public or private is accomplished by setting an attribute value on the object accordingly. Figure 9.3 illustrates the logical view of object types contained in a cryptoki token.

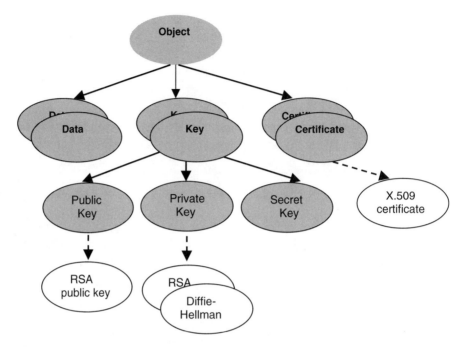

**FIGURE 9.3**
Cryptoki object hierarchy

## Cryptoki Sessions

Before an application begins interacting with a cryptoki token, it needs to establish one or more sessions with the token. A cryptoki session is a logical connection between an application and the token. In Read/Write sessions, an application can create, read, write, modify, or destroy session and token objects. Read-only sessions allow an application to manipulate session objects in any way possible, but limit access to the read operation only. Recall that access to private token objects is subject to authenticating the application. Session objects created within a particular session are automatically destroyed when that session is closed.

## The Programming Model to Cryptoki

The high-level cryptoki programming model can be summarized by the following steps:

- Initialize cryptoki.
- Perform zero or more slot and token management functions; for example, obtain information about a particular slot.

- Open one or more sessions and perform a session management function such as obtaining information about the session.

- Authenticate to the token in order to gain access to private objects.

- Perform object management functions as needed; such as, obtain an attribute value of a particular object, create one or more objects, or modify an attribute of a particular object.

- Issue cryptoki calls for cryptographic services as needed. Depending upon the cryptographic features that a particular cryptoki supports, one may perform encryption functions, decryption functions, message digesting, data signing, and so forth.

- Perform any key management functions needed by the application. For example generate a secret key, or unwrap a decrypted key.

- Close a session.

- Uninitialize cryptoki in order to clean up and release any system resources held up by cryptoki.

## About the Java Interfaces to Cryptoki

It is worth noting that currently only C-bindings are defined for cryptoki. However, there are various providers of Java wrapping interfaces to cryptoki. For example, IBM's **com.ibm.pkcs11** package provides for a set of abstract classes that encapsulate cryptoki. Implementation of these interfaces is provided in a separate package **com.ibm.pkcs11.nat** that, in turn, stands as a Java wrapper to existing native C shared-library implementing the PKCS #11 functionality. In its attempt to make this integration seamless, IBM has implemented the PKCS #11 Java Native Interface (JNI) wrapper as a cryptographic provider that plugs underneath the Java Cryptographic Extension (JCE).

# PKCS #15

Cryptoki has introduced a generic interface to performing cryptographic functions over a hardware or a software token in which PKI credentials also reside. The intent was to provide a programming layer that enables application portability. PKCS #11 shared libraries from different implementers can, therefore, be interchanged without affecting the application. The token in itself, however, remains dependent upon which PKCS #11 shared libraries are being used.

PKCS #15 takes interoperability one step further in that it defines a common structural format for the storage area of the token as well as the objects it may contain [RSA00a]. As a result, a token that contains a private key or a certificate can be successfully used by any application running in a PKCS #15 capable environment. The approach undertaken by PKCS #15 yields portability of the cryptographic constructs such as secret keys and PKI credentials. In order to achieve these objectives PKCS #15 specifies a file and a directory format for storing security constructs such as private keys, secret keys, digital, and certificates. Furthermore, the details of ASN.1 data types representing each of the PKCS #15 objects are specified. While the token can store PKCS #15 applications as well, our focus remains on objects representing security constructs.

## PKCS #15 File Structure

The proposed top-level directory and file structure of a PKCS #15 token is depicted in Figure 9.4. Two elements of this structure are required to be present, the Object Directory File (ODF) and the Token Information file (TokenInfo). The ODF directory is the top-level directory containing PKCS #15 constructs. Five directories reside under the ODF directory:

- Public Key Directory
- Private Key Directory
- Certificate Directory
- Authentication Object Directory
- Data Object Directory

## PKCS #15 Object Model

Four types of objects can be stored in a PKCS #15 token:

- **Key object**. This can be a private key, a secret key, or a public key. The presence of each of these keys is structurally mandated by the standard.
  - A private key can be an RSA private key, a private elliptic curve object, a private Diffie-Hellman key, a private DSA key, or a private Key Exchange Algorithm (KEA) key object.
  - Similarly, a public key object can be a public RSA key object, a public elliptic curve key, a public Diffi-Hellman key, a public DSA key object, or a public KEA key object.
  - A secret key object may contain a secret key for most of the common secret key encryption algorithms such as DES, RC2, RC4, RC5, and Triple-DES.

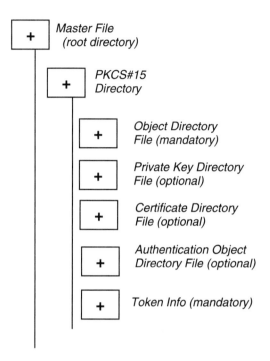

**FIGURE 9.4**
Top-level file and directory structure of a PKCS #15 token

- **Certificate objects**. These may represent X.509 or other forms of digital certificates. The presence of certificate objects is not a structural requirement of the token format. Certificate objects can represent various forms of certificates including **X.509**, Simple Public Key Infrastructure (SPKI), Pretty Good Privacy (PGP), and Wireless Transport Layer Security (WTLS) certificates as well as X.509 Attribute Certificates (**AC**).

- **Data objects**. May contain any security-related data constructs other than the ones explicitly mentioned here. Based upon the scope of interpretation, data objects can be classified into:

  - **Opaque objects** whose interpretation is left to the application at hand.

  - **External data objects** have an interpretation scope that may span one or more industries.

  - **Data objects identified by OIDs** provide a way to store and retrieve data values associated with an object identifier.

- **Authentication objects**. These objects contain information about how a card-holder is to establish an authenticated session with the token. In many cases this authentication involves a PIN object, although a biometric template can be used as well.

# PKI-Based Security Applications

A PKI is considered to be a core enabling technology. It is intended to generate certificates and manage their lifecycles. It also makes those certificates, along with corresponding revocation statuses available for consumption by various applications and security protocols. Running PKI-based business applications are indeed the main reason behind a PKI deployment. This chapter discusses several core applications that are enabled through PKI constructs. ▪

## Introduction

The main goal of a PKI is to build a high level of assurance needed in a publicly available cryptographic key. Such assurance becomes the foundation for using the certified public keys in various cryptographic services. A PKI intended goals are met when the trust in a public key it certifies is established and verified by a business application or a security protocol that is based on PKI. Several such enabling security protocols and applications have emerged in recent years. The PKI paradigm adopted in these applications evolves around the fact that data constructs in the form of secured private keys, PKCs, and certificate revocation lists are consumed in the process of performing cryptographic operations and establishing secure associations.

Applications that are fully integrated with PKIs go beyond simply consuming PKI constructs in that they interact directly with the elements of the infrastructure for services such as certificate and CRL lookup, as well as online certificate validation.

# PKCS #7

PKCS #7 forms the building block for many techniques that present data in a form nested within cryptographic wrappers. It does not represent a specific PKI-based application; rather it is considered to be a generic application of PKI for building other higher level security applications or protocols. It is mainly for that reason that we choose to list it at the top of common PKI applications.

PKCS #7 is a cryptographic wrapping format that exports a single ASN.1 data type, **ContentInfo**, and defines various object identifiers. The basic data type that is defined here has the following structure:

```
ContentInfo ::= SEQUENCE {
   contentType  ContentType,
   content      [0] EXPLICIT ANY DEFINED BY contentType OPTIONAL
}
ContentType ::= OBJECT IDENTIFIER
```

In essence a PKCS #7 format, commonly referred to as an envelope, is simply a parameterized content. The **contentType** field of the above sequence is what represents the parameterization variable, thereby allowing for various cryptographic wrappers to be used. The flexibility and perhaps at the same time the complexity aspect of a PKCS #7 content is its recursive nature. By definition the outer cryptographic enveloping may contain inner envelopes of arbitrarily nested levels. Figure 10.1 provides a high-level view of the PKCS #7 enveloping technique.

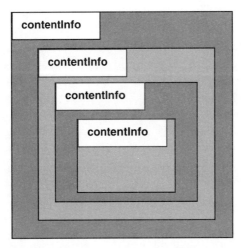

**FIGURE 10.1**
A high-level view of PKCS #7 nested enveloping

# Content Parameterization _____

The **contentType** parameter of a **contentInfo** is an OID used to indicate the type of content being wrapped. PKCS #7 content types are object identifiers derived from the arc:

**pkcs-7 OBJECT IDENTIFIER ::=**
    **{ iso(1) member-body(2) US(840) rsadsi(113549)  pkcs(1)  7 } -- {1.2.840.113549.1.7}**

Six content types are defined:

## Data
The Data content is the simplest of all PKCS #7 contents. Being of **OCTET STRING** type it may contain any stream of bytes wrapped within an ASN.1 octet. Although the type of data that is wrapped within the octet string is subject to an a-priori knowledge by the processing application and thus can be of any type, it is recommended that it represent plain data as opposed to data subjected to a cryptographic transformations.

**Data  ::=  OCTET STRING**

## Signed Data
This type of content is intended to assume a data payload of any kind; plain or one resulting from applying cryptographic transformations (see Figure 10.2). The content payload here is digitally signed by first digesting the payload into a hash value, then encrypting the result using the private key of the signer. The format allows for multiple signers of the same payload. This feature lends itself to affirming the signing action as might be required in an electronic business application. A Signed Data envelope is identified by the following content type:

**signedData   OBJECT IDENTIFIER  ::=  { pkcs-7  2 } -- { 1.2.840.113549.1.7.2}**

It includes the following information:

- **Signer information**. This is a collection of zero or more elements, each representing one particular signer. This information is used in the signature verification process performed by the recipient. Signer information identifies the digest algorithm used, the digest encryption algorithm, as well as the signer's certificate serial number and the name of its issuer. It also includes the signature and an optional set of

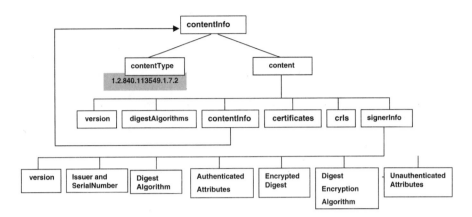

**FIGURE 10.2**
PKCS #7 signed data type

attributes that can be associated with the signer. The certificate of the signer along with the entire trust path that it requires is found in a separate field of the **SignedData** type. Signer information can be absent altogether in a special form of **SignedData** referred to as the degenerate case. This form is intended for the dissemination of certificates and CRLs using the **certificates** and **crls** field (see the ASN.1 definitions). In this case the content payload of the **SignedData** is irrelevant. It is recommended that it be omitted and the **contentType** be simply set to **data**. The syntax for **ContentInfo** permits such omission as the content is an optional filed.

```
ContentInfo ::= SEQUENCE {
          contentType  ContentType -- {pkcs-7  1}
}
```

- **The payload content**. This is the content over which the signature is computed.
- **Signers Certificate Trust paths**. A set of X.509 or extended X.509 certificates as defined by PKCS #6. The certificates found in this field should be sufficient to form a complete trust chain for each certificate as identified by its issuer and serial number in the signer's information.
- **Signers Certificate Revocation Information**. This field contains a set of CRLs that are assumed to contain revocation information for the signer's certificates. There is no provision for a network lookup of this information along the syntax and semantics of the **GeneralName** data type.
- **Digest Algorithms**. Contain a set of OIDs associated with each digest

algorithm used by the signers. Even though each signer's information includes the respective digest algorithm, this field can be useful in knowing all the digest algorithms used a-priori so that all of the verifications can proceed on a single pass.

```
SignedData ::= SEQUENCE {
    version             Version,
    digestAlgorithms    DigestAlgorithmIdentifiers,
    contentInfo         ContentInfo,
    certificates        [0] IMPLICIT ExtendedCertificatesAndCertificates
                            OPTIONAL,
    crls                [1] IMPLICIT CertificateRevocationLists OPTIONAL,
    signerInfos         SignerInfos
}

DigestAlgorithmIdentifiers ::= SET OF DigestAlgorithmIdentifier
SignerInfos ::= SET OF SignerInfo

SignerInfo ::= SEQUENCE {
    version                    Version,
    issuerAndSerialNumber      IssuerAndSerialNumber,
    digestAlgorithm            DigestAlgorithmIdentifier,
    authenticatedAttributes    [0] IMPLICIT Attributes OPTIONAL,
    digestEncryptionAlgorithm  DigestEncryptionAlgorithmIdentifier,
    encryptedDigest            EncryptedDigest,
    unauthenticatedAttributes  [1] IMPLICIT Attributes OPTIONAL
}

EncryptedDigest ::= OCTET STRING
```

The **ExtendedCertificatesAndCertifcates** data type is a set of X.509 certificates and/or extended certificates.

```
ExtendedCertificatesAndCertificates ::= SET OF
ExtendedCertificateOrCertificate
ExtendedCertificateOrCertificate ::= CHOICE {
    certificate          Certificate, -- X.509
    extendedCertificate  [0] IMPLICIT ExtendedCertificate
}
```

An extended certificate consists of an X.509 public-key certificate.

```
ExtendedCertificate ::= SEQUENCE {
    extendedCertificateInfo ExtendedCertificateInfo,
    signatureAlgorithm      SignatureAlgorithmIdentifier,
    signature               Signature
}

ExtendedCertificateInfo ::= SEQUENCE {
    version       Version,
```

**certificate    Certificate,**
**attributes     Attributes**
**}**

# Encrypted Data

This represents a basic form of wrapping encrypted data. The encrypted content is parameterized using a **contentType** field. Thus, it can be of any type known to PKCS #7. Information about the encryption algorithm is also included using the generic data type of **AlgorithmIdentifier**. The encrypted data content type is described by the following ASN.1 definitions.

```
EncryptedData ::= SEQUENCE {
    version Version,
    encryptedContentInfo EncryptedContentInfo
}

EncryptedContentInfo ::= SEQUENCE {
    contentType                ContentType,
    contentEncryptionAlgorithm ContentEncryptionAlgorithmIdentifier,
    encryptedContent           [0] IMPLICIT EncryptedContent OPTIONAL
}
EncryptedContent ::= OCTET STRING
```

Figure 10.3 depicts the layout of the **EncryptedData** type.

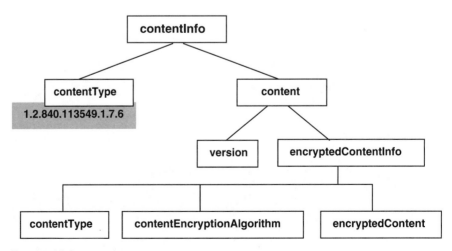

**FIGURE 10.3**
PKCS #7 encrypted data type

# Enveloped Data

The **EncryptedData** type assumes that the encryption key is to be distributed to the recipient through other means. The **EnvelopedData** type, on the other hand, exploits public key cryptography for the distribution of the secret encryption key as part of the PKCS #7 envelope. The principal employed in enveloped data consists of encrypting a data payload of any type and supplying the information about the encryption algorithm as well as the secret key material used in that encryption. Basically this can be termed as the distribution of the decryption information. This distribution is securely performed by way of encrypting the pertinent information separately for each recipient using the recipient's public key. Only a recipient is capable of using his/her corresponding private key in order to unravel the secret encryption key. The latter is then used to decrypt the envelope's payload. PKCS #7 enveloped data allows for multiple recipients so that a single envelope can be disseminated to multiple targets.

Note that the recipients of enveloped data remain anonymous even when they all receive the same envelope. For the semantics of the envelope to hold, it has to be addressed to at least one recipient. The field in which the encrypted payload appears is optional. Its absence indicates that the encrypted data is to be supplied to the recipients through other means. The corresponding ASN.1 definitions follow. Figure 10.4 shows the layout of a PKCS #7 enveloped data structure.

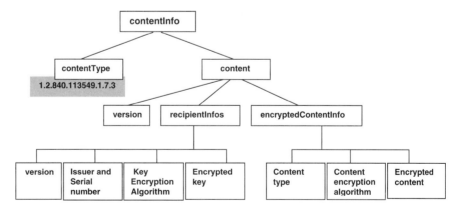

**FIGURE 10.4**
PKCS #7 enveloped data type

```
EnvelopedData ::= SEQUENCE {
    version                 Version,
    recipientInfos          RecipientInfos,
    encryptedContentInfo    EncryptedContentInfo
}

RecipientInfos ::= SET OF RecipientInfo
EncryptedContentInfo ::= SEQUENCE {
    contentType                 ContentType,
    contentEncryptionAlgorithm  ContentEncryptionAlgorithmIdentifier,
    encryptedContent            [0] IMPLICIT EncryptedContent OPTIONAL
}

RecipientInfo ::= SEQUENCE {
    version                 Version,
    issuerAndSerialNumber   IssuerAndSerialNumber,
    keyEncryptionAlgorithm  KeyEncryptionAlgorithmIdentifier,
    encryptedKey            EncryptedKey
}

EncryptedKey ::= OCTET STRING
```

# Signed and Enveloped Data

This essentially combines signed and enveloped data with the distinction that the payload digest is doubly encrypted. First, the digest is encrypted with the private key of the originator. The result is then encrypted using the secret key used to envelope the payload. Figure 10.5 illustrates the structure of a signed and enveloped content. Boxes with dashed lines are contributions from the signed data while those with solid lines are from the enveloped data. The ASN.1 definition of the signed and enveloped type is as follows:

```
SignedAndEnvelopedData ::= SEQUENCE {
    version               Version,
    recipientInfos        RecipientInfos,
    digestAlgorithms      DigestAlgorithmIdentifiers,
    encryptedContentInfo  EncryptedContentInfo,
    certificates          [0] IMPLICIT ExtendedCertificatesAndCertificates
                              OPTIONAL,
    crls                  [1] IMPLICIT CertificateRevocationLists
                              OPTIONAL,
    signerInfos           SignerInfos
}
```

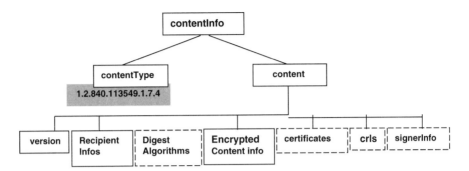

**FIGURE 10.5**
PKCS #7 signed and enveloped data structure. Dashed boxes represent the signed data while solid boxes represent enveloped data

# Digested Data

Digested data consists of a data payload of any type accompanied with its digest. This basic PKCS #7 content type is intended to add integrity to the content. Digested data is defined as follows:

```
DigestedData ::= SEQUENCE {
    version              Version,
    digestAlgorithm      DigestAlgorithmIdentifier,
    contentInfo          ContentInfo,
    digest               Digest
}
Digest ::= OCTET STRING
```

Note how the fields of a **DigestedData** are required to be present. Figure 10.6 illustrates the layout of a PKCS #7 **contentInfo** having a digest data type.

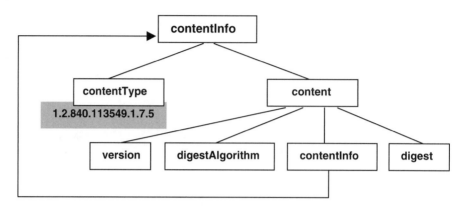

**FIGURE 10.6**
PKCS #7 digested data type

# PKCS #7 Security Services

The Data content type is intended to add a **ContentInfo** wrapper around a stream of octets. Thus it does not enhance the security of the payload in any way. Digested data is used to add a verifiable integrity check to the payload. However, digest data alone cannot guarantee the integrity of the payload as data can be modified and an appropriate digest value may be substituted for the original one. Signed data enhances its payload with data origin authenticity, and securely achieves the integrity of the payload. Unlike digested data, the payload and the signatures cannot be simply replaced without the recipient's detection. Furthermore, signed data serves the nonrepudiation property when the private key of the signer is shown to be tamperproof. Encrypted data allows the confidentiality of the payload but the secret encryption key has to be distributed to the recipient in some secure fashion. Enveloped data achieves data confidentiality without the risk of distributing the secret encryption key through external means.

For the details of the message digesting process, digest encryption process, content-encryption process (for enveloped data) that are applicable to PKCS #7 content types refer to the PKCS #7 specification [KALI98c].

# CMS

CMS is to a great extent derived from PKCS #7 version 1.5 as specified in RFC 2315 [KALI98c]. Following along the same process that IETF applies when adopting technologies originating elsewhere, CMS represents a refined superset of PKCS #7. It exports the encapsulating **ContentInfo** data type as defined by PKCS #7, and defines six content types: data, signed data, enveloped data, digested data, encrypted data, and authenticated data. We outline the differences between PKCS #7 and CMS wherever applicable below.

## Signed Data

CMS signed data takes the same form as in PKCS #7. However, CMS uses the **CertificateSet** data type instead of the **ExtendedCertificatesAndCertificates** type used in PKCS #7. A **CertificateSet** is defined as:

```
CertificateSet  ::=  SET OF CertificateChoices
CertificateChoices ::= CHOICE {
    certificate             Certificate,  -- X.509
    extendedCertificate   [0] IMPLICIT ExtendedCertificate,  -- Obsolete
    attrCert [1] IMPLICIT  AttributeCertificate
}
```

The use of **ExtendedCertificate** type became obsolete in the CMS specification; Attribute Certificates (AC) are used instead. An AC is a digital certificate signed and issued by an AC authority certifying the binding between a set of authorization privileges and the subject of the AC [FARR01].

Another difference relates to the signer information. In CMS it is defined by:

```
SignerInfo ::= SEQUENCE {
    version             CMSVersion,
    sid                 SignerIdentifier,
    digestAlgorithm     DigestAlgorithmIdentifier,
    signedAttrs         [0] IMPLICIT SignedAttributes OPTIONAL,
    signatureAlgorithm  SignatureAlgorithmIdentifier,
    signature           SignatureValue,
    unsignedAttrs       [1] IMPLICIT UnsignedAttributes OPTIONAL
}
```

Note the generalized form of the signer identification information that includes one more option as defined by:

```
SignerIdentifier ::= CHOICE {
    issuerAndSerialNumber    IssuerAndSerialNumber,
    subjectKeyIdentifier     [0] SubjectKeyIdentifier
}
```

```
SubjectKeyIdentifier  ::= OCTET STRING
SignedAttributes      ::= SET SIZE (1..MAX) OF Attribute
UnsignedAttributes    ::= SET SIZE (1..MAX) OF Attribute
```

The **subjectKeyIdentifier** is the value of the signer's subject key identifier extension when applicable. Naturally, PKCS #7 having been originated at RSA, Inc., lends itself primarily to RSA-based digital signatures. CMS signed data type, on the other hand, is applicable to any signature algorithm, such as the DSA, and not just those that are based upon encrypting a digest of the signed content.

## Enveloped Data

The CMS enveloped data type is defined by the following ASN.1 structure:

```
EnvelopedData ::= SEQUENCE {
    version                 CMSVersion,
    originatorInfo          [0] IMPLICIT OriginatorInfo OPTIONAL,
    recipientInfos          RecipientInfos,
    encryptedContentInfo    EncryptedContentInfo,
    unprotectedAttrs        [1] IMPLICIT UnprotectedAttributes OPTIONAL
}
```

```
OriginatorInfo ::= SEQUENCE {
    certs   [0] IMPLICIT CertificateSet OPTIONAL,
    crls    [1] IMPLICIT CertificateRevocationLists OPTIONAL
}
```

```
RecipientInfos ::= SET OF RecipientInfo
```

```
EncryptedContentInfo ::= SEQUENCE {
    contentType                 ContentType,
    contentEncryptionAlgorithm  ContentEncryptionAlgorithmIdentifier,
    encryptedContent            [0] IMPLICIT EncryptedContent OPTIONAL
}
UnprotectedAttributes ::= SET SIZE (1..MAX) OF Attribute
```

```
RecipientInfo ::= CHOICE {
    ktri    KeyTransRecipientInfo,
    kari    [1] KeyAgreeRecipientInfo,
    kekri   [2] KEKRecipientInfo
}
```

The differences between PKCS #7 and CMS with respect to the enveloped data type can be summarized as:

- CMS adds an extra optional field, **originatorInfo**, to pack a set of certificates associated with the originator. The associated CRLs may also be part of this field. It is expected that the certificates contained in this field to be used by the key management algorithms describing the content-encryption key for each recipient.
- While per-recipient information in PKCS #7 encrypts the content encryption key using the public key of the recipient, CMS provides a much more generalized means of using different methods of key management. These include:
  - **Key transport**. In this case the content-encryption key is encrypted in the public key of the recipient.

    ```
    KeyTransRecipientInfo ::= SEQUENCE {
        version                   CMSVersion, -- always set to 0 or 2
        rid                       RecipientIdentifier,
        keyEncryptionAlgorithm    KeyEncryptionAlgorithmIdentifier,
        encryptedKey              EncryptedKey
    }

    RecipientIdentifier ::= CHOICE {
        issuerAndSerialNumber     IssuerAndSerialNumber,
        subjectKeyIdentifier      [0] SubjectKeyIdentifier
    }
    ```

  - **Key agreement**. A key agreement protocol is used to generate a pair-wise symmetric key which is then used to encrypt the content-encryption key. This option is not available in PKCS #7.

    ```
    KeyAgreeRecipientInfo ::= SEQUENCE {
        version                   CMSVersion, -- always set to 3
        originator                [0] EXPLICIT OriginatorIdentifierOrKey,
        ukm                       [1] EXPLICIT UserKeyingMaterial OPTIONAL,
        keyEncryptionAlgorithm    KeyEncryptionAlgorithmIdentifier,
        recipientEncryptedKeys    RecipientEncryptedKeys
    }

    OriginatorIdentifierOrKey ::= CHOICE {
        issuerAndSerialNumber     IssuerAndSerialNumber,
        subjectKeyIdentifier      [0] SubjectKeyIdentifier,
        originatorKey             [1] OriginatorPublicKey
    }

    OriginatorPublicKey ::= SEQUENCE {
        algorithm                 AlgorithmIdentifier,
        publicKey                 BIT STRING
    ```

```
}

RecipientEncryptedKeys ::= SEQUENCE OF RecipientEncryptedKey

RecipientEncryptedKey ::= SEQUENCE {
    rid                     KeyAgreeRecipientIdentifier,
    encryptedKey            EncryptedKey
}

KeyAgreeRecipientIdentifier ::= CHOICE {
    issuerAndSerialNumber   IssuerAndSerialNumber,
     rKeyId                 [0] IMPLICIT RecipientKeyIdentifier
}

RecipientKeyIdentifier ::= SEQUENCE {
    subjectKeyIdentifier    SubjectKeyIdentifier,
    date                    GeneralizedTime OPTIONAL,
    other                   OtherKeyAttribute OPTIONAL
}

SubjectKeyIdentifier ::= OCTET STRING
```

- **Symmetric key-encryption key**. Here a previously distributed symmetric key is used to encrypt the content-encryption key. This option is not available in PKCS #7.

```
KEKRecipientInfo ::= SEQUENCE {
    version                 CMSVersion,  -- always set to 4
    kekid                   KEKIdentifier,
    keyEncryptionAlgorithm  KeyEncryptionAlgorithmIdentifier,
    encryptedKey            EncryptedKey
}

KEKIdentifier ::= SEQUENCE {
    keyIdentifier   OCTET STRING,
    date            GeneralizedTime OPTIONAL,
    other           OtherKeyAttribute OPTIONAL
}
```

- In contrast to PKCS #7, CMS optionally allows an originator to include unprotected information as part of the envelope. This feature lends itself well to communicating with multiple recipients where each may or may not impose any data protection constraints.

## Encrypted Data

The structural difference between PKCS #7 and CMS with respect to the encrypted data type is exhibited by an additional optional field used in CMS to carry unprotected content. This difference is reflected by the following ASN.1 definition:

```
EncryptedData ::= SEQUENCE {
    version                 CMSVersion,
    encryptedContentInfo    EncryptedContentInfo,
    unprotectedAttrs        [1] IMPLICIT UnprotectedAttributes OPTIONAL
}
```

## Authenticated Data

While signed data binds the signing entity to the content payload, CMS authenticated data enables the use of any MAC algorithm to provide the integrity of a content of any type. One might argue that signed data already serves this purpose. The difference, however, lays in the fact that signed data fundamentally relies on the PKI elements of a private key and its corresponding public key certificate. Authenticated data, a CMS defined type, provides an alternative to supporting data integrity and origin authenticity without using public key constructs, although they can also be used to protect the per-recipient message authentication key. Authenticated data is designated an OID that is not defined by the PKCS #7 specification. The value of this OID is:

```
id-ct-authData OBJECT IDENTIFIER ::=
    { iso(1) member-body(2) us(840) rsadsi(113549) pkcs(1) pkcs-9(9)
smime(16) ct(1) 2 }
```

Authenticated data is governed by the following syntax:

```
AuthenticatedData ::= SEQUENCE {
    version                  CMSVersion,
    originatorInfo           [0] IMPLICIT OriginatorInfo OPTIONAL,
    recipientInfos           RecipientInfos,
    macAlgorithm             MessageAuthenticationCodeAlgorithm,
    digestAlgorithm          [1] DigestAlgorithmIdentifier OPTIONAL,
    encapContentInfo         EncapsulatedContentInfo,
    authenticatedAttributes   [2] IMPLICIT AuthAttributes OPTIONAL,
    mac                      MessageAuthenticationCode,
    unauthenticatedAttributes [3] IMPLICIT UnauthAttributes OPTIONAL
}
EncapsulatedContentInfo ::= SEQUENCE {
    eContentType   ContentType,
    eContent       [0] EXPLICIT OCTET STRING OPTIONAL
}
AuthAttributes ::= SET SIZE (1..MAX) OF Attribute,
UnauthAttributes ::= SET SIZE (1..MAX) OF Attribute,
MessageAuthenticationCode ::= OCTET STRING
```

The details of the MAC generation steps are described in [HOUS99c].

# CMC

Certificate management using CMS, referred to as CMC, is yet another format protocol for the PKIX certificate management operations [MYER00]. The protocol is a direct application of CMS in that each protocol request and response message, respectively, consists of a canonical data type wrapped in a CMS encapsulation. Request messages use the **PKIData** type, while response messages use the **ResponseBody** data type. Figure 10.7 shows the overall structures of a CMC request and response messages.

The CMS encapsulation of **PKIData** and **ResponseBody** introduces two OIDs reflecting the payload contents of **PKIData** and **ResponseBody**, respectively. These OIDs are:

**id-cct-PKIData  OBJECT IDENTIFIER      ::= { id-cct  2 }**
**id-cct-PKIResponse OBJECT IDENTIFIER ::= { id-cct  3 }**

where

**id-cct OBJECT IDENTIFIER ::= {id-pkix 12}  -- CMC content types**

**PKData** has the following ASN.1 structure:

```
PKIData ::= SEQUENCE {
    controlSequence     SEQUENCE SIZE(0..MAX) OF TaggedAttribute,
    reqSequence         SEQUENCE SIZE(0..MAX) OF TaggedRequest,
    cmsSequence         SEQUENCE SIZE(0..MAX) OF TaggedContentInfo,
    otherMsgSequence    SEQUENCE SIZE(0..MAX) OF OtherMsg
}
```

request

response

**FIGURE 10.7**
The basic content of a CMC request and response messages

while **ResponseBody** is defined by:

```
ResponseBody ::= SEQUENCE {
    controlSequence     SEQUENCE SIZE(0..MAX) OF TaggedAttribute,
    cmsSequence         SEQUENCE SIZE(0..MAX) OF TaggedContentInfo,
    otherMsgSequence    SEQUENCE SIZE(0..MAX) OF OtherMsg
}
```

The elements defining **PKIData** and **ResponseBody** are briefly described below. Refer to the CMC specification for complete details.

## TaggedAttribute

This data type is used to convey a sequence of control attributes that essentially determine the type, state, and context information for the CMC encapsulated message. Such information may include a transaction identifier, a status, a sender nonce, a recipient nonce, as well as the message type (e,g., certification request, or a revocation request). Refer to the CMC specification for a complete list of control attributes [MYER00]. CMC control attributes are assigned OIDs that emanate from the following arc:

```
id-cmc OBJECT IDENTIFIER ::= {id-pkix  7}   -- CMC controls
```

## TaggedRequest

This data type is used to encode a sequence of zero or more certificate requests. Such requests can be either a PKCS #10 certificate request or one that is based on the CRMF specification [MYER99b].

## TaggedContentInfo

This type is used to convey a sequence of zero or more CMS objects that can be either  EnvelopedData, SignedData, or EncryptedData.

## OtherMsg

The use of this type adds a dimension of flexibility to CMC in that it can be used to include arbitrary data items. Zero or more of such items can be encoded in a CMC message. Each item is identified by a particular OID.

# Further Protections of CMS Messages

While the basic CMC message is already encapsulated within a CMS **SignedData**, further protection can be applied to it. The message can be wrapped in a CMS **EnvelopedData** in order to provide confidentiality. Furthermore, the CMC specification recommends that in this case the envelope be wrapped in an additional outer **SignedData** encapsulation. Figure 10.8 illustrates further nesting of CMS encapsulations used in supporting confidentiality of CMC messages.

It should be noted that by supporting a simple form of request and response messages, CMC preserves backward compatibility with PKCS #10. In this special case, a request message is signed using the private key of the requesting entity. Appropriate POP can be provided.

# S/MIME v3

S/MIME, an acronym for Secure/Multipurpose Internet Mail Extension, provides security services for Internet electronic mail. It can also be used as a method of securing any transport mechanism that can transmit MIME data types such as HTTP. S/MIME in its version 2 form had originated at RSA, Inc. Subsequently IETF adopted it, and added further enhancements, thus becoming an Internet standard [RAMS99]. IETF enhancements in many cases seek to generalize the applicability of a particular specification. For instance S/MIME

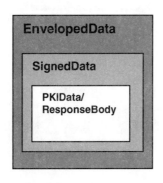
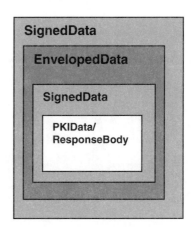

**FIGURE 10.8**
Adding further protection to a CMS message

v3 allows use of additional signing algorithms besides the RSA signature algorithm as specified in S/MIME v2. It also mandates the use of the SHA-1 digest although MD5 is maintained for compatibility with v2.

S/MIME v3 is a direct application of CMS encapsulations to MIME body parts and, thus, provides the security services of integrity, data origin authenticity, confidentiality, and nonrepudiation to MIME message parts. The CMS crypographic wrappers used to support such services are **Signed-Data** and **EnvelopedData**.

Public key plays a central role in providing those security services in that the cryptographic transformations applied to a MIME part rely on the binding of an e-mail address to a public key. The e-mail can be included in the certificate in two ways. It can be the subject alternative name extension, or simply an **emailAddress** attribute of the subject distinguished name.

S/MIME v3 defines a new MIME type, the **application/pkcs7-mime,** used for the transport of MIME-protected elements. It also specifically defines the **application/pkcs7-signature** MIME type used for the transport of S/MIME signed messages. Signing MIME parts can be accomplished in two ways.

- The signature can be applied to a MIME part that is transformed using an earlier method of protecting MIME parts as specified in RFC 1847[GALV95]. The protection here uses the multipart/signed MIME type.
- The signature can be applied natively to the MIME parts using the **application/pkcs7-mim**e type.

# SSL/TLS

SSL is a security protocol developed by Netscape Communications Corporation [FREI96]. SSL provides transport security for stream-oriented communications and has most notably evolved as the mechanism of choice for securing Web browser to Web server communications. Later, Netscape released the SSL specification to the IETF where it has undergone several improvements, the result of which is a protocol specification for the Transport Layer Security (TLS) described by RFC 2246[DIER99].

TLS is intended to provide three main security services to applications communicating over a reliable connection-oriented communication protocol such as TCP/IP. These services are:

- **Authentication**. Two communicating entities may engage in a mutual authentication to confirm one another's identity, or they may establish a one-way authentication; usually the receiving end of the communication is the one that is authenticated. The widely adopted practice is for the server to authenticate itself to the client using an X.509 digital certificate. Once a secure cryptographic channel is established, the client then sends its authentication credentials, generally in the form of a user identifier and a password, to the server. Authenticating the client to the server is performed at the application level. TLS authentication can be achieved using either secret key or public key cryptography.

- **Integrity.** Information being exchanged under a TLS session is protected from undetected modification. The sending end of the protocol attaches an integrity check value to the exchanged data. The receiving end verifies the integrity check value based upon the cryptographic parameters negotiated during protocol initialization steps. The value of the message integrity check is based on a keyed MAC algorithm.

- **Confidentiality.** Exchanged information is protected using a confidentiality session. During its initialization steps, the TLS protocol establishes a symmetric encryption key, which is then used to encrypt the communications channel. Various secret key encryption algorithms can be used (e.g., DES and RC4).

TLS is composed of two protocol layers: Record and Handshake. The Handshake protocol is a higher level client of the Record protocol. By that it is meant the Handshake protocol steps are carried over the Record protocol which exists in the stack layer that is below the Handshake protocol. Once the Handshake protocol steps are executed, application data becomes the direct user of the Record layer of the protocol. Figure 10.9 illustrates the layered TLS protocol.

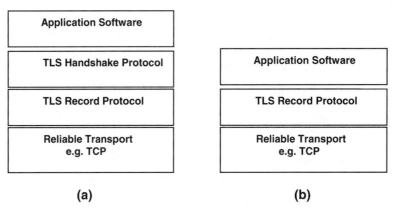

(a)                                        (b)

**FIGURE 10.9**

Layered TLS protocol. (a) during protocol initialization using the Handshake layer, and (b) the direct use of the Record layer by an application

## Record Protocol

The Record protocol is, in turn, layered into sub-protocols as follows:

- **Fragmentation.** This sub-layer breaks information such as application data into manageable records of $2^{14}$ bytes or less.

- **Compression.** This sub-layer uses the compression algorithm that has been agreed upon during the Handshake protocol in order to compress records of the Fragmentation sub-layer.

- **Record Protection**. The compressed record is subjected to a MAC calculation so that the receiving entity verifies the integrity of the data payload. Optionally the entire compressed record can be encrypted when confidentiality is enabled.

## Handshake Protocol

The Handshake protocol steps are used to initiate a TLS connection and establish the cryptographic parameters that will subsequently govern the security of the communications channel. The execution of the handshake protocol steps results in establishing the security context for the TLS session. This context is defined through the following set of parameters:

- **session identifier**. An arbitrary byte sequence chosen by the server to identify a particular session.

- **peer certificate.** X509v3 certificate of the peer. This element of the state may be set to a null value when the peer is not authenticated. Recall that authenticating the peer is an optional step.

- **compression method.** The algorithm used to compress data prior to the application of any cryptographic protection.

- **cipher spec.** Specifies the bulk data encryption algorithm; e.g. DES, and a MAC algorithm such as MD5 or SHA-1. It also defines cryptographic attributes such as the hash size.

- **master secret.** A 48-byte secret value shared between the client and server and is used as an entropy source for generating keys and MAC secrets. The master secret is computed at each end of the TLS protocol from initially exchanged random data and a pre-master secret value. The latter is sent from the client to the server in an encrypted form. For instance when RSA is used for server authentication and key exchange, a 48-byte pre-master secret is generated by the client, encrypted under the server's public key, and then is sent to the server. The server uses its private key to decrypt the pre-master secret and uses it to generate the master secret key.

- **is resumable.** A flag indicating whether the TLS session can be used to initiate new connections with the same target server. This option allows multiple TLS sessions to be established using a single handshake. It is particularly useful in reducing the overhead of a repeated TLS handshake. Note that the resumption feature implies the use of the same security parameters already established.

TLS handshake messages are submitted to the Record layer of TLS for transmission in the form for of TLS plaintext structures. The handshake consists of a protocol sequence that uses a combination of messages shown in Table 10.1.

**TABLE 10.1**

| Message Type | Description |
| --- | --- |
| Client Hello | Sent by the client when it first connects to the server. It may also be sent in response to the server's Hello Request. |
| Server Hello | Sent by the server to the client in response to a client hello upon a successful match with the client's requested algorithms. |
| Certificate | Used to exchange certificates. It can be sent by the client or the server. |
| Server Key Exchange | Sent by the server to the client only when the server certificate message is not sufficient for the client to send a protected pre-master secret key to the server. |
| Certificate Request | Used by the server to optionally request a certificate from the client. |
| Server Hello Done | Sent by the server to the client to signal the end of the server hello and its associated key exchange messages. |
| Certificate Verify | This message may be sent following a client key exchange message. It is used to verify the client certificate with a signing capability. |
| Client Key Exchange | This message is always sent by the client to the server following the client certificate message, if it is used. Otherwise it is the first message sent by the client after the server hello done message. |
| Hello Request | |
| Finished | Is sent by the entity requesting a change cipher spec ( a sub-protocol of the TLS handshake) to verify that the key exchange and authentication processes were successful. |

Figure 10.10 illustrates an instance of the TLS handshake exchange between a client and a server.

PKI support for SSL/TLS is exhibited throughout the Handshake protocol steps. The client and server certificates can be used to establish a one-way or a two-way authenticated session based upon the verification of signed protocol messages by the authenticating entity. Thus, the certificates must carry the digital signature key usage. Additionally, exchanged certificates may provide the basis for a key agreement protocol such as Diffie-Hellman. For this to happen, the certificates key usage of key agreement must be set. Finally, the key encipherment key usage must also be set in the target certificate, for instance, so that key exchange by way of enciphering the shared

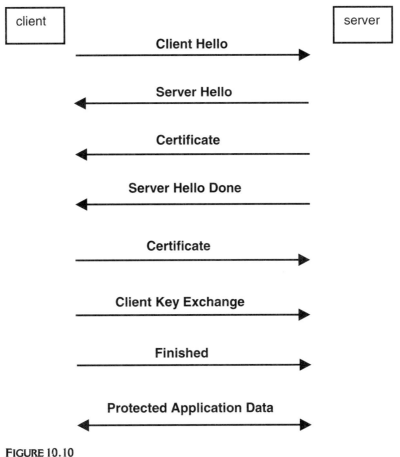

**FIGURE 10.10**
An example of the TLS handshake protocol exchanges

key using the RSA algorithm can take place. The identity that is bound to a public key certificate consumed by SSL/TLS is generally drawn from the subject alternative name extension in the form of a domain name service (dNSName). This type of identification lends itself well to hosting systems as well as Web servers. It is not, however, suitable for client or application level identification.

It is worth noting that the TLS protocol is secure, in that any negotiated cipher suite offers its promised level of security. For instance if any exchanged certificates are subjected to a reliable validation procedure, and one end of the protocol negotiates a Triple-DES using a 1024-bit RSA key exchange, you can expect the established TLS session to be accordingly that secure. The fundamental rule is that the application layer must be aware of what their security requirements are and never transmit information over a channel less secure than what is required.

# References

[ADAM99]   Adams, C., and Farrell, S., *Certificate Management Protocols*, IETF RFC2510 1999.

[ANSI85]   ANSI X9.17, *American National Standard for Financial Institution Key Management (Wholesale)*, American Bankers Association, 1985.

[BALE85]   Balenson, D., *Automated Distribution of Cryptographic Keys Using the Financial Institution Key Management Standard*, IEEE Communications Magazine, vo. 23, no. 9, pp. 41-46, 1985.

[BECK82]   Becker, H., and Piper, F., *Cipher Systems: The Protection of Communications*, John Wiley & Sons, New York 1982.

[BOEY99]   Boeyen, S., Howes, T., and Richard, P., *Internet X.509 Public Key Infrastructure LDAPv2 Schema*, IETF RFC 2587, 1999.

[BORE92]   Borenstein, N., Freed, N., *MIME (Multipurpose Internet Mail Extensions): Mechanisms for Specifying and Describing the Format of Internet Message Bodies*, IETF RFC 1341, 1992.

[CCIT88]   *The Directory: Overview of Concepts, Models and Service*, CCITT Recommendation X.500, 1988.

[CCIT98]    CCITT, *Recommendation X.208: Specification of Abstract Syntax Notation One (ASN.1)*, 1998.

[CHOK99]    Chokhani, S., and Ford, W., *Internet X.509 Public Key Infrastructure Certificate Policy and Certification Practices Framework*, IETF RFC 2527, 1999.

[CROC82]    Crocker, D., H., *Standard for the Format of ARPA Internet Text Messages*, IETF RFC 822, 1982.

[DARP81]    DARPA Internet Program, *Internet Protocol*, IETF RFC 791, 1981.

[DAVI89]    Davies, D. W., and Price, W. L., *Security for Computer Networks*, John Wiley & Sons, New York, 1989.

[DENN83]    Denning, D. E., *Cryptography and Data Security*, Addison-Wesley, Reading, Massachusetts, 1983.

[DEER95]    Deering, S., Hinden, R., *Internet Protocol, Version 6 (IPv6) Specification, IETF RFC 1883*, 1995.

[DIER99]    Dierks, T., and Allen, C., *The TLS Protocol: Version 1.0*, IETF RFC 2246, 1999.

[DIFF76a]   Diffie, W., and Hellman, M. E., *Multiuser Cryptographic Techniques*, Proceedings of AFIPS National Computer Conference, AFIPS Press, Montvale, NJ, pp.109-112, 1976.

[DIFF76b]   Diffie, W., and Hellman, M. E., *New Directions in Cryptography*, IEEE Transactions on Information Theory, vol. 22, pp. 644-654., 1976.

[DSS94]     *Digital Signature Standard*, National Institute of Standards and Technology Publication 186, 1994. See http://www.nist.gov/public_affairs/releases/digsigst.htm.

[ELGA95]    ElGamal, T., *A Public-Key Cryptosystem and a Signature Scheme Based on Discrete Logarithms*, Advances in Cryptology: Proceedings of CRYPTO 84, vol. 196 of Lecture Notes in Computer Science, Blakley, G. R., and Chaum, D., Editors, Springer-Verlag, Berlin, pp. 10–18, 1995.

[ETH92]     ETH Series in Information Processing, Massey, J. L., editor, vol. 1, Hartung-Gorre Verlag Konstanz, Zurich, 1992.

[FARR01]    Farrell, S., and Housley, R., *An Internet Attribute Certificate Profile for Authorization*, IETF Draft RFC, 2001.

[FIPS81]    FIPS 81, *DES modes of operation*, Federal Information Processing Standards Publications, 81, U. S. Department of Commerce/ National Bureau of Standards, Springfield, Virginia, 1981.

[FREI96]    Freier, A., Karlton, P., Kocher, P., C., *The SSL Protocol Version 3.0, Netscape Communications*, 1996.

[GALV95]    Galvin, J., Murphy, S., Crocker, S. and N. Freed, *Security Multiparts for MIME: Multipart/Signed and Multipart/Encrypted*, IETF RFC 1847, 1995.

[GORD85]    Gordon, J. A., *Strong primes are easy to find*, Advances in cryptology, Proceedings of Eurocrypt 84, Springer-Verlag, pp. 216-223, 1985.

[HILL29]    Hill, L. S., *Cryptography in an algebraic alphabet*, American Mathematical Monthly, 36 (1929), pp. 306-312. 1929.

[HOUS99]    Housley, R., Ford, W., Polk, W., and Solo, D., *Internet X.509 Public Key Infrastructure Certificate and CRL Profile*, IETF RFC 2459, 1999.

[HOUS99b]   Housley, R., and Hoffman, P., *Internet X.509 Public Key Infrastructure Operational Protocols: FTP and HTTP*, IETF RFC 2585, 1999.

[HOUS99c]   Housley, R., *Cryptographic Message Syntax*, IETF RFC 2630, 1999.

[HOWE95]    Howes, T. and Smith, M., *The LDAP Application Program Interface*, IETF Informational RFC 1823, 1995.

[ISOI88]    *Information Processing Systems—Open Systems Interconnection—The Directory: Overview of Concepts, Models and Service.* ISO/IEC JTC 1/ SC21, International Standard 9594-1, 1988.

[KAHN67]    Kahn, D., *The Codebreakers*, Macmillan Publishing Company, New York, 1967.

[KALI98]    Kaliski, B., *PKCS #1: RSA Encryption Version 1.5*, IETF Informational RFC 2313.

[KALI98b]   Kaliski, B., *PKCS #10: Certification Request Syntax, Version 1.5*, IETF RFC 2314,1998.

[KALI98c]   Kaliski, B., *PKCS #7: Cryptographic Message Syntax, Version 1.5*, IETF Informational RFC 2315, 1998.

[KENT93]    Kent, S., *Privacy Enhancement for Internet Electronic Mail: Part II: Certificate-Based Key Management*, IETF RFC 1422, 1993.

[KENT98b]   Kent, S., Atkinson, R., *Security Architecture for the Internet Protocol*, IETF RFC 2401, 1988.

[KOBL87]    Koblitz, N., *Elliptic Curve Cryptosystems*, Mathematics of Computation, vol. 48, no. 177, pp. 203-209, 1987.

[KOBL94]    Koblitz, N., *A Course in Number Theory and Cryptography*, Springer-Verlag, New York, 1994.

[KOBL98]    Koblitz, N., *Algebraic Aspects of Cryptography*, Springer-Verlag, New York, 1998.

[KOHL83]    Kohl, J.T., and Neuman, B. C., *The Kerberos Network Authentication Service*, IETF RFC1510, 1993.

[KOHN78]    Kohnfelder, L. M., *Toward a practical public-key cryptosystem*, B.Sc. thesis, MIT Department of Electrical Engineering, 1978.

[KONH81]    Konheim, A. G., *Cryptography, A Primer*, John Wiley & Sons, New York 1981.

[KRAW97]    Krawczyk, H., Bellare, M., and Canetti, R., *HMAC: Keyed-Hashing for Message Authentication*, 1997, IETF Informational RFC2104.

[LAI91]     Lai, X., and Massey, J. L., *A proposal for a new block encryption standard*, Advances in Cryptology-EUROCRYPT-1990 (LNCS 473), pp. 389-404, 1991.

[MENE96]    Menezes, A. J., Oorschot, P. C., Vanstone, S. A., *Handbook of Applied Cryptography*, CRC Press, 1996.

[MERK78]    Merkle, R. C., *Secure Communications Over Insecure Channels*, Communications of the ACM, vol. 21 no. 4, pp. 294-299, 1978.

[MERK79]    Merkle, R.C., *Secrecy, Authentication, and Public Key Systems*, UMI Research Press, Ann Arbor, Michigan, 1979.

[MEYE82]    Meyer, C. H., and Matyas, S. M., *A New Dimension in Computer Data Security*, John Wiley & Sons, New York, 1982.

[MILL86]    Miller, V. S., *Use of Elliptic Curves in Cryptography*, Advances in Cryptology, CRYPTO'85 Proceedings, Springer-Verlag, pp. 417-426, 1986.

[MOCK87a]   Mockapetris, P., *Domain Names—Concepts and Facilities*, IETF RFC 1034, 1987.

[MOCK87b]   Mockapetris, P., *Domain Names—Implementation and Specification*, IETF RFC 1035, 1987.

[MYER99]    Myers, M., Ankney, R., Malpani, A., Galperin, S., and Adams, C., *X.509 Internet Public Key Infrastructure Online Certificate Status Protocol—OCSP*, IETF RFC 2560, 1999.

[MYER99b]   Myers, M., Adams, C., Solo, D. and Kemp, D., *Certificate Request Message Format*, RFC 2511, 1999.

[MYER00]    Myers, M., Liu, X., Schaad, J., and Weinstein, J., *Certificate Management Messages over CMS*, IETF RFC 2797, 2000.

[NEED78]    Needham, R. M., and Schroeder, M. D., *Using Encryption for Authentication in Large Networks of Computers*, Communications of the ACM, vol. 21, no. 12, pp. 993-999, 1978.

[NIST01]    National Institute of Standards and Technology (NIST), *Draft Advanced Encryption Standard*, Computer Security Resource Center (CSRC), http://csrc.nist.gov/encryption/aes/, 2001.

[NYST00]    Nystrom, M., and Kaliski, B., *PKCS #9: Selected Object Classes and Attribute Types*, Version 2.0, IETF Informational RFC 2985, 2000.

[POST85]    Postel, J., and Reynolds, J., *File Transfer Protocol (FTP)*, IETF RFC 959, 1985.

[PRAF00]    Prafullchandra, H., and Schaad, J., *Diffie-Hellman Proof-of-Possession Algorithms*, IETF RFC 2875, 2000.

[PREN93]    Preneel, B., *Information Authentication: Hash Functions and Digital Signatures*, Preneel, B., Govaerts, R., and Vandewalle, J., editors, Computer Security and Industrial Cryptography: State of the Art and Evolution (LNCS 741), pp.87-131, Springer-Verlag, 1993.

[RAMS99]    Ramsdell, B., *S/MIME Version 3 Message Specification*, IETF RFC 2630, 1999.

[RIVE92]    Rivest, R. L., *The MD5 message-digest algorithm*, IETF RFC 1321, 1992.

[RSA93a]    *PKCS #8: Private-Key Information Syntax Standard*, RSA Laboratories Technical Note Version 1.2

[RSA99a]    *PKCS #11 v2.10: Cryptographic Token Interface Standard*, RSA Laboratories, 1999.

[RSA99b]    *PKCS #5 v2.0: Password-Based Cryptography Standard*, RSA Laboratories 1999.

[RSA99c]    *PKCS 12 v1.0: Personal Information Exchange Syntax*, RSA Laboratories, 1990.

[RSA00a]    PKCS #15 v1.1: Cryptographic Token Information Syntax Standard, RSA Laboratories, 2000.

[SCHN91]    Schneier, B., *One-Way Hash Functions*, Dr. Dobb's Journal 16, No. 9, pp.148–151, 1991.

[SCHN96]    Schneier, B., *Applied Cryptography*, John Wiley & Sons, 1996.

[SHS95]     *Secure Hash Standard*, Federal Information Processing Standards Publication 180-1, 1995. See http://www.itl.nist.gov/fipspubs/fip180-1.htm.

[SIRB88]    Sirbu, M., *A Content-Type Header Field for Internet Messages*, IETF RFC 1049, 1988.

[WAHL97]    Wahl, M., *A Summary of the X.500(96) User Schema for use with LDAPv3*, IETF RFC 2256, 1997.

[WIEN94]    Wiener, M. J., *Efficient DES Key Search*, TR-244, School of Computer Science, Carleton University, 1994.

[YEON95]    Yeong, W., Howes, T., Kille, S., *Lightweight Directory Access Protocol*, IETF RFC 1777, 1995.

# Index

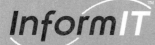